A Life on FRINGE

The Memoirs of EUGENE FORSEY

Toronto
OXFORD UNIVERSITY PRESS

Oxford University Press, 70 Wynford Drive, Don Mills, Ontario, M3C 1J9

Toronto   Oxford   New York   Delhi   Bombay   Calcutta   Madras   Karachi
Petaling Jaya   Singapore   Hong Kong   Tokyo   Nairobi   Dar es Salaam
Cape Town   Melbourne   Auckland

and associated companies in
Berlin   Ibadan

Canadian Cataloguing in Publication Data
Forsey, Eugene A. (Eugene Alfred), 1904-1991
A life on the fringe

Includes bibliographical references.
ISBN 0-19-540720-2 (bound) ISBN 0-19-540868-3 (pbk.)

1. Forsey, Eugene A. (Eugene Alfred), 1904-1991.
2. Canada – Politics and government – 20th century.
3. Canadian Labour Congress – Biography.   4. Canada.
Parliament. Senate – Biography.   5. Legislators –
Canada – Biography.   I. Title.

FC601.F67A3 1990   971.06'092   C90-094761-6
F1034.3.F67A3 1990

Printed in Canada by Webcom

To the memory of

HARRIET

who was responsible for most of the good I have done, and none of the harm, and who, till almost the very end of her earthly life, took the keenest interest in the book's progress.

THE
ILLUSTRATIONS
APPEAR
BETWEEN
PAGES
122
AND
123

Contents

Preface

When another publisher, a dozen years ago, suggested I write my memoirs, I replied that I'd sooner be sentenced to penal servitude: the thing wasn't worth doing; it would mean an appalling amount of work; and I could not endure the thought of yet another editor determined to correct my English.

I stuck to this till two things happened. First, my two grandsons showed a keen interest in my accounts of various events in my life, and I realized that I might put some of them on paper for the boys' diversion. Second, my wife had to go into a chronic care hospital, my expenses shot up, my income didn't. Then it occurred to me that if I put something on paper, a publisher might be interested, and I might get in a little extra cash. The very morning this idea entered my head I got a letter from the Oxford University Press suggesting, in effect, that I might reconsider my preference for penal servitude. I sent the Press a sample chapter. They said to go ahead.

My original opinion of the value of the work is reinforced when I read the memoirs of various eminent friends who have done great things as scholars, diplomats, politicians, mandarins. They have taken a leading part in decisions of great moment. They have been at the centre of great events. I have been only on the fringe: in scholarship, in trade unionism, in politics. I have been around a long time. I have known a great many interesting people. I have had three careers (all minor): academic, union, and political. I have belonged to three political parties and to two churches (and been deeply influenced by a third). I have been blessed with an astonishing number of wonderful friends, far beyond my desserts. And I have had a lot of fun, some of which I have tried to pass on. Whether that is enough to warrant my going public is a matter for my readers to decide.

One of my friends actually did a Ph. D. on me. (I have never seen it.)

He said his supervisor and colleagues could not make out what made me tick: too many glaring contradictions in what I had said and done. I doubt if this book will give them any clues.

Much of the book will probably be dismissed as frivolous: a fair number of good stories, but little else, and that little pretty thin. Some readers may wonder how I chose what to put in and what to leave out. Why, for example, is there almost nothing about the Second World War? The answer to that is that I did nothing in it except to try to preserve and enhance democracy and freedom at home. Looking back, I think I ought to have volunteered, though I should probably have been no use as a combatant, and not much as anything else. Remnants of pacifism and isolationist nationalism clung to me, and I stayed put.

Lack of space is responsible for the omission of my trip to India in 1953, my year at Harvard, my year at Queen's, my long connection with Trent University, my debts to many cherished friends, and a great many of my best stories. Some of the cuts I made may simply betray my lack of sense of proportion. I am sure I have left unsaid many things I ought to have said, and probably said some things I ought not to have said. Some of my failures may be put down to original sin and senility, or at least laziness and an increasingly erratic memory. I have never kept a diary, and I have checked very few of my recollections. Nevertheless, I hope some readers will get as much entertainment out of this book as I got out of writing it. And I hope some of it may be useful for historians' footnotes — particularly the chapters on the Board of Broadcast Governors, the Senate, the rule of law, and Quebec nationalism. Finally, I hope I have not caused anyone more than tolerable pain by anything I have said.

Two of my previsions of what writing this book would mean have been fulfilled. The third was not. William Toye has been an editor beyond my dreams. Some of the others I have encountered nearly drove me crazy (as perhaps I did them!). Bill has been a joy, a very gentle, parfit editor. His patience has been limitless, his ingenuity inexhaustible, his judgement beyond reproach, his kindness unfailing. He has, incidentally, corrected my English.

Ottawa, Ont.   E.F.
13 June 1990

1

My Background
and
Early Years

I was born in Grand Bank, Newfoundland, on 29 May 1904, the son of
Eugene Forsey of Grand Bank and Florence Elvira Bowles of Ottawa. My
father's people were all Newfoundlanders. The Forseys came from the
West Country of England in 1775; family tradition says from Devon, but
recent research by a Memorial University professor says more probably
from Dorset. I am descended also from another West Country man,
Jonathan Hickman, who arrived in Grand Bank in 1763 from St Pierre
when that island was handed back to the French. Jonathan had been born
prematurely on a vessel coming from England to Halifax in 1747. He was
so weak that the crew shook their heads, put him in a box, packed him in
oakum, and were about to throw him overboard when his mother called
out in the Devonshire speech: ' 'E's not deed yit!' It proved to be a classic
case of English understatement. They unpacked him and he lived for 100
years and five months old and begat ten children. He was buried right beside the house where I was born. The present Chief Justice of the Supreme
Court of Newfoundland, Alex Hickman, and I are among his numerous
descendants. Another Newfoundland ancestor was Ann Tibbo, my great-
great-grandmother. This name, clearly a corruption of Thibault, came from
the Channel Islands. It constitutes my only claim to French blood.

My father died when I was just under six months old and my mother
came back to her family in Ottawa, where I was brought up. I have spent
most of my life in Ottawa and Montreal. But my mother inculcated in me
a strong sense of my Newfoundland origins, and maintained close ties
with my Newfoundland family. Accordingly I have always felt myself intensely a Newfoundlander; and in the province, which I still find it hard

to think of as part of Canada, I feel myself in my own country (where I had one ancestor in 1620) and among my own people.

This feeling is reinforced by the fact that my numerous Newfoundland relations always treat me as if I had left yesterday. That they are numerous results from the fact that Newfoundland outports, till well into my time, were often very isolated. Grand Bank, though one of the larger and more prosperous, had, till after I was grown up, almost no communication with the outside world except by vessel and telegraph. There was a road in one direction to the next town, Fortune, about four miles away, and a road up the shore in the other direction for a few miles. That was all. One consequence was an almost incredible degree of intermarriage. As my grandmother once said to me: 'When I was a girl, you had your choice. You could marry a cousin of some sort or stay single.' She and my grandfather were first cousins, both Forseys. Across the street lived my grandfather's half-sister, married to another first cousin of my grandmother's, a Hickman. When I took my New Brunswick wife to Newfoundland in 1966, one of my Grand Bank cousins lavished hospitality on us, and my wife asked me what the precise relationship was. 'Well, on three sides of the family her great-grandfather was my great-great-grandfather, and on a fourth side her great-great-grandfather was my great-great-great-grandfather.' The Chief Justice and I are related at least three times over.

My grandfather, George Robert Forsey, a rather quiet man, was something of a power in Grand Bank and Fortune. He had been a merchant, a shipbuilder, and a shipowner; when I knew him he was Resident Magistrate, Port Warden, and Customs Officer for both towns. There was no municipal government in those days. He was the civil authority. He had had very little formal education. When he was a boy the town was so poor that all the people could do for education was to hire one teacher, to whom each youngster of the large families was able to go for six months. Happily the teacher was excellent. My grandfather became a very well-read man, in both English and French. He did a good deal of business in St Pierre and was for years a subscriber to the Montreal newspaper *La Presse*. He was also very gifted mechanically (a bent, alas, of which I have inherited nothing). He built some of his own farm machinery and tile-drained his farm (where he planted apple, pear, plum, and cherry trees). He set up the first telephone line in Newfoundland, after the General Post Office in St John's, and this only seven years after the invention of the instrument. He bought the apparatus in St Pierre, wrote Alexander Graham Bell for instructions, and installed a system of three instruments, connecting his home, his shop, and his farm. The Premier, Sir James Winter, a friend, came to Grand Bank to speak the first words over them.

My grandfather was the first Master of the Masonic Lodge, in 1876. (I, though not a Mason, gave the main speech at its centennial celebration.)

He once ran for the Legislature but was narrowly defeated (a precedent I was to follow in contests for the Montreal City Council, the Ontario legislature, and the House of Commons, though my defeats were never narrow).

My grandmother was in many respects a striking contrast to her husband. He was tall, she was short. He spoke little, she was eloquent, with a vocabulary of great richness and pungency. Some of this she undoubtedly inherited from her maternal grandfather, John Symes, always known in the family simply as 'Granfer'.

Granfer was a character. An Englishman, reputed to be the son of a general, he had failed to get into the army because he was too short. He had quarrelled with his father and never referred to him except as 'Jim's father' (Jim was his brother). He held strong views on sanitation and insisted on building his house well outside the town to be sure of a pure water supply.

He was capable, when he chose, of speaking very good French. When he did not choose, he spoke it not at all. Once he sailed his vessel to St Pierre. When he arrived a French official came aboard and asked the name of the vessel. This was one of Granfer's 'no French' days, so he replied briskly: 'What's that to thee?' The official, in high dudgeon, went ashore to fetch a higher official. While he was gone, a bystander said to Granfer: 'You're in for trouble. Since you were last here there's a new law: you must have the name of your vessel and its home port painted on the stern. You haven't.' Quick as lightning Granfer got a can of paint, a brush, and a block and tackle, let himself down over the stern, and painted on it: 'What's That to Thee? Grand Bank, Newfoundland'. The higher official came aboard, full of the majesty of the French state. 'What do you mean, insulting my subordinate?' 'Insulting? I insulted no one.' 'He asked you the name of your vessel and you replied, "What's that to thee?" ' 'Well, that's the name.' 'A likely story!' 'Well, go and look.' The official rowed round in his dory and there it was!

Granfer's originality, and his trenchant style, have persisted in later generations. One of his sons decided to change the spelling of his name from Symes to Simms—a decision on which, at any hour of the day or night, my grandmother could be roused to a pitch of invective that Swift might have envied. His brother kept the original spelling. They moved to Kingsclear, New Brunswick, and opened a shop. Over the door was the sign 'Simms and Symes'. Often my grandmother, or one of my aunts, would come out with something that was pure Granfer; for example: 'Look at Edith [our servant], walking as slow as if she was driving a snail ahead of her!'

My Newfoundland family were staunch and active Methodists. My grandmother's mother, Granfer's daughter, was a saintly local Methodist whom everyone in the town called 'Grandma Forsey'. She learned to read, though never to write anything more than her own name. But she was a power in the community. True to her inheritance of Granfer's individual style, she was determined not to die in her own house. So whenever she took ill she promptly betook herself to my grandparents' home—where, in fact, she died. She left no will, merely giving instructions to my grandmother as to which of her children should get which pieces of her considerable property; and such was her imperial sway that not one of them questioned her fiat. After her death my aunts said they heard her praying for them.

Coming from such a background, my father almost inevitably felt a call to the Methodist ministry. After achieving a brilliant record at the Methodist College secondary school in St John's, he went to Mount Allison University in Sackville, New Brunswick, where he met my mother and where they both graduated in 1899, my father in Arts and Theology, my mother in Arts. My father was valedictorian. He and my mother left the reputation of being the most brilliant graduates of the university to that time.

My father had a memory like Macaulay's and his eloquence was legendary. As a youth he was exceptionally strong physically, 'a young Hercules', and he grew up in the belief that nothing was too much for his strength. He also shared the common conviction that to admit to any illness or weakness was a disgrace. This turned out to be his physical downfall. He was sent, as a 'probationer' for the ministry, to the Petites Mission, the toughest in Newfoundland. He threw himself into his work with utter abandon, neglected the most elementary precautions against illness, swam half-frozen lakes ('ponds', in our Devonshire idiom), and gave away his warm clothing to the poor (who were legion). He naturally won the devotion of his people, but he knocked out his heart and was never ordained.

After his marriage he taught briefly in Nova Scotia at Acacia Villa school (where Sir Robert Borden had been a pupil, and later a teacher). But for his health he was ordered to Mexico, where he and my mother lived for two years. His health was improving when he sent my pregnant mother north, insisting that I be born in Newfoundland. While she was away he got caught in a tropical storm, neglected to change his clothes, came down with bronchitis (to which he was subject), and knocked out his heart again. My mother came back to find him on the verge of death, and he died in the railway station in Mexico City. His sister, my Aunt Blanche, a nurse, stayed on in Mexico for the eight years required by Mexican law so that she might bring his body home to Newfoundland.

At the age of eight months I became an involuntary immigrant to Canada and began my life in Ottawa, to which my mother had taken me to live with her parents. My roots on the 'Mainland' were already deep. My mother's mother, Letitia Norton Shaw, was born in Granville Ferry in

1844. The Shaws had come from Halifax, Yorkshire, to West Barnstable, Cape Cod, in 1634. (I recently discovered I had an ancestor, a Brewster, on the *Mayflower*.) 'The great Chief Justice Shaw of Massachusetts' was one of the same family. One branch came to the Annapolis Valley of Nova Scotia in the 1760s. My grandmother was the daughter of Joseph Shaw and Mary Thorne. The Thornes had come to Massachusetts, probably from the West Country of England, in the 1630s, but had moved to New York when it was taken from the Dutch. They intermarried with the Dutch settlers, notably the Lefferts family (who had been among the original grantees of Long Island). Mary Thorne's mother, Anna Sneden, was of Dutch ancestry. The Thornes and Snedens, United Empire Loyalists all, came to the Annapolis Valley in 1783.

Joseph Shaw was a shipping and lumber man of some substance. Lured by his brother Alfred's tales of the forest riches of Gaspé, he immigrated to Canada in 1851 and set up a lumber mill and shop in Gaspé Basin. He died in Gaspé about three weeks after Confederation. In those days Gaspé had a considerable population of Irishmen and Jerseymen. Great-grandfather occasionally enjoyed teasing an old Irishman, Mr Doolan. One day he asked him: 'Mr Doolan, do you understand Latin?' 'No, Mr Shaw.' 'Do most of the people in your church understand Latin?' 'No, Mr Shaw.' 'But you have all your services in Latin.' 'Yes, Mr Shaw.' 'Well, how do you explain that?' 'Well, Mr Shaw, I'll tell ye: Latin is the only language that myshtifies the Devil.'

Great-grandmother lived on in Gaspé Basin till 1894, at least in the summers, and my mother and her brother and sisters spent their summers there till 1895. This was the beginning of what I call my 'semi-Anglican bringing up', which has made me an Anglican 'fellow-traveller' and a member and patron of the Prayer Book Society. For Great-grandmother Shaw retained a fondness for her old church, and it was her custom to take the whole family to the Methodist church in the morning, every Sunday, and to the Anglican church for Evensong. This continued well into my mother's time, and was reinforced by the fact that when my Grandfather Bowles came to Ottawa, with the Parliament of the Province of Canada in 1866, and found Sparks Street Methodist Church 'full' (all the pews already rented), he betook himself to the Anglican Church of St Alban the Martyr and stayed there till 1876, when he and my grandmother became founding members of Dominion Methodist Church. Later one of my mother's sisters married an Anglican in Montreal; they moved to Richelieu, across the Richelieu River from Chambly, and for most of my sixteen years at McGill University I spent the week-ends there and attended the old garrison church in Chambly.

Grandmother Bowles got her secondary-school education first at the Mount Allison Ladies College in Sackville in 1861, then at the Wesleyan Female Academy, Hamilton, Canada West (it was on the site of the present

Royal Connaught Hotel). During her time there she paid a visit to a school friend in Quebec City. Grandfather Bowles sat behind her in church there, and used to say he fell in love with the back of her head! She had the magnificent 'Shaw hair', though in fact it was rather the Sneden hair: Great-great-grandmother Anna Sneden Thorne died at 84 without a grey hair in her head.

My grandmother married William Cochrane Bowles in 1869. Grandfather Bowles was born in Quebec City and brought up there and in Three Rivers (as he always called it). His father, John Bowles, Anglo-Irish, came from Cork; his mother, Margaret Cochrane, from Belfast—'black Protestants' both. He grew up completely bilingual. He began his official career as a page in the Assembly of the Province of Canada in 1855, and retired in 1915 as Chief Clerk of Votes and Proceedings of the House of Commons of the Dominion of Canada. As far as I know, no one else in our history has served Parliament so long. He knew all the Fathers of Confederation well. Sir John A. Macdonald used to say to him: 'Willie, Willie, you're indispensable in this House!' For many years he doubled as secretary to Sir John Bourinot, and after Bourinot died he probably knew more about parliamentary procedure than anyone else in the country.

Just before the Great War began (so we heard long afterwards), probably during the great Naval Bill debate of 1913, a very knotty problem of procedure arose on which my grandfather found himself Athanasius *contra mundum*. Everyone else in or about the House said the point should be decided one way; my grandfather thought the other. He felt so strongly about it that he appealed to Sir Robert Borden to ask the opinion of the Clerk of the House of Commons at Westminster. 'Well, Mr Bowles, I wouldn't do it for anyone else. But in view of your long experience and vast knowledge, I will.' The reply came back: 'Mr Bowles is right.' When he retired at 74, after two paralytic strokes, Borden and Laurier paid tribute to him in the House. Borden said: 'When I came to the House of Commons in 1896, Mr Bowles was already an institution.'

I was fascinated by his stories of early days. The first time he went from Quebec to Toronto with the Parliament of the Province of Canada, the Grand Trunk Railway was finished only as far as Brockville, and he had to get out there and ride the rest of the way by stage coach in a howling blizzard. When he first came to Ottawa it had only a volunteer fire brigade, of which he was a member. When, about 1878, he built our house on Lisgar Street, just east of Bank Street (it is still there, with a false front, and the Bible House is on what was our lawn), his friends at the House of Commons said: 'Willie, why are you going out into the country to live?' It was only nine blocks from the House, but it was on the very edge of Ottawa, the first house on the street (all the others numbered from it). Even by 1911 Ottawa was still a small city. I can remember my grandparents, contemplating the census figures of that year, saying: 'Eighty-six thousand! It's getting too big.'

To be brought up in my grandfather's house was almost to be brought up within the precincts of the House of Commons. I went to the old Centre Block from the time I could walk; I went to the interim Parliament Buildings in the Victoria Museum for the three years the House sat there after the fire of 1916; I have been going to the present Centre Block ever since it was built. I have listened to innumerable debates and most of the great orators of the last seventy years and more, and I have loved every minute of it. I remember one man who was elected to Parliament in 1867 (Sir Mackenzie Bowell), half-a-dozen who were elected in 1874, a dozen in 1878, and every Prime Minister who has held office since 1894 except Sir Charles Tupper.

The Borden Naval Bill of 1913 gave me, vicariously, my first taste of the rigours of parliamentary debate. In those days there was no limit on the length of speeches, and in Committee of the Whole every Member could speak as long as he liked and as often as he liked on every clause of a bill. On the Remedial Bill of 1896 the Liberals, and dissident Conservatives, had used this form of the filibuster to kill the bill. On the Naval Bill of 1913 the Liberals could not quite repeat that (in 1913 Parliament was not within weeks of its end by the efflux of time, as in 1896), but they did their best to rival if not surpass their previous record. Finally Borden introduced the first Canadian closure rule, and in order to pass the bill kept the House sitting, day and night (barring Sundays and the dinner recess each day), for a solid fortnight. I have good reason to recall this, for it disrupted our household arrangements. My grandfather ordinarily came home to supper soon after six o'clock, then returned to the office until the House rose (which might not be till the small hours of the next morning, for there was no fixed hour of adjournment in those days). During that fortnight he got home for supper about eight o'clock, left immediately afterwards for the office, came back the next morning for breakfast (having worked incessantly all night), took two hours' sleep, then repeated the performance. All this at 72 years of age.

The old Centre Block was in many respects very different from its successor. One entered from the grounds into a vast hall, extending to the Senate in one direction, to the House of Commons in the other. In the stone floor were shields bearing the Arms of the various provinces. One shield was blank. I was informed that it had been left blank for the Arms of Newfoundland when that country came into Confederation.

I missed the fire of 1916 because I was having my appendix out. As soon as I was well enough I went up the Hill and carefully inspected the ruins. For years I kept a fist-sized piece of glass and wire, all that was left of one of the windows.

The fire was capricious. My grandfather's office, I supposed, had been reduced to ashes and rubble like the rest. But it had not. After the new building was finished I paid a call on his successor. He drew my attention to a photograph of my grandfather on the wall. He said: 'Do you notice anything odd about it?' 'Well, there is a small mark in one corner that looks as if it had been made by a drop of water.' 'Correct. And that is the only damage that was done to our office. Everything on either side was burned to a crisp. In our office not so much as a single paper was even curled.'

I have lived most of my life in the midst of political discussion, and not merely Canadian. My first political recollections are of the Mexican Revolution of 1910. My father's brother and sister were in Mexico, along with the scores of friends my father and mother had made during their two years there. So we were deeply concerned. One result is that even now, if I were wakened in the middle of the night, I could reel off instantly the names of all the leading figures on both sides.

Then there were British and Irish politics. My grandfather was of course intensely interested in both, and I have the liveliest memories of the Third Home Rule Bill, the Irish Volunteers, the Ulster Volunteers, John Redmond, Sir Edward Carson, F.E. Smith (the 'Galloper', later Lord Birkenhead), the Curragh mutiny, the Ulster Covenant, the Mountjoy Arch, the gunrunning. I remember also, vividly, the two Balkan Wars of 1912-13.

My mother and my grandfather gave me my first lessons in constitutional government. They must have been superb simplifiers, for I have never had to unlearn anything they told me. Mother told me what a Cabinet was the morning after the election of 1911. My grandfather answered countless questions with unequalled clarity, and, I may add, wit: he was not Irish for nothing!

My Grandfather Bowles' main interests, apart from the House, were his magnificent garden (for which he won several prizes) and Dominion Methodist Church, where he held several of the chief offices. It was then a central institution in Ottawa, counting among its members and adherents such notable figures as Sir Clifford Sifton and the Honourable Frank Cochrane. The church officers all wore frock coats or Prince Alberts, and top hats.

Those were the days of great preaching and great preachers, and Dominion Church provided an outstanding example in Dr James Henderson. He was an extraordinarily handsome man, tall, with a great mane of white hair and a patriarchal white beard, a magnificent voice, a mastery of the Scriptures and of Methodist theology; and he filled the church (which held well over a thousand people) morning and evening. 'Filled' is the word. The doors had to be locked and police stationed at them to keep people out. Under an earlier minister the building was the scene of a series of revival meetings by two other great Methodist preachers, Crossley and Hunter. Among those who attended were Sir John and Lady Macdonald, and my grandfather had the task of reserving, and guarding, a pew for them.

All the family were great readers, and my mother and grandfather read aloud superbly and tirelessly: Dickens, Thackeray, Galsworthy, Arnold Bennett, British political biography, E.O. Somerville's and Martin Ross's Irish stories, Joseph Lincoln's New England stories, and much else I have now forgotten. The family also loved the theatre and seldom missed seeing, at the Russell, the great British actors and actresses whom the Governors-General brought to Ottawa. I was too young for most of these; but I did see a performance by Harry Lauder (on one of his 'farewell tours'), Maude Adams in Barrie's *A Kiss for Cinderella*, and Sarah Bernhardt in an evening of short scenes. I even did a bit of acting myself: as the boy Shakespeare in *Master Will of Stratford* (put on by the Junior Drama League for the Shakespeare Tercentenary), and in a French school play, where I acted the part of a veterinary surgeon to the accompaniment of much hilarity when, though notorious for my shyness and ill-success with girls, I had to kiss the prettiest girl in the class.

I was rather more at home at the House of Commons, where I heard the Anglo-French War Mission heads, Arthur Balfour and René Viviani, speak and where I shook hands with the celebrated Captain (by then Major) Dreyfus.

I lived with my grandparents and my mother at 311 Lisgar Street till 1922, and had all my schooling within four blocks of it: first at the Normal Model School (Elgin and Lisgar), then at the Ottawa Collegiate Institute (now Lisgar Collegiate, Cartier and Lisgar), which until 1922 was the only public high school in the city.

I had a very happy childhood, marred only by a long series of 'bilious attacks', finally diagnosed as appendicitis and cured by the first of my seventeen operations. In retrospect I think I was spoiled. My Grandfather Bowles was a second father to me, and a most indulgent one. My grandmother and my two aunts were so devoted that at the various summer places we visited I was called 'the baby with the four mothers'. In general I was very biddable. But I had (and still have) a violent temper. My mother used to din into me, 'Greater is he that ruleth his spirit than he that taketh a city'; and various treats conditionally promised were withheld because I had yielded to the Devil's seduction into my besetting sin.

We never had a cottage. We went to a different summer resort, or to relatives and friends, every year down to the outbreak of the war. Because the House of Commons had then no fixed hour of adjournment, and often sat far into the night and on into the small hours of next day, Grandfather Bowles could ordinarily take two months off in the summer, unless there was a 'summer session' (words that fell on our ears like a knell). So almost every year off we went, the whole family, on July 1 and stayed away till the end of August.

By 1911 Mother had entered the civil service, so the family was reduced to my grandparents, Aunt Hazel, and myself. We went first to Yarmouth, Nova Scotia, where one of the attractions was the Canadian cruiser *Niobe*. Her presence was perhaps not unconnected with the Dominion general election. Everybody in town looked forward to going aboard. But the *Niobe* ran on the rocks. We moved on to the Milford Lakes, and then to Annapolis Royal. We saw the Temperance Hall great-grandfather had built, and met a few old people who remembered my grandmother as a child. One of them greatly amused my grandfather (who was of some importance in the small Ottawa of those days) by saying: 'There goes Dolly Shaw's husband.'

At Annapolis also I heard my first political speech: Sir Wilfrid Laurier, from the back of his private car. Of the speech, alas, I remember nothing. What I do recall is the reception it got. Annapolis was a hive of Conservatives, and when Sir Wilfrid finished, from away back in the crowd came one feeble, barely audible, 'Hurrah!' My grandfather was startled: 'Letitia, I've never seen anything like this with Sir Wilfrid. They're going to be defeated' — as indeed the Liberals were, resoundingly.

In 1912 Mother and I went to Newfoundland to stay for three weeks with my Forsey grandparents and my aunts in Grand Bank. We took one Reid Newfoundland Company steamer from North Sydney, Cape Breton (where we had a short visit with Mother's cousins, the Salters), to Port-aux-Basques, then another steamer along the south coast of Newfoundland, landing and taking on passengers and cargo at a series of outports: Grand Bruit (pronounced 'Grand Brit', where a stream hurled itself into the harbour in a magnificent waterfall), Rose Blanche, Rencontre ('Ren-counter'), François ('Fransways'), Barrachois ('Barrashways'), Hermitage, Pushthrough, Harbour Breton. The voyage took several days, and at the head of Fortune Bay we saw some splendid fjords. Grand Bank lies at the southern end of the Bay, almost at the tip of the Burin Peninsula, about thirty miles from St Pierre.

I had a wonderful time. Grandfather Forsey gave me a beautiful model of a Newfoundland fishing schooner, about a yard long and two feet high to the top of the mainmast. He also taught me the names of all the parts and how to box the compass. One of my aunts was the postmistress and telegraph operator (the post office had been in the family for a whole generation, and my aunts and uncle had been sworn in as children, as the office was at first in the family home). This aunt taught me the Morse code, though I don't think she ever let me touch the telegraph keys. Of this learning, I am sorry to say, no vestige remains. My grandmother admitted me to her garden, where none of my aunts dared set foot, and fed me superb 'white' strawberries, almost as large as small apples, topped off with Devonshire cream. We had our own cows, and one of my aunts operated the De Laval cream separator. The garden supplied also gooseberries and currants, and of course vegetables and flowers. I remember especially the white roses, and the peonies on either side of the front door.

We had neither electricity nor running water (I don't think anyone in the town had), and there were no motor cars. We kept two horses, a black one for driving and a white one for the cart that brought home the hay from our various scattered fields. Just short of Fortune, the nearest town, there was Clawbonny, a large, well-wooded property my grandfather had bought at an auction when his children were small.

Clawbonny had been their delight, and it was mine. That was where the orchard was, and the stream, with its high waterfall and its pool, deep enough to swim in. It was also the delight of the white horse, who, the moment he got there, had to be unharnessed instantly so that he could roll without taking the cart with him. Just at the entrance gate, looking out over the Bay, was Strawberry Hill. When my father lay dying in Mexico, he said to Aunt Blanche, his nurse-sister: 'Bury me on Strawberry Hill, facing the Atlantic.' He was indeed buried there, but the body was later moved to the graveyard beside our house, where it now lies with the bodies of my grandfather and of old Jonathan Hickman and other relatives.

Grand Bank in those days did a flourishing trade in salt cod, mainly to Oporto, Portugal. The cod, laid out to dry on the stony beaches, were handled entirely by women in picturesque sun-bonnets, of a shape effectively mimicked by one of our small yellow Newfoundland orchids, popularly called 'old women's bonnets'.

During our three weeks, one day held some excitement when the Governor, Sir Ralph Shrapney Williams, was paying an official visit to the South Coast. Of course my grandfather had to give him an official welcome, with a speech in the Masonic Hall, almost across the street from our house. The turn-out was smaller than might have been expected because almost none of the women came; it was washing day, a day of overmastering importance from which not a moment could be spared.

We invited Sir Ralph and Lady Williams and their staff to lunch, but they returned to the official yacht and ate while they sailed along the coast to Fortune. We had a hurried lunch at home then drove pell-mell to Fortune, where my grandfather made a second speech of welcome, moving our family, and the Governor and his party, to some quiet amusement.

At the end of the three weeks Mother and I set off for Canada. My Bowles grandparents, and my Aunt Hazel, had gone to Prince Edward Island, where I was now to join them. (Mother's statutory summer leave was over.) Grandfather Bowles met us in Moncton, with my grandmother's sister and brother-in-law, Aunt Molly and Uncle George Trueman. Uncle George was of course one of the old New Brunswick Truemans, a family that has given Canada two university presidents. Years before he had suffered from some internal ailment, for which his doctor told him the remedy was to get a job where he would have to do a great deal of walking. So he got a post as conductor on the Intercolonial Railway. The treatment worked, and he went on to become station-master in Moncton. (Another great-uncle by marriage, Joseph Salter, had been the first mayor of that city, before moving to North Sydney.) Uncle George had retired in 1911, but he was still a power in the local offices of the Intercolonial.

In those days there was no ferry to the Island. You had to take a lo-cal train from Moncton to Pointe-du-Chêne, and a steamer from there to Summerside, and then, to get to Charlottetown, the narrow-gauge Prince Edward Island Railway. When we got to the station in Moncton there was the local train to Pointe-du-Chêne waiting for us. But it was a most dilapidated-looking old scarecrow. Uncle George gave it one look, then summoned his successor: 'Those cars won't do at all. My brother-in-law is a most important man in Ottawa, a high official of the Government. Take those cars off and put on some decent ones!' 'Yes, Mr Trueman.' I was tremendously impressed by this evidence of Uncle George's still-imperial sway.

We passed a tranquil summer at Stanhope, just outside Charlottetown.

Mother was a gifted artist. When she was at Mount Allison the head of the Art School, John Hammond, RCA, wanted her to give up her university work and become a professional painter. When I was six she went into the civil service, at first into the Census Branch, but soon after into the library of the Geological Survey and the Victoria Museum as cataloguer. When her chief became a VAD (Voluntary Aid Detachment) worker in the First World War, Mother became, for two years, acting librarian. When her chief returned — but only to marry one of the geologists — mother applied for the librarianship. The Library Committee, the two Directors, and the Deputy Minister all recommended her. But the Civil Service Commission insisted she must write the examination that was used for the post of librarian of the Public Archives, including papers in French, German, and Italian. The French was easy, the German easier. Of Italian she knew nothing, but in three weeks she mastered it, in spite of excruciating neuritis, and topped the list for the whole country.

This, she thought, meant she'd get the librarianship of the Survey and the Museum forthwith. Months passed; nothing happened. One Sunday, Tom Tweedie, MP, an old Mount Allison friend, came to tea. 'Well, Florence, have you got the promotion?' 'No, Tom, I haven't.' 'What! I thought the examination had settled it.' 'So did I, but it didn't.' 'Humph. I'll have to see to this.'

Tom Tweedie was a power in the Conservative Party who had once re-fused Cabinet office. (He later became Chief Justice of Alberta.) He went to see Dr Roche, Chairman of the Civil Service Commission, and put the facts of mother's case before him. Roche said he could do nothing at the moment. 'Very well. I shall sit outside until you make the appointment.' Roche laughed, and Tweedie sat down in the outer office. He was about six feet four in height and weighed over 200 pounds. It would have taken a derrick to move him.

After some time Roche appeared. 'What, Tom! Are you still here?' 'I am. I meant exactly what I said. Here I sit till you make that appointment.' This scene was re-enacted several times. Finally Roche caved in.

Mother became very deaf. I realize now how much she had to struggle against, though deafness never impaired her efficiency, or affected in the slightest her sunny disposition or soured her wit.

Aunt Hazel, the youngest of the family, was from 1913 its mainstay. She had a fine mezzo-soprano voice and had studied at the New England Conservatory of Music in Boston, but severe eye trouble put an end to any hope of a professional career. The doctors said she must absolutely avoid ever getting overtired. My grandfather's strokes, my grandmother's weak heart, my illnesses, and Mother's being away at her office most of the day—six days a week in those times—meant that the whole burden of running the house, and looking after her parents and me, fell on Aunt Hazel. Except for her eyes, she had an iron constitution, and executive ability enough to run a large corporation. She not only ignored her disability but came very near denying it. She was Mother's ears, Mother was her eyes, especially after Mother retired from the Geological Survey.

Aunt Hazel was determined that Mother should hear everything; when she didn't, Aunt Hazel repeated what was said, even if it was only an exclamation from me that, having mislaid my gloves, I had now found them. This produced in me a determination that if ever I got deaf I'd let a great deal go because much of what everybody said was just not worth repeating. This resolve, to which I have steadfastly adhered, has the happy by-product of curbing my garrulousness. When I can't hear I just smile—unless I have some reason to think that the person speaking to me has asked me to agree that, let us say, Hitler was a great benefactor of mankind.

Aunt Hazel would not tolerate any reference to disability or advancing age. Once a professor writing a history of the Geological Survey wanted to interview Mother. I warned him that he should ring up beforehand because she was 89 and was sometimes more tired than at other times; also, that he must speak out, as she was deaf. He rang my aunt and said: 'I understand that Mrs Forsey is 89.' My aunt replied, with dignity: '*We do not* discuss our age.' 'And I believe Mrs Forsey is rather deaf.' 'My sister wears a hearing aid.' If anyone warned Aunt Hazel that either of them might trip over some obstacle, she would reply frigidly: '*We do not* trip.'

Aunt Sybil, the middle one of the three Bowles sisters, was a charmer. She radiated sweetness and light, *élan vital*, boundless generosity. I spent many holidays in her home, and during my years at McGill she and her family were my sheet-anchor. Her wedding, in 1909, was one of the most memorable events of my early childhood. We had superb weather, the garden was ablaze with hundreds of flowers, everything was done in style. I was a page, and a young third cousin was the flower girl. Great-aunt Molly Trueman came from Moncton and after the wedding held the young men enchanted with her wit.

I got on well at school, where I had excellent teachers. French I had from the beginning, in the Normal Model School. In high school the teaching I got fitted me to enter second-year French at McGill, in a class conducted entirely in French by the late Associate Chief Justice Tyndale, a master of the language. In competition with two students who were half French Canadian, I headed the year.

In my five years at the Ottawa Collegiate—where my mother, her brother and two sisters had all been pupils—I rarely got less than a first class in any subject, and usually led the class, winning the General Proficiency Medal in each of my first four years. In the Fifth Form (Grade 13), which I did in one year instead of the customary two, I narrowly missed the General Proficiency Medal, which was won by a brilliant girl in her second year in the Form. I headed the list in Classics (which I loved), English, French, and barely missed the top mark in History. These subjects came easily to me. At Mathematics I was a duffer, but I slogged hard enough to get a First Class in Algebra, Geometry, and Trigonometry. I wrote thirteen papers and got a First Class in the lot. I believe no one else in the province had done it up to then, and it soon became impossible, as no one could write thirteen papers in a single year. The credit belongs wholly to a set of superlative teachers: 'Col' Stothers in History; Mr Hardy and Mr Mabee in Classics; Mr Gilchrist, Mr Mann, and Miss Kellock in English; Miss Muir and Mr Latour in French; Mr Norris, Mr G.B. Stewart and Miss Tomkins in Mathematics; Mr Smeaton, Mr F.A. Stewart, and Mr MacKay in Science. Their standards were stiff, but they took endless trouble over us. Mr Hardy, giving 85 per cent in Greek, would comment 'Satisfactory'. Mr Gilchrist read every essay with meticulous care, filled the pages with red ink, and made us rewrite the whole thing, with the corrections. Miss Kellock (a sister of Mr Justice Kellock of the Supreme Court of Canada) did not use red ink or make us rewrite but was equally thorough. The highest mark I ever got from her was 78 per cent and I felt it to be the equivalent of a gold medal. Such merit as my writing may have it owes in no small measure to 'Gilly' Gilchrist, 'Hank' Mann, and 'Corn Flakes' Kellock (a nickname for which I confess responsibility).

My most memorable teacher at the Collegiate was the redoubtable Miss Tomkins ('Sis') in Algebra. In person she was the schoolmarm of cartoons:

tall, gaunt, angular, hair drawn tightly back, steel-rimmed spectacles. She had, in the Irish phrase, 'a tongue that would clip a hedge'. But she was a teacher of genius, and she took infinite pains. Her comments on poor work, except when an Inspector was present, could be blistering, though I think they never blistered. But it was at least chastening, when I made a mistake with a problem on the blackboard, to have 'Sis' glare at me, one eyebrow raised, the other lowered, and say: 'Murder! Would you look at that for a solution! Get away out of that, you lunatic, and rub that abomination off the board!' When the Inspector came there was a sea-change: blushes and twitters, and: 'Now, Forsey, I don't think that's *quite* the solution.' She was respected, feared, and loved. I can remember only one pupil who ever resented even her most scathing comments.

One subject that never failed to rouse her was the alleged superiority of the masculine mind in mathematics. Once our class gave her a golden opportunity. We were a mixed class, half boys, half girls. On this particular day, when we reported on our homework, it soon became evident that the boys had not distinguished themselves. Sis's eyes lit up. 'How many boys got all their homework right?' A mere handful stood up. 'How many girls?' Nearly all stood up. 'These superior male creatures! They're such wonderful mathematicians! We poor dust and dirt beneath their lordly feet! And now LOOK at them!' *Pax cineribus.*

Did I ever have any fun, any pleasures? I did indeed, lots. For one thing the family was very hospitable and we had a constant succession of friends coming in for meals, the evening, or for a few days (from Montreal, the Maritimes, Newfoundland, even occasionally from Toronto). They were of all kinds, all ages. My grandmother, of course, had her 'day' when she received callers — everyone did. Then every Sunday evening people would come in after church for hymns and other sacred music and refreshments (strictly teetotal, of course). By the time I was in high school I was subjected (that is the word) to dancing lessons, and to dances, which I loathed. I was a miserable dancer; I was scared stiff of girls and I bored them stiff. I also took piano lessons, which produced no lasting effect. I had a good ear; I enjoyed listening to others playing or singing. (I even composed a few melodies myself.) Like all good Methodists I sang hymns lustily, and generally in tune, a good many of them without the aid of the hymn-book. (I still have a repertoire of about forty hymns — half of them, learned in more recent years, in French.) But I never really mastered the art of reading music. I remained in music almost illiterate, though until my ears went back on me I greatly enjoyed listening to concerts of classical music, and to opera — especially Wagner, that stupendous genius.

I kept moderately fit and had a good deal of fun bicycling, snow-shoeing, skiing, playing tennis, and swimming. Grandfather Forsey gave me a bicycle in the fall of 1912 and I can still remember its number: 417263. It accompanied me to Oxford in 1926. Snowshoeing I did mainly at Rockcliffe (which in those days had very few houses) and (I think) at Fairy Lake, in what is now the Gatineau Park. Skiing was at Rockcliffe, tennis in Ottawa South. Rockcliffe and Britannia were the two standard places for recreation. Both were reached by streetcar. The Rockcliffe line went clear out to the Rifle Ranges, though after some years the main line ended at Cloverdale Road, where one could transfer to a small car that ran the rest of the way. The line to Britannia—where there was a fine beach, a dock for the river steamers, and bathing rooms at the end of the pier—ran for miles and miles through farms and pastureland, past the summer resorts of Woodroffe and Westboro.

There were special cars for summer, and extra-special cars for the Britannia line, all manufactured by the Ottawa Car Company on Albert Street. Most of the summer cars were open on both sides, with heavy leather thongs along the sides to protect the passengers, and running-boards along which the conductor came with the fare-box. At the end of the line the conductor and the motorman changed ends, the leather thongs changed sides, and the car went back to the other end of the line. The Britannia cars, in contrast to all the others, were long, and enclosed on both sides like the ordinary cars in winter. In summer the Britannia cars were glorious affairs, bright red and yellow, and they set a thrilling pace for the crowds of children who went to Britannia Beach for birthday parties and Sunday School picnics. The special winter cars were named the Duke and Duchess of York because they had been built for, and used by, the future King George V and Queen Mary when they visited Ottawa during the reign of Edward VII. They were done up in style, the windows decorated with the royal initials etched in the glass.

We were heavily dependent on streetcars to get anywhere beyond easy walking distance from Lisgar Street. Of course we walked to church, and to the House of Commons, and to Sparks Street and the part of Bank Street between Lisgar and Wellington, and to the two schools; and we took a horse-drawn cab when we went to Government House. Otherwise it was the streetcar. We never had a motorcar; very few people had one when I first remember the city. Those who did had to be very rich, and very venturesome, because the cars scared the horses and often led to runaways. In winter, of course, sleighs replaced carriages and delivery wagons—sleighs with magnificent buffalo robes to keep one warm, drawn along streets enclosed by great banks of snow, the horses decorated with the traditional bells of the nursery song. It was all wonderfully picturesque and stimulating. Much of this lasted till my children's time.

Incidentally, Ottawa was the first Canadian city to have electric street-cars. All the experts had said it couldn't be done in a Canadian winter. But Ahearn and Soper—the ubiquitous owners of three Ottawa Services, plus the Ottawa Car Manufacturing Company—did it.

Two of the tourist attractions of Ottawa in those days were the Chaudière Falls and J.R. Booth, the lumber magnate. My grandfather was once able to display the two simultaneously. He had been told to show the sights to a visiting VIP. When he asked the visitor what he most wanted to see he was told 'J.R. Booth'. Grandfather got a cab and drove across the bridge to the Falls, where a crew of men were working. The visitor asked: 'Well, where's Mr Booth?' 'You see those men down there on the logs?' 'Yes.' 'Which would you say was the roughest and worst dressed of the lot?' 'That one' (pointing). 'That's Mr Booth.'

Many years later my wife and I were visiting friends in Foster, Quebec, not far from Waterloo, where Booth was born. A man passed the window. Our hostess said: 'You come from Ottawa; you must know, or have heard of, J.R. Booth.' We said we had. ' That's one of his family, a cousin of some sort. J.R. was the only one of the whole crew who ever amounted to anything. They all were notoriously "poor pay". When J.R. was in his teens, he went into a shop in Waterloo to buy a hammer or a saw or some other simple tool. He wanted credit. The answer was, "Not to a Booth." J.R. left, vowing never to darken the door again till he could buy the shop; which eventually he did.'

Booth is immortalized in Booth Street. A good many other Ottawa lumber tycoons have given their names to streets; for example, Rochester, Gilmour, MacLaren, and Bronson. Other streets commemorate pioneer land-owners or their households. The Sparks family are said to have named not only Sparks Street, but various others after members of the family or even after family servants. This perhaps accounts for Anne Street (which became Gladstone Avenue), Maria Street (which became Laurier Avenue), Biddy Street (which became Lisgar). Other British statesmen besides Gladstone received this tribute, notably Rosebery and Chamberlain (not Neville, but his father). So did the Royal Family: the Dukes of Sussex, Clarence, Cambridge, Gloucester, York; Queen Charlotte; the Prince Consort; the King of Würtemberg (usually misspelled); the Cobourg family. Lisgar, of course, was named for a Governor-General.

All this brings back to me the old Ottawa railway stations of my boyhood. The oldest was just off Sussex Street, not far from where the City Hall now stands. It was the only station when my grandfather arrived in Ottawa in 1866. It lasted, at least as a freight-shed, till well into my time. On the site of the present Conference Centre was the Grand Trunk station, originally belonging to the Canada Atlantic, J.R. Booth's line from Parry Sound to Côteau Junction (where it joined the main line of the Grand Trunk). This old wooden station, which I remember, was replaced by the present building when I was six or seven. It, and the Château Laurier, were part of the great expansion of the Grand Trunk under Mr Hayes, who was drowned on the *Titanic*. Till very recently it was still possible to make out, over the door of the building, graven in the stone, the words

'Grand Trunk Central Station'. The CPR station, a dismal white brick affair, was on Broad Street, just off Albert. The day came when the CPR leased Track 3 in the Central Station for its afternoon train to Montreal. Gradually it borrowed other tracks, and finally the station became the Union Station. The cross-town tracks of the Canada Atlantic passed just behind the Victoria Museum, at the end of Elgin Street, and, just west of Elgin Street, there was a special platform for unloading sheep.

I have included these things among my youthful pleasures because they were part of the framework of my happiness for the first eighteen years of my life.

2

McGill

With my Ontario honour matriculation I entered second-year Arts at McGill University in the fall of 1922. McGill was a natural choice. Mother's sister and her husband (Sybil and Ernest Latter) lived in Montreal, and I stayed with them for my first year at the university. Mother had a number of cousins there, and the city had always been our metropolis: we went there shopping, we even went there for holidays. It never occurred to us to go to Toronto.

The Montreal, and the McGill, I knew as a student from 1922 to 1926, and as a teacher from 1929 to 1941, were of course both much smaller than they are today. Montreal was the largest city in Canada, but when I first knew it, long before I went to McGill, it was not more than about half the size it is now. McGill, however, was one of the 'big' universities, especially by comparison with those in the Maritimes, which were the ones I compared it with.

The Montreal I knew was 'English' Montreal — in numbers, though not in power, far the lesser of the 'two solitudes'. In my years at McGill I scarcely ever set foot in the other. I had no occasion to, nor as far as I could tell had most of the 'English'. I belonged to a generation that remembered when it was the custom to alternate the mayoralty between English and French. I was there, visiting my aunt and uncle, when the custom ended. In 1913 it was the English turn, and they put up Major George Washington Stevens, afterwards Commissioner of the Saar Territory. The French put up Médéric Martin. He won, hands down.

I had been brought up as very much part of the old order. My maternal grandfather's uncle-by-marriage had built one of the first houses on St Catherine Street West. (I think it is there still, turned into a shop.) One of my grandfather's cousins had a beautiful old stone house on Dorchester Street, where my mother and I visited her when I was about four years old. Dorchester was then in the last days of its glory as *the* residential street of the city. (It has now been renamed Boulevard René Lévesque, a sad reward for Lord Dorchester's services to French Canadians.) This cousin moved later to Sherbrooke Street, next door to the Ritz-Carlton Hotel. In my student days she regaled me with stories of her early youth, when there was a fence across the top of Beaver Hall Hill, and young couples used to go courting in the woods where Christ Church Cathedral now stands, and people shook their heads over the folly of poor Henry Morgan, moving his shop from St James Street north to St Catherine. The artist John Hammond, a family friend, described to me how he had witnessed the burning of the old Parliament Buildings in 1849.

In my own time it was Sherbrooke Street that was *the* residential street, one of the great streets of the world. It was lined by the stone mansions of the rich and powerful, or at least those of them who did not live in the legendary Square Mile, which ran from Sherbrooke Street up the slope of the 'Mountain' to the edge of Mountain Park, and from Guy Street to an eastern limit that I have forgotten, and was crowned by Sir Hugh Allan's house, Ravenscrag (now the Neurological Institute). Ravenscrag had a special suite of rooms reserved for visiting members of the Royal Family. (The old Montreal English families were as much at home in London as in Montreal, and moved easily from one to the other as the fancy took them.) Lady Allan, after one very large party to which she had bidden an unusually motley array of guests, is said to have remarked to a friend: 'My dear, there were people from *Westmount* there!' Westmount was no doubt very respectable. But it was not the Square Mile, or the Sherbrooke Street of Sir William Van Horne.

McGill, when I was an undergraduate, had about 3,000 students. My graduating class had about 300 members. Dalhousie, the largest of the Maritime universities, had in those days, we were told, about 800 students. The University of New Brunswick, as late as 1941, had only two buildings, one of which included the President's residence. I know: my wife and I stayed there, guests of Larry MacKenzie and his wife. (Larry was an old friend of my wife's at Dalhousie.) By the time I got my UNB honorary degree in 1962, UNB had a graduating class as big as mine had been at McGill, and an imposing array of new buildings.

McGill itself, when I entered it, had several buildings: Arts, Engineering, Physics, Biology, and of course Medicine, and the Royal Victoria College (the women's residence) are the ones I remember. I had very little to do with any of them except the Arts building. Its exterior was very much the same as it is now. Its interior was very different. It was, I think, the original university building (except for the western end, Moyse Hall, named after a Dean of not very long before my time). The floors were wooden. So were the staircases, which moved gently up and down when more than a handful of people trod them. Some of the corridors were so narrow that even very thin people could pass each other only if one of them squeezed his back against one of the walls. The Principal's office, at the east end, had been Sir William Dawson's residence, and still had the remains of the speaking tube through which he had ordered the servants to bring up his meals or perform other domestic duties.

We loved our city, and our university, and were proud of both.

I had stated my intention of being a candidate for the Methodist ministry. But a B.A. was a prerequisite, and I enrolled in Honours Economics and Political Science, with half-Honours in English. I had a successful three years, winning in each year the top scholarship in Economics and Political Science and a scholarship in Economics and English. At graduation I won the Allen Oliver gold medal and a graduate fellowship in Economics and Political Science. I was valedictorian, president of the Economics Club and the History Club, vice-president of the Newfoundland Club and the Conservative Club. I then had a year of graduate study, writing my MA thesis (*magna cum laude*, if my memory serves) on economic and social aspects of the Nova Scotia coal industry. I ended my McGill student career by winning one of the two Rhodes scholarships from Quebec. Looking back on it I wonder why, with such a start, I have accomplished so little.

At McGill, as at Ottawa Collegiate, I was blessed with exceptional teachers. Stephen Leacock, head of the department of Economics and Political Science, was one of the most brilliant men I have ever known. He could have reached the top in any career he chose. He was a magnificent public speaker, a master of English, French, and German. If a foreign student had difficulty with English, Leacock could instantly summarize a theory or an argument in French or German. He never, to my recollection, used a note. His knowledge was encyclopaedic, and he had an unsurpassed gift for opening our minds, awakening our critical faculties, shaking us up. He was an ardent Conservative and Imperialist (though also, like Sir Sam Hughes, a fierce Canadian nationalist), but never a propagandist in the classroom.

His only fault was an occasional easy-goingness about poor work by students from what would now be called the low-income group. I remember one case that occurred after I had joined the staff. A Jewish student, a thoroughly nice boy and a hard worker, had failed in an Economics paper. Leacock set the supplemental paper and asked me to mark it. It was abysmally bad. One question, on Adam Smith's theories of wages, produced a copperplate half-page under that heading, which contained not one syllable with even the faintest relation to Adam Smith, to wages, or to theories of any kind on any subject. (Like all my best stories, this is incredible, but true.) Of course I ploughed him. Leacock was devastated: 'Such a nice boy! And he's had such a hard struggle to get here at all! He's hardly had money for shoe-leather.' Leacock, I think, would have passed him. I couldn't. It was perhaps a case of Bernard Shaw's 'hard, kind hearts and soft, cruel ones' (though Leacock would not have been impressed by any quotation from 'that elderly jackass', as I once heard him call Shaw).

Leacock had some endearing personal quirks. His gown was a thing of tatters. For years his watch-chain hung in two pieces, joined by a large safety-pin, from which hung his house door-key. In response to a question (not from me), he said he kept the key there because otherwise he forgot it and got locked out. He insisted that members of the staff wear dinner jackets at meetings of the students' Political Economy Club. But one sloppy spring evening he appeared with the regulation jacket and stiff shirt front, a black tie (not in a bow but simply hanging down at each end), and a pair of loud check grey trousers turned up at the ends to keep them out of the slush. I am sure he had been interrupted while dressing and had simply forgotten to change the trousers.

His lectures were eloquent, but serious. There was some fun (inevitably), but not much. The fun came at other times; for example, at meetings of the Political Economy Club. I think the most hilarious thing he ever wrote was for a meeting of that body in 1936. Whether it was ever published I do not know. In December 1935 thirteen senior professors, some of them of international reputation, had received a letter from the administration. Leacock was one of them. The letter read: 'Dear Professor —— , Under the statutes of the university, members of the staff retire at age 65 [this was true, but it had not been enforced for years], the university reserving the right to retain the services of those it considered of sufficient value. You will retire June 1, 1936. Yours truly,—— , Secretary, Board of Governors.' Not one syllable of thanks, appreciation, regret, or even of common politeness. Leacock was furious. A *Montreal Star* reporter asked if he had any comments. 'Yes, and I shall spend eternity shouting them down to the Governors.' Sir Edward Beatty, Chairman of the Board, was a personal friend. He wrote Leacock: 'Dear Stephen, I cannot understand why you are so upset.'

Leacock did better than shout his comments down from high heaven. He wrote 'The Executions for Senility at McGill University', and read it aloud to us, with tears of laughter streaming down his cheeks. Each of the Governors' victims was celebrated in turn. I can remember, alas, only one passage, on Professor Walter, head of the department of German: 'The old Walter was accused of putting on a German play. His plea that it was not really German was thrown out, on sworn evidence of one witness that he had distinctly heard the words "Ein Glas Bier" '. The whole performance went with a roar, the audience helpless with mirth.

Leacock's second-in-command, and later successor as head of the department, was J.C. Hemmeon, as different a man as could well be imagined, but devoted to Leacock and for many years doing much of his administrative work. A Nova Scotian from Wolfville, descended from a Hessian soldier who settled in the province after the Revolutionary War, Hemmeon had none of Leacock's spellbinding eloquence or wit. His was a Harvard So-cratic method. He too made us think. Politically he was at the opposite pole from Leacock: a socialist (I have even heard him call himself a Communist), but in fact far too intense an individualist to belong to any party. He can perhaps be best described as an agnostic Christian nationalist anarchist, a true skeptic.

Hemmeon seldom went public. His battles, and they were corkers, were with the administration: with at least one Dean and a succession of Principals. A.E. Morgan and Cyril James he detested, Lewis Douglas he despised. When Morgan offered him the deanship, he declined. 'Why?' 'Because I do not wish to hold any such position while you are Principal.' 'Well, that's frank!' 'It was meant to be.' 'Whom would you suggest?' 'What about Adair [a brilliant historian]?' 'Dr Hemmeon, have you ever met a ruder man than Professor Adair?' 'Yes, and he's sitting opposite me at this moment.' When Hemmeon resigned as chairman of the Library Committee because he couldn't endure James, James started on a eulogy. He got out part of one sentence, when Hemmeon interrupted: 'Stop! Stop right there! I know what you think of me, and you know what I think of you. Stop!'

He took retirement a year early on full pension — an arrangement as ar-dently desired by the Principal as by Hemmeon himself. In Wolfville he lived alone, except for his dog, in a house surrounded by a steel fence sunk in concrete, the gate firmly locked. He had been greatly loved by his old students, but rare indeed was the one who passed that portal. Carl Goldenberg repeatedly, when he was in Nova Scotia, wrote asking for a chance to see him. He was always put off on various pleas, some of them wholly fictitious, as mutual friends in Wolfville told me. (So was I, except once when my wife was with me and he actually had us to dinner.) Finally Goldenberg went to Wolfville and telephoned. Hemmeon's unmistakable voice answered: 'Oh, I'm so sorry he's away. He'll be very disappointed to have missed you. I've often heard him speak of you.'

The third man in the department was J.P. Day, an excellent teacher and a wit who supplemented his lectures on money and banking with lively sketches on the blackboard, illustrating, for example, 'A Run on the Bank'. He enjoyed jokes on himself. Once he went to Moncton to speak, arriving just about noon. The first thing that caught his eye in the hotel was a sign: 'Dr J.P. Day, of McGill University, will speak at 8:00 o'clock on the Gold Standard.' A second line added: 'The Bore will arrive at noon.' A man of imposing presence (in an academic procession he eclipsed even Sir Arthur Currie), he was quintessentially English. In the spring he left on the first boat for England, in the fall he returned on the last from that country. He never officially recognized the Canadian dollar. He always spoke of the fee for an extension lecture as 'three guineas', not fifteen dollars.

For a few years we had a fourth professor in the department, John Farthing, son of the Bishop of Montreal. Jack was a genius. In both Economics and Political Philosophy he had no equal. He worked for years on a massive reformulation of economic theory and on a book on political philosophy. Neither ever saw the light of day, for Jack was a perfectionist. If, arriving at chapter ten, he noticed a sentence in chapter one that, on second thoughts, left unsaid something that suddenly seemed essential, he started all over again. I wonder what became of his MSS. He probably destroyed most of them. His health broke down, and after his death in 1954 Judith Robinson and Margaret Blackstock collected fragments he had written, and letters, and published them under the title *Freedom Wears a Crown*. It is a small masterpiece on constitutional monarchy.

In the Department of English I also had the good fortune to study under a remarkable group of teachers. The head of the department was Paul Lafleur, one of a trio of brilliant French-Canadian Protestant brothers. Eugène was the leading Canadian constitutional lawyer of his day, Henri the greatest heart specialist, and Paul was probably the greatest scholar of English and comparative literature. His learning was almost intimidating. He began his first lecture to the second-year class, of which I was a member, with: 'It is, of course, quite impossible to have any real understanding of English literature without a thorough knowledge of French, German, Italian, and Spanish literature, to say nothing of Latin and Greek' — all of which Paul had. This might have scared us stiff. But Lafleur's lectures held us enthralled. Every word was perfect, every sentence immaculate; the whole delivered with a fire I have never heard equalled. He read aloud better than anyone I have ever known. I can still hear his voice declaiming Bacon on intolerance: 'Surely this is to bring down the Holy Ghost instead of the likeness of a dove in the shape of a vulture or raven; and set out of the bark of a Christian church a flag of a bark of pirates and assassins.' The mere recollection still sends chills up and down my spine.

Paul had a deservedly high opinion of himself, and immense dignity. In that same first lecture he told us: 'Attendance at my lectures does not constitute a social introduction. I do not wish to be accosted by undergraduates in the public street.' But if you were fortunate enough to win his approval, he was kindness itself, and students who knew him well were devoted to him. Felix Walter, one of the best, burst into tears on hearing of his death, and I was not far from doing the same.

I was considered to be a very competent mimic of Lafleur's voice and manner. Years after his death Professor Walter, Felix's father, would every now and then rush into my office with: 'Forsey, I've an old student of Polly's here. Come up and give him your act.'

Leacock, who did not like Lafleur, used to call him 'Even I'. 'Ask Lafleur if Portuguese is a difficult language and he'll reply: "Oh, very difficult. *Even I* find it difficult."' But Lafleur must have been the only person who ever scored off Leacock. One day they had a spat in a Faculty meeting. Next day Leacock wanted to make it up. He slapped Lafleur on the back (this was like slapping Queen Victoria on the back), and said: 'Hello, Lafleur. Come to dinner tonight.' 'No, thank you.' 'All right, go to hell.' 'I should much prefer it.'

I never had classes with Lafleur's successor, Cyrus Macmillan. But I had several with the third man in the department, George W. Latham, a Harvard man and a close friend of Hemmeon's. Latham had a staccato mode of utterance and a highly individual style. Several examples recur to me. On Carlyle: 'There is an impression [pause] that Carlyle was rather a brute to his wife [pause]. But I don't think Carlyle was any more a brute to his wife than any man has to be.' In a course on English prose from Bacon to Stevenson, he lectured one day on Bunyan. Next day it was Defoe. But Latham persistently called Defoe Bunyan: 'Now when Bunyan wrote *Robinson Crusoe*' or 'As Bunyan said in *The Adventures of Moll Flanders* . . .' Halfway through the hour he took off his glasses, looked hard at us, and said: 'Have I been saying "Bunyan" in this lecture?' Some hardy soul said: 'Yes, sir.' 'Well, now, see here. For the rest of this lecture when I say "Bunyan", I mean "Defoe"'; and for the rest of the lecture Bunyan it was.

He once gave me a comparison between the former head of the department, Dean Moyse, and Lafleur: 'The Dean knew everything about everything. But he wasn't always sure where he had put it. So if you asked him a question, you were sure to get an interesting answer. But it might not have anything to do with the question. Paul was different. Paul knew everything about certain subjects, and he knew exactly where he had put it. So if you asked Paul a question on one of those subjects, he would reach into the proper pigeon-hole in his mind and give you the perfect answer.'

Years later, when I was on the staff, Latham came one day to the Faculty Club for lunch and sat at a table with three of us. He said: 'I have been thinking . . . that it was a pity . . . that there were no more characters left at McGill.' We kept our countenances with difficulty. Then the old gentleman's eye twinkled: 'And then . . . it suddenly occurred to me . . . that perhaps *we* were the characters now, you know!' Latham was a fine teacher, and beloved. He was often referred to as 'Daddy' Latham.

A third member of the English department was Harold Files, also Harvard. He had a gentle Harvard manner, and Harvard learning and polish, and was not without wit. Commenting on a highly improbable case of death-bed conversion in one of Smollett's novels (I am ashamed to say I have forgotten which), he noted that Smollett himself had recognized its improbability by saying: 'But the mercy of God is infinite' — and, said Files, 'the mercy of Smollett is more so.'

Files' lectures were first-rate. His examinations could be terrors. I wrote one for his course on the English novel. I had thoroughly enjoyed it and worked hard at it. Usually on examinations the questions were on parts of the course that I had reviewed intensively, almost never on the parts I had not. This time my luck failed. I wrote so poor a paper that I was afraid I also had failed. To my astonishment I got a first class. I confessed to Files my fear and my astonishment. He replied: 'Oh, you didn't see the other papers.'

A fourth professor of English in my time was Algy Noad, who became one of my closest friends. Noad never got the recognition he deserved because he was too modest. His scholarship was as encyclopaedic as Lafleur's, but his lectures, though impeccable in content and style, lacked fire. He was full of fun, which often took the form of what he called 'glimericks'. I remember one: 'There was a young man in a fjord/ Who tied up two clams with a cord./ He remarked, "When they wake/ They'll be certain to make/ A fuss if the team hasn't scored!"'

I asked Algy once whether he knew Portuguese. He replied: 'Very little, very little. But it's interesting you should ask that, because only a few days ago I was reading an obscure Portuguese poet of the fourteenth century, who said . . .' Here followed what for anyone else would have been the beginning of a Ph.D. dissertation.

When the war broke out in 1939 Algy, an ardent anti-Fascist, volunteered. He was assigned to naval intelligence. After Japan came in, one of his superiors asked if he knew any Japanese. 'No.' 'Would you be willing to learn it?' 'Yes.' He took the course, came out marginally behind the top candidate, who had been born and brought up in Japan, and spent the rest of the war deciphering Japanese code messages. He died young, an irreparable loss to Canadian scholarship.

In History I took one course from Professor Fryer—Harvard again, a fine teacher, and 'the glass of fashion and the mould of form.' Curiously he had a flawless English accent.

I got to know all three other professors in history: Basil Williams, the head of the department; W.T. Waugh; and E.R. Adair. Williams, an Englishman, aristocratic to the core, was a supporter of the British Labour Party. After a distinguished career at McGill he went on to the University of Edinburgh. Waugh was an Ulsterman. His original ancestors had been Scottish Border folk, 'who made their living crossing the Border and stealing English cattle. I am also descended from a pirate, and a rather eminent pirate.' Waugh's lectures were excellent and gained, rather than lost, from the fact that he suffered from asthma, which caused him to speak slowly and with emphasis. He could be caustic. After visits to Washington and Ottawa, he told me: 'In Washington I visited the gallery of the House of Representatives. They were a most deplorable-looking lot of blackguards. Your House of Commons is vastly superior. For one thing, its members chew much less *gum*.' Adair was English, descended from an American Southerner who, on the defeat of the Confederacy, exiled himself to England. Adair's lectures were among the best at McGill, and his individual attention to his students included having them to tea, where he regaled them with entertaining tales of his experiences. One of these had to do with a friend in the India Office who had got a job for a young Indian. Then difficulties arose from an unexpected quarter — the young man's grandmother — and Adair's friend got a letter from the boy's father lamenting that the whole thing was off: 'The grandmother of the Bipin, she is lady of supreme mental robustity, a chip of the large log, an old one of the school. All my tears will not avail to dissolve the large chest of this so light-brained lady, turning always to all my protestations the addled ear.' There was more, which I have forgotten, the whole ending with, 'May God preserve Your Honour in the choicest spirits!'

In my sixteen years at McGill we had four Principals: Sir Arthur Currie, Arthur Eustace Morgan, Lewis Douglas, and Cyril James.

Currie was head and shoulders above the other three. He was a big man in every sense, not least because he would listen, and was ready to admit mistakes. On one occasion some student organization had invited Scott Nearing, the American socialist, to speak and secured the YMCA hall. Currie promptly told Major Beaton, the YMCA secretary, that he was cancelling his subscription. Beaton called J.M. Macdonnell, of the National Trust Company. Macdonnell was horrified. He went to see Currie and remonstrated. Currie listened, banged the table, and rang Beaton: 'Beaton, I take it all back. Jim Macdonnell is here and he's proved to me that I acted like a damn fool.'

Currie, I discovered a few months ago, had a very low opinion of me. He had me on the carpet once when I was on staff. I had made a very dull speech to the St James Literary Society; so dull that I nearly put myself to sleep. I did put the *Montreal Star* journalist, Austin Cross, to sleep, and he wrote a report (so he told me years later) of what he thought I must have said. It was not wholly accurate, and one phrase, which I had not uttered, caught Currie's eye and roused his ire. I was summoned to the presence. The Principal began by telling me that one could not believe a word printed in the *Star*. He was eloquent on the subject, especially on a headline purporting to give his view on Honolulu: 'Hoola-hoola dance not immoral, says Sir Arthur Currie.' At the end of half an hour he turned to what the *Star* had reported me as saying. I told him I had not said it. 'Oh, but Forsey! It's right there in black and white in the *Star*.' I must have convinced him of my innocence, for Cross told me Currie had raised Cain at the *Star* and it nearly cost him *his* job.

Currie came to a premature end. The commander of the Canadian Corps in the Great War, he was criticized for his handling of the campaign during the last 100 days, first by Sir Sam Hughes, then by W.T.R. Preston, whom Currie sued for libel in 1928; he was successful, but the case broke his health. He was ill-advised to launch the action. Preston had been for years a Liberal Party handyman (to use no stronger term) and in that capacity had established a reputation that it would be flattering to call dubious. Laurier had had to bundle him out of the country after one election scandal, and veracity was not among his virtues. But he was not without imagination. In a book he wrote he achieved, against formidable competition, an astonishingly mendacious account of the constitutional crisis of 1926. It included a motion no one had ever moved, and placed it at a date when Parliament had been dissolved. Currie ought to have known that Preston's word was worthless, and that the Canadian law of libel was virtually useless. (Years later, when I considered suing J.W. Dafoe of the *Winnipeg Free Press*. Arthur Meighen told me to forget it, saying that in England I could have got £5,000; in Canada I'd get nothing.)

Currie's successor, Morgan, an Englishman—former Principal of University College, Hull—didn't last long. He succeeded in antagonizing everyone except the students: governors, professors, old and young, men and women, Englishmen, Scots, Americans, Canadians, radicals, and conservatives. After Morgan left, Robert George, of the English department, said to me: '*You* know what was the matter with Morgan, Forsey.' 'There were a great many things.' 'Yes, yes, yes, but there was one fundamental thing, and you know as well as I do what it was.' I disclaimed any knowledge. 'Well, you probably wouldn't want to say it to me, because I'm English. But because I *am* English, I can say it. All Englishmen know that we are superior to everyone else in the world. But some of us have enough sense to keep it under our hats. Morgan hadn't.' The amazing thing is that a close friend of mine in England, who had known Morgan well there, said his behaviour at home was totally different from his behaviour at McGill. I have seen at least one other conspicuous example of the same thing: the Englishman abroad who is the antithesis of the Englishman at home. This perhaps accounts for the fact that any Canadian of Scots or Irish ancestry can say proudly, 'I'm Scotch', or 'I'm Irish', and not an eyebrow is lifted. But woe betide the Canadian of English ancestry who says 'I'm English'. I did it once, proclaiming myself 'solidly and stolidly English, alike by ancestry and cast of mind', and got away with it, but I think only because it was in the context of the 'two nations', 'French' and 'English'.

Lewis Douglas did not last long either. Hemmeon's verdict on him was that he did less damage than Morgan or James because he was so seldom there.

Of Cyril James I had little personal experience, though I suspect he had not a little to do with my departure. His own end at McGill was bizarre. He fell foul of the Governors on some question of academic freedom (where he was wholly in the right), and they gave him his come-uppance. They then appointed a successor, who, however, promptly had a change of heart and bowed out. The Governors had to beg James to stay until they could find another replacement, which he very decently agreed to do.

It is hardly surprising that Leacock once said that McGill offered a short course for Principals.

I had four years at McGill as a student. When I came back from Oxford in 1929 I joined the staff as sessional lecturer in economics and political science, and a sessional lecturer I remained for the whole of my twelve years there. Four times Hemmeon recommended me for promotion. Four times I was turned down. After the fourth time my wife suggested I ask the Dean why. I did. The interview, a long one, remains green in my memory. The Dean, C.W. Hendel, was an eminent authority on Rousseau (and, I think, Hegel). He was by all accounts a first-rate teacher. But making him Dean had turned his head. He habitually referred to himself in the third person, like Queen Victoria: 'The Dean feels', 'The Dean thinks', 'The Dean' this, 'The Dean' that.

He had had one whack at taking me down a peg, telling me that my lectures were not popular, instancing particularly one course that I had taken over on Leacock's retirement. I said: 'That is very interesting. In Dr Leacock's last year that course had sixty students. This year it has a hundred and twenty.' He nevertheless returned to the task. I was, he explained, 'injudicious'. I asked for examples. He gave four.

First, in a letter to the Montreal *Gazette*, answering one accusing me of 'favouring' unemployment relief, I had said that 'no one outside a lunatic asylum considered unemployment relief a good thing in itself, but it was better than letting people starve.' The phrase 'no one outside a lunatic asylum' was 'injudicious'.

Second, at a meeting of student advisers two years before, I had 'raised a point of order'. 'Yes, I did, and my point of order was correct.' 'Oh, yes. It was correct. But it reflected on the Dean's conduct of the meeting.' 'But you weren't in the chair. Professor Hughes was in the chair.' 'Oh, yes. So he was.' 'By no stretch of the imagination could my point of order have been a reflection on you.' (What had happened was that, after a considerable debate, a motion had been carried, but a senior professor *then* made a long speech on it. My wife and I were expecting a very distinguished astro-physicist for dinner, and it began to look as if I'd not get there, especially if people were going to start discussing motions that had already been carried.)

The third exhibit I have forgotten, though it ranked with the other three.

The fourth was a gem: 'You have been heard, in this building, speaking in an excited tone of voice.' 'Well, that takes the cake! What am I reported to have said?' 'Oh, the Dean could not tell you that. It was told to the Dean in confidence. Besides, it wasn't what you said. It was the tone of voice.' From then on, when anyone spoke to me in the building I was careful to refrain from an expression of opinion in any but the flattest tone of voice. As I told the Dean, my motto thenceforth would be: 'Méfiez-vous! Taisez-vous! Les oreilles de l'ennemi vous écoutent!'

I went upstairs to Hemmeon and told him I had something to report that I couldn't expect him to believe. No one could; it was too preposterous. I then recounted exhibit four. He said: 'I have no difficulty at all in believing it. The damn fool put his complaint in writing over his own signature.' He pulled out a drawer, took out a paper, and there it was, verbatim, on official stationery.

Later I had another series of encounters with the Dean, lasting six months. The daughter of two friends of my wife and myself (and of my mother and aunt) had, in her fourth year, turned in an abysmally bad paper on British and American government. During the year I had repeatedly called her attention to the advisability of listening to lectures instead of reading the *McGill Daily*—to no effect. Her father, having failed to reach me by telephone (we had left for the Eastern Townships for a short vacation, and the telephone had been disconnected), went to the Dean alleging that I was 'prejudiced' against his daughter. This was doubly absurd, since the questions were wholly on matters of fact—the composition and powers of the House of Lords and the American Senate, that sort of thing. The girl's father threatened to appeal to Sir Edward Beatty, the Chancellor.

Of course I said: 'Have the paper re-read by someone else.' Hemmeon re-read it and said it was worth precisely what I had given it, 34 per cent. The Dean professed to be satisfied.

But in a week or so he summoned me back, by letter, from the Townships. The irate parent had returned to the charge. I offered to give up my job at the University of British Columbia Summer School and stay in Montreal to coach the girl for a supplemental examination. This was rejected: 'Miss —— is going away for a two-month vacation.' Would I coach her in September when we'd both be back? Of course.

I set the supplemental: ten questions, of which the candidate could choose five. By September I had completely forgotten which questions I had set. I coached the girl remorselessly, making her write answers to old questions, and going over the answers with her. (As it turned out, I covered every one of my ten questions.) Her paper was a fresh disaster. I gave her 37 per cent.

Back came her father, with the same accusation and the same threat. Back came the Dean to me: 'The case of Miss —— has arisen again, in a very troubling way.' Again I said: 'Well, have the paper re-read by someone else.' Hemmeon re-read it and said it was worse than the first one: I had given her too high a mark! Again the Dean professed to be satisfied. Again the father blustered. Again the Dean shook in his shoes and summoned me.

I said: 'Twice, now, you have assured me that this case was settled. Now it bobs up again. How much oftener is this going to happen? What do you expect me to do now?'

The reply staggered me: 'The Dean wishes to peruse the paper himself.' I said: 'I'll have to think that over.'

I consulted my wife, who asked me if he had any right to ask for the paper. 'None.' 'Then tell him you'll hand it over only if the Faculty orders it.' Hemmeon and another senior colleague at first favoured letting the Dean have the paper. But when I repeated what my wife had said, they changed their minds and emphatically endorsed her advice.

I went to the Dean and told him I'd hand over the paper only if the Faculty ordered me to. It was his turn to be staggered: 'Oh, the Dean would not like to do that. He feels that would be very bad for you.' I replied that I'd risk it. I knew the Faculty loathed him and were just waiting for the chance to give him a swift kick on the spot indicated. His vanity had kept him from having any inkling of this, so he agreed to take the matter to a Faculty meeting. I put the paper in a safety-deposit box at my bank, as both Hemmeon and I were sure that the Dean was capable of rifling my office.

The Dean drew up an enormous bill of particulars, including the precise texts, dates, and addresses of his and my letters. He had the decency to show the document to Hemmeon and me. We corrected a few minor errors and the great day arrived.

I was, of course, not present. I did not have tenure—I occupied only an academic footstool. But I received full accounts of the meeting from three heads of departments.

The Dean read his bill of particulars, with the complete text of letters (e.g., 'From the Dean, Brandon, Vermont, to Mr Forsey, Anglican Theological College, University of British Columbia, Vancouver, British Columbia, July ——, 1939', and the rest, verbatim). The reading took three-quarters of an hour and was repeatedly interrupted. 'What was the hour that letter was written?' 'Did Eugene go to UBC for the summer?' 'Yes.' 'Did he enjoy it?' 'Very much.' 'Did he travel CPR?' When he had finished the Dean said he felt he deserved the sympathy of Faculty for having to read all this. One of the professors said it was the Faculty that deserved sympathy for having to listen to it. Then came the debate.

Mrs Grant, Warden of the Royal Victoria College, the women's residence, challenged head-on the Dean's tale of Miss —— in his office in tears, alleging 'prejudice'. Mrs Grant said the young lady had spoken to her after the result of the first examination: 'There were no tears; on the contrary, she said Mr Forsey had been perfectly fair.' The Dean switched round in his chair: 'The Miss —— you describe is not the girl I saw in my office.'

I was given two versions of Mrs Grant's reply. To those who knew Maud Grant, who could have run the whole British Empire at the height of its power single-handed, the livelier version is the more likely: 'That I can well believe. But I saw the real Miss ——. What you did to her in your office I don't know.' Shocked silence.

The head of one department then drew attention to Miss ——'s record, which was a mass of red ink. She had rarely passed any course except by a supplemental examination. Another head of department said: 'She's a moron.'

Then came the dénouement. The Dean asked the Faculty to hand over my paper to him for his 'perusal'. This time it was Faculty that was staggered. Three heads of departments spoke.

Professor Murray, Bacteriology and Immunity: 'Mr Dean, do I understand that if I plough a student in bacteriology and immunity, you claim the right to re-read his paper?' 'Oh! yes.' 'Do you know anything about bacteriology and immunity?' 'Oh! no.' 'But you claim the right to re-read his paper?' 'Oh, yes.'

Professor Sullivan, Mathematics, and Professor Clark, Geology, each had a similar exchange with the Dean.

Then came the vote. The Dean had one supporter. The future Principal, Cyril James, was on his side, but he had not yet formally taken office as director of the School of Commerce, so he could not vote.

But the vote was not the climax. The Principal, Lewis Douglas, had a final touch to add: 'Well, ladies and gentlemen, I think I may now entertain a motion that henceforth the Dean should have a right to re-read all papers.' Professor Clark: 'Mr Principal, have you or have you not been present for the last two hours? Faculty has just turned down precisely that proposal.' Silence.

The Dean resigned next day. His resignation was refused. Somewhat later his class at Princeton honoured him with a gold medal as the most distinguished man of his year.

My mark stuck. But it had taken six months, May to November, to make it stick.

This was only one of several affairs that did not endear me to the administration. Some years earlier, before Leacock retired, there had been a fracas. One of our graduate students, a good one, had done an M.A. thesis on some subject that I have forgotten. It was a very feeble effort and I failed it. Leacock wrote me in a fury and I discovered that I was supposed to have supervised the student's work. No one had ever told me so—not by one syllable, in writing or by word of mouth. I had the distinct impression that it was to be supervised by my very senior colleague Dr Day. Leacock said I should seek employment elsewhere. I did, but without success. (I wrote one acquaintance, head of another university, asking him to be kind enough to let me know if he heard of any openings. He replied that I could scarcely expect him to 'intervene in a matter internal to McGill.' I wrote again, pointing out that I had not asked him to do anything of the kind, adding that I hoped to retain my senses to the last.)

This storm blew over. But I dare say that as the years went on my activities in the CCF, the League for Social Reconstruction, the Fellowship for a Christian Social Order, the Montreal Civil Liberties Union, and my visit to Russia in 1932 — plus the rumpus over my ploughing the student whose examination paper the Dean wanted to re-read — built up a backlog of exasperation in the administration, which was no doubt under considerable pressure from a Montreal élite badly frightened by the Depression.

The Depression that began in 1929 aroused my interest in the distribution of the national income and I decided to make this the subject of a Ph.D. thesis. My teaching load was very heavy, the statistical work involved was considerable, and my extra-curricular activities were numerous. So my progress was slow. However, I was getting to the end of the job when the Rowell-Sirois Commission (the Royal Commission on Dominion-Provincial Relations, 1937-40) published its admirable special study, which completely cut the ground from under my feet. I went to my supervisor and said so. Clearly I must chuck the thing. He said no. So very foolishly I finished it. The outside examiner rightly ploughed it. I promptly received from the university authorities a letter informing me that, as the attainment of a Ph.D. was the acid test of academic competence and I had failed it, my sessional lectureship would end the next year, 1941.

Some time after I received this I saw another letter — shown me by, I think, the head of the department — in which some official, probably the Dean, said plainly that the administration wanted to get rid of me and was looking for a credible, and respectable, ground for doing so. The news of my failure must have seemed heaven-sent.

My prospects looked dim. Then, on the initiative (I am convinced) of Professor Frank Scott, I was awarded in 1941 a Guggenheim Fellowship to work on a book on the Canadian cabinet system. And in the spring of that year, just as I was being removed for being unable to win a Ph.D., I earned that degree for my book on the power of dissolution of Parliament.

The administration had one shot left in its locker. A few days before the Convocation that was to confer the degree, the Registrar met me in the corridor of the Arts Building. He said: 'We want proof that you have an M.A. degree from Oxford.' I blew up: 'I've been through a good deal here, but this puts the tin hat on it. Go and look in the Library at the list of people who got the M.A. at Oxford in 1932.' 'We have looked, but we can't find your name in it.' 'You'd better look again. It's there. I've seen it. Besides, you've had it in the McGill Calendar for nine years. I suppose I could cable the Master of Balliol for confirmation.' The Registrar went scarlet in the face. A day or so later he told me they had found my name in the list.

I remain convinced that this was a deliberate attempt to prevent my getting the degree. After the Convocation I went to see the Dean of Graduate Studies and asked for an explanation of the performance. He happened to be an old colleague of my mother's at the Geological Survey, so he knew me. He looked most uncomfortable, and finally said: 'We wanted to be sure it was accurate in the Convocation Programme.' I said icily: 'I see', looked at him, as P.G. Wodehouse would say, 'in a rather marked manner', and left.

In 1966 I returned to McGill to receive an honorary LL.D. and to deliver the Convocation address.

3

Oxford

In 1926 I was chosen as one of the two Quebec Rhodes Scholars. Fortunately for me the selection process was nothing like as stiff as it is now. I don't think I'd stand a chance today.

As a prelude to my McGill undergraduate years I had spent a whole glorious summer in Grand Bank. There was not enough time to repeat this before Oxford, but I did get there for two weeks and sailed from St John's for Liverpool. On the boat there was one future celebrity, Charles Ritchie, who became a distinguished diplomat, ambassador, and diarist. I never got to know him really well on the voyage (I think I stood rather in awe of him), though in one of his delightful books he was kind enough to mention me, too favourably. Other fellow-passengers were the Newfoundland delegates to the Imperial Conference, who took me under their wing. They all knew my family, and Newfoundlanders are a very clannish people. After we got to London they continued their kindness. I drove all over the city in a car with an Imperial Conference sign on the windshield, and bobbies saluting as we passed. I spent some time at the offices of the Newfoundland High Commission and there met Sir Patrick McGrath, who was preparing Newfoundland's case on the Labrador boundary for the Judicial Committee of the Privy Council. As far as I know Sir Patrick did not have a university education, but his research was masterly and enabled Sir John Simon, who had taken the case for Newfoundland, to run rings around the lawyers for Canada.

During the short time I was in London I stayed with one of our Montreal Ulster cousins, Evelyn Warwick, who had married the English architect Septimus Warwick. He practised in Montreal for years before going to London, where he was the architect for Canada House. Evelyn was very proud of our Cochrane ancestry. She said we were related to the famous admiral Thomas Cochrane, Earl of Dundonald (1775-1860). But Evelyn, a strong Conservative, was somewhat ambivalent about him. He had been a Radical MP and had once arrived at a Radical meeting with a barrel of gunpowder. Evelyn was also apprehensive about my going to Balliol College, whose Master, A.D. Lindsay, was a prominent member of the Labour Party. The College had the reputation (unjustified) in Conservative circles of being a 'hotbed of socialism'.

The Reverend Richard Roberts (later Moderator of the United Church of Canada, whom I had known well in Montreal) had given me a letter of introduction to John Macmurray, a philosophy don at Balliol. He became my 'moral tutor' (I never quite discovered what this meant). It was taken for granted that I would 'read' Modern Greats — that is, Philosophy, Politics, and Economics. I foolishly put Economics first and Politics last. Still more foolishly, by John's persuasion I put Philosophy second. This turned out to be worse than a mistake: it was an absurdity. I had never studied a word of philosophy in my life and I was a dunderhead at it. My essays for Macmurray were disasters, emphasized by the fact that the man who shared tutorials with me, Harry Hodson, was a philosophical genius. He read Kant (Macmurray's favourite philosopher) when riding on an omnibus.

I think John had given me up as hopeless. Then suddenly, when Hodson was reading one of his brilliant essays, he quoted Bertrand Russell on a passage in Kant. I burst in with: 'Oh, but that's nonsense! That's not what Kant meant at all. He's completely wrong.' I shall never forget Macmurray's look of utter incredulous astonishment, or his 'You're perfectly right. Russell *is* wrong.' At last, in a phrase of P.G. Wodehouse, 'between the collar and hair-parting, something had stirred.' I was not after all the imbecile I had hitherto seemed. I never shone in my Philosophy tutorials, nor, I think, in my final examination. But John's burden did become lighter.

Macmurray was not only a distinguished philosopher but a devout man with a very strong social conscience. When I knew him at Balliol this last had not, as far as I know, come to its full flowering. A few years later he left Balliol to become Grote Professor of Mind and Logic at University College, University of London. He produced, in the 1930s, a series of books — *Freedom in the Modern World, Creative Society, Reason and Emotion, The Structure of Religious Experience* — that set forth, among other things, the necessity of a synthesis of Christianity and Communism, which provided a ground for co-operation between Christians and Communists. The Communists were of course delighted. So were many Christians of the Left, of whom I was one. We were horrified and terrified by Fascism. We were impressed by the Communists' battle against it. We welcomed the possibility of co-operating with them if we could do so without compromising our faith. We had yet to learn that for Communists, co-operating meant the co-operation of the cannibal and his victim. I suppose Macmurray learned this too; he must have. But I lost touch with him in his later years, by which time he had become a Quaker.

Meanwhile he had an immense influence in Christian Left circles. I think this had a good deal to do with the founding of the Fellowship for a Christian Social Order and the writing of its book, *Towards the Christian Revolution*. It certainly must have been the main reason why the Student Christian Movement of Canada brought Macmurray to Canada for one of its annual conferences. I attended, with my wife, who took copious notes, which were afterwards transcribed and circulated in mimeographed form. (I ran across my copy a year or so ago.) Some at least of his philosophical ideas have survived. There is a John Macmurray Society in Toronto, and among those passionately interested in what he wrote is at least one Jesuit priest. But the number of those who now believe in a synthesis of Christianity and Communism must be small indeed.

In Economics my first tutor was A.B. Rodger, a Scot. Of him I remember little, except one thing that reveals my incurable frivolousness. Reading essays aloud, I was repeatedly baffled by the pronunciation of English proper names. For poor Rodger this was an affliction. When I pronounced 'Congresbury' as it is spelt, he wearily told me it was 'Coomsbury'. I gave up. From then on, whenever I came to a proper name I simply spelt it. A friend told me that Rodger had said to him: 'Forsey's a very nice fellow, but a French-Canadian with a very imperfect knowledge of English.' Later I was sent to Lionel Robbins, one of the greatest economists of his day, then teaching at New College. I don't think I profited from my good fortune as I should have.

For Politics I had Humphrey Sumner. He also formed a very poor initial opinion of my knowledge and capacity. After one or two tutorials he gave me to read Kenneth Pickthorn's little book on the British Constitution. It wasn't quite the Constitution shown to children, but very nearly. Everything in it I had known for years. He had one habit that distracted my attention from much of what he was trying to teach me. He incessantly smoked a pipe, which kept going out and which he kept re-lighting from a 'spill' (a rolled piece of paper). He invariably let the spill burn to his finger-tips, as I watched with horrified fascination. When Humphrey came to Canada he surprised and very much pleased me by looking me up.

Most of the lectures I attended at Oxford were very inferior to what I had been used to at McGill. (Whenever I have said this, the invariable response has been: 'Oxford prides herself on her poor lectures.') The one notable exception was provided by G.D.H. Cole, the Guild socialist economist. Though I went to his lectures, and also to a study group at his house, I was never one of his inner circle, a brilliant set of left-wing members of the Labour Party. I was greatly surprised when Mrs

Cole, visiting Montreal many years later, looked me up, and still more surprised when she said her husband had had a high opinion of me.

Cole was not only a Labour economist and scholar but also a writer of detective stories, which he wrote whenever and wherever he had a moment free. Once, when I was going up to London, he got into my compartment. After saying 'How do you do?' he explained that he could not talk to me as he was in the middle of writing a chapter for one of his thrillers. He was also the author of an operetta on the General Strike of 1926, produced by the Oxford Labour Club in the fall of that year. I had joined the club immediately after my arrival and was given a small part as a member of a chorus of Liberals outside the gate of Heaven. Our song began:

> We are the Liberal Party, the chosen people we,
> The country is behind us, it backs our policy.
> At least we feel quite certain our rule it would prefer
> If we knew what we wanted, or who our leaders were.

I marvel that I got through any of the papers in 'Schools', on which my degree depended. One of them was a sight translation from the German. I never studied German, at school or later, but I had mugged up enough at Oxford to read some German works in economics (nothing in philosophy or politics). What was my horror to be confronted by a passage from Thomas Mann's *Der Zauberberg*, which the knowledgeable tell me is one of his most elusive novels. The first words were etched on my memory: 'Kann man die Zeit erzählen, die Zeit, wie sie ist, an und für sich?' (roughly, Can we describe time, time as it is, in and for itself?) This was followed by one of those German sentences where about seventeen adjectives and adjectival phrases intervene between the definite article and the noun. I nearly threw in the towel. However, I persisted. But I was scared stiff I'd fail the whole exam. I had only one hope: that in the oral, some weeks later, I'd be able to cope with questions on German. So I set to work with a very kind and learned Canadian lady, Mrs Gerrans, a friend of two years' standing, who coached me remorselessly, using a novel, a 'Roman des militär Lebens'.

My luck with examinations held. The examiners had set the stiffest paper ever in German, and felt they must therefore be rather lenient in marking it this first year. In the oral examination, on the German paper I got not a single question, but in the whole oral exam I got off very easily. The only searching question was in Economics, from Professor Edwin Cannan, who asked me to explain why something or other had produced a certain effect in England but not in Ireland. I replied candidly: 'I haven't the faintest idea.' Cannan, in his rather high voice, said: 'Potatoes!'

When the results came out I had miraculously got a First. I am less and less able to understand why.

I stayed on at Oxford, as Rhodes Scholars were then entitled to do, for another year. Robbins persuaded me to do a B.Litt. on the economics of migration. Nothing came of it. I cannot even recall doing much work on it. Robbins had left Oxford and I was nominally supervised by a genial, easy-going scholar who put me under no pressure.

The Fellows of my College, apart from my tutors, I knew scarcely at all. This was a great loss and largely my own fault. There were three I could have known who would have done a great deal for me.

The Master, A.D. Lindsay, a Scots Presbyterian (Balliol has of course a long connection with Scotland, beginning with its founders, John de Balliol, and Devorguilla, his wife), was an authority on Kant and a Christian socialist. He had known Keir Hardie, one of the first Labour MPs. Lindsay occasionally made speeches. I remember one, in which he quoted a seventeenth-century radical with the startlingly appropriate name of Mr Wildman: 'The poorest he that is in England hath a life to live as the richest he,' adding his own: 'The poorest baby born in a Glasgow slum has a life to live as the baby born in the most exclusive residential district.' (He put it more crisply, but I have forgotten the name of Glasgow's equivalent of Forest Hill, Toronto, or Montreal's Square Mile.) That belief has been the basis of much of my own small contribution towards social justice.

The Master once invited me to lunch. It didn't come off. I overstayed a leave in London with very old senior friends from Ottawa, and arrived back in Oxford to find the invitation—missed. I was lucky to escape a penalty; but the invitation, naturally, was not repeated. Lady Scott's Life of her father, the Master, made me realize how much I might have profited from even slightly more knowledge of the man if I had not blotted my copybook.

Two other Fellows I knew slightly, and certainly could have known better. Both were almost institutions of the College in their time.

One was the Senior Dean, Francis Fortescue Urquhart—universally known, to colleagues and undergraduates, old and young, and universally addressed, as 'Sligger'. Where the name came from, and what it signified, I never found out and was too diffident to ask. Sligger's father had, I believe, been a British diplomat with one unusual eccentricity. When Sligger was a boy, his father took him across Europe naked; when other passengers came into the train compartment and did a double-take, Mr Urquhart would say: 'Here, Francis, take this copy of the *Times* and wrap yourself in it.'

Sligger had a chalet at Aix-en-Provence. Invitations to it were much prized. I got one and went, but the visit fell flat. I had no idea what to say or do. I did not even know whether I was expected to contribute to the expenses, and was too shy to ask. The chalet is still there, and I recently received an appeal to contribute to its preservation. After my visit I cannot recall ever exchanging a word with its owner. He was a very saintly looking man, and very handsome, with curly white hair. I admired, even revered, him from afar. Scores of undergraduates were devoted to him, and I think with ample reason.

The other Fellow whom I might have known well, but didn't, was Kenneth Bell. He was a history tutor, with a large family, who kept open house. At the front door was a big sign with a number of bells on it (six, I think, when I first saw it; each new baby got a fresh bell on the sign) and the inscription, 'Balliol men enter'. Most of those who knew Kenneth at all took this literally, as indeed they were expected to do. I did not. Kenneth Bell was a 'hearty', and with hearties I felt at a loss. Amazingly, he ended up as an Anglican clergyman and must have provided a classic example of muscular Christianity.

I enjoyed almost every moment at Oxford (as who would not?). But my first winter was not wholly comfortable. I never was so cold, before or since. English friends would say: 'But you come from such a far northern country. How can you possibly find England cold?' My reply was twofold. First: 'Do you realize that I am now about 350 miles farther north than I've ever been in my life? Oxford is in the latitude of southern Labrador; Ottawa is in the latitude of Venice.' Second: 'We have central heating. You don't.'

This deficiency I experienced to an extreme degree. I had a sitting-room and a bedroom. They were separated by a corridor about twenty paces long. The bedroom had no heat whatever. Neither had the corridor, whose walls literally dripped water: it ran down their face like a gentle rain on a windowpane. The large sitting-room had a very small fireplace. By heaping on coal I could make myself reasonably comfortable, but only by sitting with all my winter clothes on and wrapped in an eiderdown, with the two front legs of my chair in the fender. In damp weather — that is, most of the time — the chimney smoked majestically. The college authorities had put in the chimney a gadget that was supposed to cure this but didn't. All it did was beat a steady, rapid tattoo and make the fire belch forth at frequent intervals, emitting clouds of dense smoke. One afternoon Hodson came to see me and I was quite invisible: smoke filled the room from about three feet above the floor clear to the ceiling. Harry actually asked: 'Are you there, Forsey?' When I assured him I was, he had to bend double to make me out!

Fortunately I got so used to the chill that in my second and third years, when I was in a building with central heating, I complained of the heat. And when I returned to McGill I made a nuisance of myself by throwing up windows in Montreal winter weather.

The chill was not the only discomfort of Balliol in those days. There was just one set of latrines, and to reach them from my rooms I had to cross two quadrangles. This was well enough in the daytime, but in the middle of a cold night the trip was a horror. Undergraduates always called the latrines 'the Lady Perihan'. Lady Elizabeth Perihan was one of the College benefactors who was always named in the College prayers of gratitude for 'our exhibitions and maintenance here'.

At McGill the influence of Dr Hemmeon and of my minister, the Reverend Allworth Eardley — an English Methodist old-fashioned radical — had knocked the props from under my Conservatism and I arrived at Oxford ready to join the Labour Party, which I did. Except for the university Labour Club, I took a very small part in undergraduate activities. I was on the executive of the Adam Smith Society, and I belonged to the Raleigh Club (Empire and Commonwealth), and the College's Fallodon Club (named after the former Sir Edward Grey, Foreign Secretary in the Asquith government). I spoke once, briefly and badly, at the Union.

I took part in the League of Nations Society and once went to Birmingham to make a speech for it. The Society asked a devout Quaker lady to billet me. She firmly refused: 'Most certainly not! A most disreputable young man. He stayed with me in Harrogate, and came in roaring drunk at three o'clock every morning!' My Oxford friends, especially my Quaker friends, were delighted. I may add, in my own defence, that I have never been in Harrogate in my life. Who this *alter ego* was I cannot imagine; perhaps a fellow West Country man with the same surname. There are plenty of Forseys in Devon and Dorset.

Those were the days when the League of Nations was new, and most people, at least in Europe, had great hopes of it. This was especially true of the Quakers, whom I had joined soon after coming to Oxford. Every year crowds converged on Geneva for the meetings of the Assembly, and I was one of them. It was in Geneva that I met two people who became among my closest and most generous friends, Dr and Mrs John Shaxby. He was English, a professor of physiology at the University College of South Wales in Cardiff; his wife was Anglo-Irish. They had a lovely home on the outskirts of Cardiff, where I was a frequent guest.

Among other Quakers who came regularly to Geneva were Mr and Mrs Jones of Manchester. Mrs Jones, a journalist, was tall, dark, handsome, and commanding, with flashing black eyes and a strong sense of the dramatic. Mr Jones was small, grey, meek, and generally silent. Mrs Jones' invariable command when addressing her husband was 'Herbert, come here at once.' Unusually for a Quaker in those days, she was a strong Conservative. But that did not prevent her from warmly welcoming J.S. Woodsworth when he came to Meeting in Geneva. After the gathering she engaged him in conversation. Suddenly her voice rang out across the meeting-room: 'Herbert, come here at once. I want you to meet this gentleman. He has been in jail. Most interesting.'

In those days there was no simultaneous translation. So every French speech had to be followed by an English translation, and every English by a French. The interpreters were incomparable. Once I arrived just too late to hear an English speech by Sir Austen Chamberlain. But I did hear the French translation. I read the original speech next day in *The Times*, and the interpretation was perfect to the last comma. This was standard.

I did a small amount of work for the Labour Party in the election of 1929, chiefly by trying to persuade married women electors to vote early, to prevent crowding at the polls towards the end of the day when the men came off work. I was never very successful. The almost invariable reply was: 'I likes to wait till me 'usband comes 'ome.'

In those days of course I was, as a British subject, entitled to vote in a British election. Indeed, long after I came back to Canada I was able to vote for the Oxford University seat and actually succeeded, for I think the only time in my life, in voting once for a candidate who won! The abolition of the university seats made that a solitary triumph.

I spent many of my vacations on the Continent, usually in France. The Easter vacation of 1928 I spent, with Escott Reid, at Les Baux in Provence, which we made our headquarters for walking tours to Avignon, Nimes, the Fontaine de Vaucluse, Arles, Uzès, Mont-Majour, Le Grau du Roi, and other celebrated places in the region. I came back to England so tanned that friends asked me when I was going to join the Indian Majlis! Many years later, in India, I was twice asked by Indians what part of India I came from. I might have been surprised if I had not become inured to being taken for so many different nationalities—fifteen by actual count; never for English, often for American, but also for French, German, Swiss, Italian, Spanish, Swedish, Polish, Hungarian, Jugoslav, Turkish, Jewish, Czech, and a couple of others that have slipped my memory. Usually it was my apparently nondescript appearance, but occasionally my accent. I once met a French-Canadian girl who insisted I was Polish: 'No English person ever spoke French as you do.'

In the summer of 1927 I had taken Mother and my Aunt Hazel pretty well all over England and Scotland for two months, arranging the whole trip without reference to any travel agency. In 1929 I repeated this, with Mother, Aunt Hazel, and my Newfoundland Aunt Mab, but this time on the Continent: France, Switzerland, Italy, Austria, Hungary, Germany, and Belgium. The hotels would ask: 'Are you with Thomas Cook and Son? Sir Arnold Lunn? American Express?' They were inclined to be incredulous at the reply: 'No. I am with myself.' I not only arranged arrivals and departures, hotels and *pensions*, but became a lightning calculator of foreign prices in Canadian dollars. For the Hungarian pengo I devised a simple method: multiply by six and divide by $1.02. As we usually spent an appreciable time in each place we visited, I had plenty of practice. On two occasions in Provence I spent the whole day acting as English-speaking guide not only to my relatives but to an American lady from California, and a Canadian from Toronto accompanied by an American from New York. All three were on American Express tours and had paid substantial sums for the guarantee of an English-speaking guide. The guide did not appear, so I filled in. Not one had a solitary word of French. I had to do everything for them: they could not order so much as a sandwich or buy a post card. The custodians of various historic sites would deliver their set speeches in French at breakneck speed, and I'd then ask them to pause a moment for the translation.

I made a great many friends among my fellow-undergraduates. George Mitchell, with whom I shared 'digs' in my last year, was an American from Virginia. (He once said to me: 'Never ask an American if he's from Virginia. If he is, he's sure to tell you. If he isn't, don't embarrass him.') George's father had been president of a small American college in Richmond, and his brother Broadus, a professor at Johns Hopkins, had been a perpetual (and of course defeated) socialist candidate for Governor of Maryland. George himself was a socialist, but he confessed to me that he found it hard to call a black man 'Mr'; 'Dr', 'Professor', yes; but 'Mr'? Years later, visiting Thomas Jefferson's house in Charlottesville, I noticed how careful the black guide was always to say 'Mr Jefferson'. George had a great-aunt who, in the 1920s, was still keeping a record of the families of her forebears' former slaves, as she was convinced she would one day get them all back! George always called 'Away Down South in Dixie' his national anthem, and the election of a Republican in Virginia shocked him to the core.

It was George who called our digs in Oxford (a loft over a garage) 'The Executive Mansion'. Anything more ludicrously inappropriate it would be hard to imagine. We had two bedrooms, toilet facilities, and a single basin. Of course we could, and did, take our baths in the College. (The College bath man, Cornell, kept us all in order in classical style: "Urry up, gentlemen, please! There are several gentlemen waiting!") During the 'great frost' of 1929 the single basin's pipes, like all the rest of the plumbing in Oxford, froze and we had to empty the water out of the window in the sloping ceiling. George used the opportunity to honour his Scots ancestors by shouting, each time, the old Edinburgh warning: 'Guardy l'eau!'

Another close friend of those years, Bernard de Bunsen, is happily still flourishing. He belonged to the great Anglo-German family and his mother was a Buxton. The Buxtons were among the Liberal intellectuals who had joined the Labour Party; one member, an Anglo-Catholic priest, flew the red flag over his church! Bernard was related to half the noble families in England and Germany. His father, as a boy, had played with the German Crown Prince. The Buxtons had been ardent supporters of Bulgaria in the Balkan troubles before 1914; so much so that when Bernard went to Bulgaria in the 1930s he found himself getting standing ovations when he went to the theatre—much to his embarrassment, for he was a naturally retiring person. The Bulgarian ovations had an aftermath, equally embarrassing: when he went to Yugoslavia, the triune kingdom, fearing that he might have been too much influenced by its Bulgarian rival, laid down the red carpet for him. We all learned to be a little careful when mentioning any prominent English or German names, because if we showed signs of disapproval of any of them Bernard would very diffidently warn us: 'He's my father's cousin', or 'She married my mother's uncle', or something of that sort. Bernard went on to become President of the University of Makerere in Uganda, in the days when Uganda was one of the richest and most peaceful countries in Africa. For his services there he was knighted.

Another great friend was Escott Reid, with whom I shared the Easter vacation of 1928. His brilliant career in the diplomatic service is one of those that make me realize how very much on the fringe my life has been. Escott has kept in touch, but not very successfully, because my inability to drive a car, my wife's long illness, and my own growing infirmities have kept me from accepting his numerous invitations to visit him up the Gatineau. When I was in India in 1953 he invited me to New Delhi; but my employer, the Canadian Congress of Labour, called me home.

Other friends were Louis MacKay, Donald McDougall, Walter Crocker, Donald Creighton, and Charles Lightbody.

Louis MacKay was a classical scholar and a poet, in both English and French. In his last year at Oxford he married a daughter of Hector Charlesworth, editor of *Saturday Night* and later Chairman of the Canadian Broadcasting Commission, the predecessor of the CBC. I was best man at the wedding.

Donald McDougall was a brilliant historian. He had been blinded in the war and had come to Balliol on a special scholarship. He had, of course, to employ a 'reader'. One of them, who did not last long, tried his patience beyond endurance by calling Georges Cadoudal 'Georges Cadoodle'.

Both Louis and Donald returned to Canada to become professors at the University of Toronto, and I kept in touch with them till Louis went to the University of California and my visits to Toronto became fewer.

Walter Crocker I knew less well, partly because I stood rather in awe of him. He was, and is, one of the most conscientious men I have ever known, and conscientious in an unusual way: it troubled him that the College servants, who, he felt, were his equals, should do things for him. He became a British civil servant in West Africa, then returned to his native Australia to a career as a professor, a diplomat, finally Lieutenant-Governor of South Australia, and a knighthood. His diplomatic career brought him to Ottawa as High Commissioner. To my surprise and immense pleasure he looked me up, and I got to know him far better than ever I had at Oxford. The better I knew him the more I admired him. We still occasionally correspond.

Donald Creighton was another fellow-student at Balliol whom I knew only slightly, though in later years he became one of my closest and most revered friends; we fought together against Quebec nationalism. I had nothing like his intellect, his depth, his learning, his passion, or his mastery of the English language. Nor had I his acute sensitivity to praise or cavil. When I wrote him to say how much I had enjoyed *Dominion of the North*, he replied with an emotion that startled me, and later repeatedly said how much my letter had meant to him. I replied that it had been a very ordinary letter from a very ordinary reader; but he insisted. On the other hand, when a rather well-known literary critic, whose knowledge of Canadian history was minimal, attacked him for what he had the temerity to call errors of history, he was sunk in gloom. I said: 'Look, Donald, this man is a literary critic. If he had criticized your style, you might have some reason to take him seriously. But he had enough sense not to try that. Instead he attacks your history, on which his opinions are worth precisely nothing. I wouldn't waste thirty seconds on him.'

Creighton was in some ways an intensely private man. At one stage he declared he would never leave his papers to the Archives, and he strongly urged me to leave nothing of mine: 'Underhill did it. God knows I have no love for Underhill. But now students are burrowing through his papers to find all sorts of personal matter. They would do the same to me, or to you. Don't do it.' He even asked me to destroy all the letters I had had from him (every one of them a gem, alike in content and style, and written in the most perfect handwriting). I refused. I told him I'd return them to him (which I did), but I could not take the responsibility of destroying them. What he did with them I do not know. But happily he relented about withholding his papers generally from the Archives. I cannot believe that even his worst enemy will ever find in them so much as a hint of impropriety.

Charles Lightbody was another historian, a very good one, and a most extraordinary personality. Learned, shortsighted, and rotund, he always struck me as more like a German professor than any real German professor. The tales of him are legion. He was as innocent as a child, and got into some mild scrapes as a result. Forgetting that he was an American citizen (though he had come to Saskatchewan as a child), he took some part in a Canadian general election that was technically illegal and I believe was hauled into court for it.

Charles had a heart of gold, and a total mastery of any subject he had ever studied. He had also a flow of speech that was fascinating but almost incessant. Even such a chatterbox as I had difficulty getting a word in edgeways. Once, at Balliol, Louis MacKay, just after lunch, invited me to come to tea the following Saturday. He said he was going to call on Charles, who lived some distance away, to invite him also. He returned about 6:00 o'clock. I asked if Charles had accepted. 'Well, I'm not sure. I'm not certain that I got a chance to ask him!' It turned out that he hadn't.

Charles was the most absent-minded person I have ever known. At one of the Couchiching Conferences I shared a room with him. I woke one morning to find him scouring the room for something. He looked in everything, on everything, under everything. Finally he turned out the wastebasket. All in vain. I said: 'Charles, what on earth are you looking for?' 'My glasses. I can't remember where I put them.' 'Well, you surely couldn't have put them in the wastebasket!' He replied, with perfect solemnity: 'It doesn't seem very likely, but I might have.' He ultimately found them on top of the bed. He had got into bed with them still on, had then taken them off and laid them on the bedclothes, gone peacefully to sleep, and slept so tranquilly that they lay undisturbed the night through.

At that same conference one of the student waitresses said to me one evening: 'I'm afraid Professor Lightbody is very cross with me.' 'Why?' 'At lunch I upset a whole glass of tomato juice over him.' 'What did he say?' 'Nothing.' 'What did he do?' 'Mopped his shirt-front with a paper napkin and went on talking.' Later in the evening, I said to Charles: 'I hear Miss —— upset a glass of tomato juice over you at lunch.' He stared at me. 'Oh, no. Nobody upset anything over me.'

When he was in Brandon, towards the end of his career, his automobile licence was briefly suspended for some minor infraction. When he got it back he started to drive home from the university. Stopped at a red light, he noticed an infirm old lady trying to hobble across the street. He immediately got out, helped her across, and walked home, leaving his car at the red light!

Charles's innocence and benevolence involved him in one traumatic experience. He got interested in Marxism. While teaching at St Lawrence College, Canton, NY, he joined the American Communist Party. In due course his career at the College ended. But he accepted this, not with resentment or fortitude but with joy; for the Party invited him to teach at its new School of Social Research in New York. This was rapture. But the rapture was short-lived. He ploughed the son of an important Party functionary. He was summoned before the Board. 'Comrade Lightbody, you cannot do this. Young X is the son of Comrade XX.' 'I know that. But I am sorry, he produced a very bad paper. So I had to plough him.' 'But Comrade Lightbody! He is the son of Comrade XX! You must pass him.' 'I won't.' 'But you must.' 'I have never yet given a pass to any student who didn't deserve it, and I do not intend to start now.' 'You *must* pass him.' 'I will not. I shall resign.' 'Oh, Comrade Lightbody, we don't want to lose you!' But lose him they did. So did the Communist Party. So did the whole movement for social change. From then on Charles would not so much as look at any kind of left-wing politics. He told me the whole story, swearing me, of course, to secrecy. From this oath I was released years later by a side-wind. Charles had gone to teach at the University of Saskatchewan, where he proved valuable but somewhat difficult. A colleague, Hilda Neatby, at a meeting of the Learned Societies, was giving me a kindly but hilarious account of some of the difficulties. Suddenly she said: 'Eugene, did you know that Charles had once been a member of the American Communist Party? He thinks no one knows it, but everyone at the University of Saskatchewan knows it.' There was no point in withholding the fact that Charles had told me so himself.

Through George Mitchell I got to know another and very different character at Oxford, George Smith, retired Vice-Warden of Merton College. He was, I think, in his eighty-sixth year when I met him. He wore on his watch-chain the insignia of the British Fascists. But he lost no time in telling me that he had resigned from the body: 'They have no spunk!' He went on to say that England was being governed by 'paupers. I don't wish the paupers any harm. But I fail to see why I should be governed by them. I suppose the Reform Bill of 1832 was all right. I *suppose* it was. I wasn't there. But that business of Dizzy's in '67 was very premature, *very* premature; and as for Gladstone in '84 — lunacy!'

Parliament had just given the vote to women over thirty — 'the flapper vote', as it was popularly called. Of course I expected Mr Smith to denounce it in almost apoplectic fury. To my astonishment he didn't. 'One of these young women said to me the other day, "Well, I suppose you think it's dreadful *our* getting the vote." I said: "No, my dear. The men have made such an appalling mess of things that I don't see how you can make them worse; and you may possibly make them better."'

Charles Ritchie has given us a lively account of his years at Oxford, which were also mine. I cannot rival his achievement, not only because I have not his literary gifts but because my life there was as different from his as chalk from cheese. I did not drink. I did not smoke. I did not gamble. Once I accepted a friend's advice to take a hot whisky toddy for a fearsome cold. It proved, of course, wholly ineffectual. Once I served mulled claret to the Fallodon Club in my rooms, quieting my conscience by telling it that the mulling would have removed most of the alcohol. Once I got involved in a bridge game because the man in the rooms next to mine on the staircase needed a fourth. I have always been a duffer at bridge. The minute I finished one of my rare games, I always forgot everything I had learned. But my neighbour could find no one else, so I accepted his invitation. When it turned out there were stakes, it was too late to draw back. My Methodist horror almost froze me, but amazingly my partner and I won. At first I refused to take my winnings (a few shillings), but I was finally prevailed upon to do so: I could give the money to missions. (I did.)

Keeping fit was *de rigueur* in Oxford. I did it in rather modest ways: walking, bicycling, punting on the river, swimming at Parsons' Pleasure — an odd name for a stretch of water where male undergraduates swam in the nude. Whether it still exists I don't know. Some years after I left it nearly came to grief. I had the story from Russell Bretherton, then a

Fellow of Wadham College. Joseph ('Juffy') Wells, Warden of Wadham, had become Vice-Chancellor of the University. He decided that Parsons' Pleasure was an offence and determined to end it. Word of this reached the Fellows, and Bretherton and one of his colleagues paid a call on Juffy. They said they had heard he was going to close the Pleasure and they were deeply thankful. It was high time. They congratulated him. Juffy was, of course, immensely pleased. He thanked them warmly and they proceeded to leave. But just before they closed the door one of them said: 'Of course, sir, you realize what the result will be?' 'Result? What do you mean?' 'Mixed bathing, sir.' 'Good God!' said Juffy, and that was the end of his plan.

For a very short time I played a little golf. But I somehow contrived to lose my clubs, an early example of an absent-mindedness that has since cost me three overcoats, a scarf, several handsome walking-sticks, and about a score of umbrellas.

These scattered scraps of memories of Oxford, and of some later events they recall, might have been ampler and more coherent if I had been able to check with the numerous letters I wrote home. My mother kept them all. But when she and Aunt Hazel had to give up their house in 1967 and move to a nursing home I threw the letters out. I was sure they could never be of any interest to anyone and I was short of space. I am still inclined to think that my original estimate of their value was correct.

A year or so ago I was asked what Oxford meant to me. I replied that the experience 'broke through language and escaped'. For one thing it opened to me subjects, ideas, languages, civilizations, some of which might otherwise have remained closed to me. For another, it reinforced my pride in England, 'her glory and her message' (to use Churchill's words), in which I had been brought up. It made me understand more fully just what that glory and that message were. It gave me a deeper devotion to parliamentary government, to the rule of law, to the freedom that 'slowly broadens down from precedent to precedent'; a stronger determination to do what I could to see that Canada also should be a 'land where, girt with friends or foes, a man may speak the thing he will'. It confirmed my 'loyal passion for our temperate kings'.

4

Montreal Extracurricular
1929-1941

During my student days at McGill I was a Meighen Conservative, a Tory Democrat — of the school of Lord Randolph Churchill, Sir Winston's father and one of my political heroes. This got me into trouble once as a 'Bolshevik'. But for the most part I was politically unimpeachable, as orthodox in politics as in religion and conduct.

I came back from Oxford a socialist. But for the first two years I gave little outward and visible sign of my change. Then things began to happen. Brooke Claxton, his brother-in-law Terry MacDermott, and a number of other friends of mine (I rather think Frank Scott was one) had set out to do a book on the distressful state of the country in the Depression and how it could be set right, and I had been given some minor part in the undertaking. Nothing came of it. The others went on to greater things, and I kept the noiseless tenor of my way as a sessional lecturer in economics and political science. But this turned out to be an overture.

F.R. Scott and Frank Underhill, and some like-minded academics at McGill and the University of Toronto, founded the League for Social Reconstruction in 1931-2, and I at once joined it. I wrote several pamphlets for it: *Dividends and the Depression, Immigration, Recovery: For Whom?.* When the LSR set to work on its book, *Social Planning for Canada,* I was assigned one chapter. But my assignment blossomed like Aaron's rod. A number of the experts whom we had relied on to do other chapters turned in such sketchy work that we simply could not contemplate printing it. As in my political career, I was a substitute for the people we really wanted. I ended up writing about a third of the whole book.

In 1935, when it was on the verge of publication, there was a curious incident. George Mooney, then the YMCA secretary in Verdun, had been chosen CCF candidate for that riding. He was, deservedly, immensely popular there and we had great hopes of electing him. Some members of our committee had the bright idea of listing him as one of the authors of *Social Planning*. I could hardly believe my ears. He had not written so much as one comma; he had never been, as far as I can recall, to a single meeting of the committee. He had had no more to do with *Social Planning for Canada* than with *The Taming of the Shrew* or *Paradise Lost*.

I protested, but my colleagues were completely unmoved. George was certain to be elected. He would be a great figure in the House of Commons. He would become a national celebrity. To have his name as one of the authors would bring us a flood of readers.

It was my turn to be completely unmoved. I warned that no one was 'certain' to be elected. I hoped George would be, but hopes were not votes. I hoped that if he were elected he would cut a great figure in the House of Commons. But the House of Commons was a peculiar place. A popular platform orator was not necessarily a success there. (I privately doubted whether the House would be impressed by George's habit of interlarding his speeches with 'if you will' every six or eight words.) I felt so strongly about the proposal that, several days later, I went to Frank Scott and said that if George's name went on the list of authors, mine would have to come off. To my enormous relief he said he had been thinking it over and had decided it would not do.

Someone had suggested that George should simply write an Introduction. I said I had of course not the slightest objection to that. In the event his name did not appear at all—and he did not get elected.

Apart from this one incident, all my recollections of the LSR are happy. I hope I was useful. When Michiel Horn's book on the LSR came out in 1980 I was astonished to find that he credited me with a variety of positions and actions in the organization of which I had no recollection at all. I wrote him saying he must have got it wrong. He replied with unimpeachable documentary evidence! Clearly, someone will say, the actions I had forgotten must have been foolish or discreditable. But, on the contrary, they had all been, at least in Horn's judgement, quite the opposite. I am grateful to all the many friends who bore patiently with my eccentricities and gave lavishly of their time, their wisdom, and their hospitality: Frank Scott, King Gordon, Joe Parkinson, Harry Cassidy, George Grube, Leonard Marsh. King Gordon was not then married. The others all were, and their wives, all of them remarkable women, were heavily involved in the hospitality. All these LSR colleagues were intellectually my superiors. Nearly all, alas, have now gone to their reward.

In the summer of 1931 I took my cousin, Billy Latter, who had just celebrated his twenty-first birthday, to Europe: England, Scotland, Wales, France, Switzerland, Italy, Austria, Hungary, Czechoslovakia, and Yugoslavia. We bicycled through Normandy, Britanny, Provence, and a good part of Italy.

For much of that summer I had to speak German every day and all day. Outside France, Belgium, Switzerland, and Italy, French was not much help. But the Germans and Austrians were great travellers; in northern Italy, where Austria had once held sway, and in the Succession States of the Austro-Hungarian monarchy, even my rudimentary German, fluent but grammatically shaky, was almost indispensable. With my German pocket dictionary and my Griebens *Reiseführer*, I was able to manage pretty well. In a Yugoslav train I even held forth for thirty minutes, in German, to a Hungarian Jew who cross-examined me on, of all things, the Canadian Senate! I couldn't do it for thirty seconds now. I can still say, competently, that I have forgotten almost all my German; which usually produces, from Germans: 'But you speak very good German!' To which I return: 'Yes, up to the end of that sentence.'

That trip took nearly four months. In 1932 I took a much shorter and very different one: I went with King Gordon to the Soviet Union for three weeks. We travelled from London to Leningrad by steamer, through the Kiel Canal; from Leningrad by train to Gorky (Nizhny Novgorod); down the Volga by boat to Stalingrad; then by train to Kharkov, Kiev, and out through Warsaw, Berlin, and Amsterdam, back to England at the Hook of Harwich. The only places where we stopped for more than a day or two were Leningrad, Moscow, Warsaw, and Berlin.

On the boat to Leningrad we were accompanied by a young Englishman, Christopher Dilke (a grandson of Gladstone's famous minister, Sir Charles), and by a very shrewd, witty, and much-travelled American newspaperman, a Mr McDermott of the Cleveland *Plain Dealer*. These two stayed with us. Two other men left at Leningrad: an English Cockney and a New York Jew. The Cockney I remember chiefly because he had a very loose set of false teeth which, when he was not talking himself, he detached and rattled in his mouth! The Jew was a dear old gentleman. He boasted: 'I speak seven languages, and all of them just as poifect like I speak English.' Describing how he had once been falsely accused of burning his house down, he lamented: 'I didn't do it! But what's the use? A Russian Jew and a fire, it's like a fiddle and a bow.'

Our guide throughout the Soviet Union was an electrician from one of the Baltic States who had worked in Boston, where he had had his own firm. In the Soviet Union this meant that he had a capitalist past; perhaps this was the reason for his rather mild and diffident manner. He did his job well, though in one crisis, when other people had taken our accommodation in a train, he proved quite helpless. We were rescued by a girl railway official who simply bundled the unfortunate Russians out of our place with what sounded like pretty strong language.

We saw the routine sights: the magnificent Hermitage Museum in Leningrad (where, among the treasures, incongruously, was a china beer mug, German, with pictures of a camel and a man, and the inscription: 'The camel can work for eight days without drinking' and, on the other side: 'There are also camels who can drink for eight days without working'); Lenin's tomb; a vast former church, converted to an anti-religious museum; Lenin's birthplace, in Ulianovsk on the Volga. The only place where the people seemed relaxed was Kharkov, perhaps because of its warmer climate. We usually stayed up pretty late, without being really fully aware of the fact, because we were so far north that we could read a newspaper by daylight at ten o'clock in the evening, and dawn came in the very small hours.

We were not conscious of being watched or steered. But I have no doubt that we were kept well away from anything that might have created an unfavourable impression. Of course there were the things that didn't work, and we soon realized that Russians had no idea of time (the expression for 'immediately' was 'this hour'). The theatres coped with this by shutting the doors at the appointed time so that if you were late you just didn't get in. We were careful to arrive on time for a performance of *Hamlet* in Russian.

In Warsaw we had our first really satisfactory breakfast for weeks. McDermott, who was mildly sympathetic with what the Russians were trying to do, nevertheless smacked his lips and exclaimed: 'Good old capitalism! But I don't take back anything I said!'

My chief memory of our single day in Warsaw is of the magnificent old square, soon to be destroyed in the Second World War—but, I hear, completely restored since.

After Warsaw, Berlin, where we arrived at a sadly historic moment. On our first morning King Gordon and I walked past the Prussian Police Presidency. Over the door, in large capital letters, was the name of its chief, Grzinski. 'One of the most powerful men in Germany,' I said to King. That night he was in jail. Colonel von Papen had just become Reich Chancellor and had sent a lieutenant and four private soldiers to arrest Herr Severing, the Prussian socialist Minister of the Interior, who, with the whole Prussian police at his disposal, simply said, with dignity: 'I yield only to force.' Papen, on taking office, had said to Hindenburg, 'At last, Field Marshal!' Hindenburg replied, 'Yes, at last!' It was, indeed, very nearly the end. Within months Hitler was in power. The socialist government of Prussia had crumpled. There seemed to be some point in the wall poster that called on all anti-Fascists to 'fight with the Communists!'

For the moment, however, liberty seemed to survive. Indeed, we went to a socialist Youth meeting of some 6,000 people, where the chief speakers were a young German socialist and a socialist member of the Austrian Parliament. The young Berliner I could follow only by very careful attention (I was not used to the Berlin accent); the Austrian I could follow as easily as if he had been speaking English or French. I remember one small bit of his speech. He was making fun of Hitler's statement that, under National Socialism, 'Interest must go, but capital must remain!' The speaker pointed to the jug of water on the table and said: 'It's like saying "The wetness must go, but the water must remain!"' He wound up with a resounding hope, or prediction, that 'We shall all be united in a single, All-German, Socialist Republic.'

After Berlin, a day in Amsterdam, where we saw a magnificent exhibition of Rembrandts gathered from all over the world.

I got back to Montreal filled with optimism about the future of the Soviet Union. In those days it was still possible to be romantic about that country. After all, the Czarist régime had been very bad. Violence had been, probably, inevitable. Russia had never had a Renaissance, a Reformation, an Enlightenment, a French Revolution (a rather simplistic view). It had been industrially backward. One had to make allowances for all these things.

At that time also socialism was much simpler and more specific than it is now. There was a simple faith in nationalization and co-operatives. It was possible for a British or Canadian socialist to believe that the only difference between the Communists and ourselves was that they believed that violence was inevitable and we didn't. We were firm believers in parliamentary democracy. Disillusionment with nationalization was still to come. So were the worst horrors of Stalinism, or at any rate the knowledge of them.

So then, and for some years after, I was ready to speak favourably of what I had seen in the USSR, though always with reservations. I even addressed one meeting of the Friends of the Soviet Union. But it convinced me that the local Communists were trying to take me into camp and I refused further invitations. I was a socialist democrat; I was a pacifist, a Quaker; I was, in constitutional matters, as I still am, a John A. Macdonald Conservative. (When I was in the Senate I used to say that I sat as a Pierre Trudeau Liberal because I was a John A. Macdonald Conservative, and it was not just a witticism.) I might add that 'democratic' was not then the all-purpose synonym for 'good' or 'desirable' that it has sometimes been since, covering a variety, if not a multitude, of sins.

In 1932 the Co-operative Commonwealth Federation (CCF) was formed in Calgary. I promptly joined what was then its only affiliate in metropolitan Montreal, the Verdun Labour Party, and from then on I was an ardent and active CCFer. I never was on the National Council. But I was President of the Quebec section (what there was of it); I was a delegate to the Regina Convention of 1933; I had a small share in the drafting of the Regina Manifesto. I have no recollection of any specific contribution. But King Gordon's family entertained a number of us at their summer home on the Lake of the Woods (we had been taking part in a western version of the Lake Couchiching Conferences), and while we were there we received a first draft of the Manifesto from Frank Scott and Frank Underhill, which we scanned with a critical eye, but in which we made, as far as I can recall, few, and only very minor, changes.

King Gordon and I drove to Regina through the United States (there was no Trans-Canada Highway in those days). The convention there was a variegated assortment of 'sondry folk, by aventure y-falle in felaw-shipe, and pilgrims were they alle' to the Co-operative Commonwealth. They were fleeing from the City of Destruction, ravaged by drought, unemployment, and bankruptcy. They all sought the Holy City. But they were not by any means united on what exactly it was or how to get there. I can't remember any Communists; if there were some they certainly had no effect on the deliberations or the decisions. Not surprisingly there were also no representatives of big business, though King Gordon, Frank Scott, and I found ourselves at least once cast in that role.

The Saskatchewan Farmer-Labour Party had adopted an agricultural policy known as 'use-lease'. The Montreal newspapers had painted it in lurid colours as virtually nationalization of the land. We felt tolerably sure that it was not that, but we couldn't make out just what it was. Here, on the spot, was our opportunity to find out. So, very respectfully, we asked George Williams, the Leader of the Farmer-Labour Party, to tell us. He literally retreated into a corner, glowered at us, and growled: 'Nobody is coming here from the EAST to take our Socialism away from us!' Accustomed to being considered in Montreal as practically Stalin's right-hand men, we hastened to deprecate the soft impeachment. But Comrade (or Brother, or Mr —— I cannot remember how we addressed him) Williams was not to be moved. For him we were the personal representatives of the CPR, the Bank of Montreal, and the Royal Bank of Canada. Not one syllable of explanation of 'use-lease' could we get out of him. Fortunately the subject sank below the horizon, and to this day I have no idea what it meant.

As far as I know there were no trade-union delegates. A.R. Mosher, President of the All-Canadian Congress of Labour, and of the Canadian Brotherhood of Railway Employees, had been at the Founding Meeting in Calgary the year before, but he did not appear in Regina; and of course the highly respectable and 'non-partisan' Trades and Labor Congress of Canada and its unions would not have touched us with a barge-pole.

The farm organizations, or some of them, were there: the United Farm-ers of Ontario (including Agnes MacPhail and the learned Utopian, W.C. Good). The United Farmers of Saskatchewan were there. So were the United Farmers of Alberta, represented by such notable figures of the parliamentary Ginger Group as Ted Garland, Bob Gardiner, Henry Spencer, George Coote, and, last but by no means least, Bill Irvine.

There were some delegates from Independent Labour parties, notably the Manitoba ILP, which sent J.S. Woodsworth himself and the former Mayor of Winnipeg, John Queen.

There were academics: Frank Scott, King Gordon, Joe Parkinson, Frank Underhill, and myself, sent by what organization or organizations I now have no notion. There was Elmore Philpott, crippled by the arthritis the war had given him, former candidate for the leadership of the Ontario Liberal party, eloquent and charismatic.

There was Lewis St George Stubbs, crusader for 'social justice' (by which he meant a judicial system with a social slant). He was something of a hero. He had been a county court judge in Manitoba and had distinguished himself by being very much the poor man's judge. A fiery character, he had not taken kindly to having his judgements reversed by a higher court. He wound up his judicial career by hiring a hall and holding a public meeting to say what he thought of one such reversal. He was of course dismissed, after the usual inquiry. He was responsible for adding to the Regina Manifesto its fourteenth point: 'Social Justice'. He was elected to the Manitoba Legislature as a CCFer, but soon, as might have been expected, became an Independent.

There were, as far as I know, no delegates at all from the Maritime Provinces.

British Columbia sent a considerable delegation, mostly, or all, from the 'Socialist Party of Canada, British Columbia Section' (the other sections were, I think, extinct). Most of these were ultra-pure Marxist international socialists. They regarded the Communist Party with disdain, heretics from the true Marxist faith. One of their stalwarts (I do not think he was at the Regina convention), Wallace Lefeaux, a Vancouver lawyer, later was a CCF candidate for Vancouver Centre in the Dominion election of 1935, and came within an ace of being elected. This was no mean feat, for his typical speech consisted of telling the electors that if they wanted to vote for him, that was all right, but it didn't really matter, because the revolution was going to happen anyway! It was this sort of attitude that provoked Tommy Douglas's famous *mot*: 'For years the people of British Columbia have been trying to elect a CCF government, but the British Columbia CCF has always managed to stop them!'

Naturally these ultra-Marxists and the United Farmers of Ontario looked on each other with suspicion, even horror. Some of the United Farmers of Alberta probably shared the feelings of the UFO. They inclined to favour Mr Good's idea of non-partisan government: representatives of various groups and interests meeting amicably in committees and working out reasonable solutions to common problems. To complicate the picture, Bill Irvine, one of the foremost UFA delegates, was a Social Credit enthusiast!

We had also one advanced (for those days, at any rate) feminist, Mrs Lucas. She was accompanied by her husband (always referred to simply as 'Mrs Lucas's husband'). Mrs Lucas was reputed to have consoled a friend, in jail as a prisoner of conscience, with: 'Don't be afraid, dear. God is with you, and She will take care of you' (thus anticipating some modern developments in certain churches). Mrs Lucas distinguished herself in the proceedings of the convention by rising, on every motion for the appointment of a committee, to move 'that there be a woman on this committee'. This went on until John Queen forestalled her by leaping to his feet to move 'that there be a man on this committee'.

Agnes MacPhail did not see eye to eye with Mrs Lucas. The ladies of the convention gave a luncheon for Agnes. Her speech was brief: 'This woman business makes me sick. From the first day I was in the House of Commons, I've never asked for anything on the ground that I was a woman. If I didn't deserve it on my merits, I didn't want it'; and, drawing her habitual opera cloak around her, she swept from the room, leaving a seething mass of infuriated feminists behind her.

In one of the Regina Convention's committees Ernie Winch, of the Socialist Party of British Columbia, proposed that the CCF should declare itself for nudism. I scotched that: 'No, no, Ernie! I can see the headline in the *Winnipeg Free Press* tomorrow morning: "J.S. Woodsworth comes out for nudism!"' Ernie went on to become a very respected and beloved member of the British Columbia Legislative Assembly, where he was the champion especially of mental patients and dumb animals.

My warning about nudism is the only thing I can recall contributing to the deliberations. My recollections seem to be almost entirely frivolous.

That such an oddly assorted collection of individualists, fully as 'sondry' as Chaucer's pilgrims, succeeded in agreeing on anything is surprising; and sometimes consensus, in the Duke of Wellington's words, was 'a damned close run thing'. That they should have produced a manifesto of Canadian Socialism seems, in retrospect, little short of miraculous. But they did. One reason, I think, was the sheer horror of the Depression and the drought. Another was the passionate earnestness of the leaders, above all of J.S. Woodsworth. Canada owes most of its present social security, social ownership, and even the fact of its central bank to these pioneers of the CCF. I am proud to think that I had even so small a part in their work. They never achieved office except in Saskatchewan. But they inspired some Liberals and some Conservatives, scared some others, shamed some more, into doing what, left to themselves, they would have done too little and too late, if at all.

They certainly scared the élite in Montreal—though not, perhaps, immediately. The first CCF candidate for any legislative body was in a provincial by-election in Alberta. She was defeated by an Independent, 'supported', as the Montreal *Gazette* sublimely put it, 'by Conservatives, Liberals and other thoughtful elements'; and the *Gazette* breathed freely again. But not for long.

Very soon we found that meetings of the LSR in Montreal were being watched by no less than four sets of police, in plain clothes of course. We owed our discovery of it to professional jealousy. At one of our meetings a member of the audience came up to a small group of us at the coffee interval and said: 'See that man over there? He's RCMP. That one is the QPP [Quebec Provincial Police]. That one's the city police subversive squad. I'm one of Duplessis's own men. Those other fellows shouldn't be here at all.' We had had plenty of indications that the three official forces were watching us. The only thing that surprised us was the presence of Mr Duplessis's own man.

It would be interesting to know what the police made of our deliberations. Any resemblance between their reports and what was actually said might well prove purely coincidental, for the officers' knowledge of socialism of any kind was neither profound nor precise. Two incidents will illustrate this.

One concerns a public meeting of the Canadian Labour Defence League held for the unemployed, somewhere in the East End of Montreal. This was undoubtedly a Communist front, presided over by a cherubic-looking elderly gentleman, the Reverend A.E. Smith. He had been a Methodist minister in Manitoba; indeed, he had been the President of the Conference that received J.S. Woodsworth's resignation from the Methodist ministry. (His son, Stewart Smith, later became a prominent Communist leader in Toronto.) At the meeting the city police made several arrests. When one of the accused came to trial, Constable Boychuk testified that the chairman of the meeting had said: 'All those in favour of the revolution, hands up.' Defence counsel asked whether he was sure it was 'revolution'. Yes, he was sure. 'Are you prepared to swear it wasn't "resolution"?' 'Oh, it might have been.'

The other incident shows that these niceties were also not well understood in a much more exalted quarter. In 1934 the Canadian Political Science Association, an early member of the now vast assemblage known as the Learned Societies, was having its annual meeting at McGill. One of the subjects to be discussed was immigration. Dr N.A.M. MacKenzie, afterwards President of the University of British Columbia, told his friend General MacBrien, Commissioner of the RCMP, that that body might be able to make a valuable contribution to the discussion and so should send a representative. The General thought he was being tipped off and hastened to assure Dr Hemmeon, who was looking after the arrangements on Dr Leacock's behalf, that he would be glad to send a man to keep tabs on the doings. Should he come in uniform or in plain clothes? (If he had come to the annual meeting in Ottawa in 1930, he could have listened to my not very subversive defence of Lord Byng's refusal of dissolution of Parliament in 1926. But of course it *was* subversive, of what Donald Creighton called 'the Authorized, or Grit, Version of Canadian history'.)

Fear and horror of the CCF probably reached their climax in the mind of J.W. McConnell, the sugar magnate who bought the *Montreal Star* from its founder, Lord Atholstan (only to discover in the fine print that the old fox had retained control of editorial policy). McConnell issued orders that the CCF was never to be mentioned in the *Star*. The paper was not allowed even to take paid advertisements for CCF meetings, as I discovered when I was provincial president of the party. Then, disaster: the CCF won the provincial election in Saskatchewan in 1944. The appalling news of course reached the *Star* newsroom very late in the evening. What was the staff to do? Print nothing on the subject? Say the Liberals had won? It was a problem almost too nice for human solution. Then some daring soul suggested ringing McConnell at home. They did. For a moment, stricken silence; then the mournful response: 'You'll have to print it.'

Another enterprise in which I took part was the Fellowship for a Christian Social Order (FCSO) and a set of leaflets written for it by King Gordon, Professor Jim Coote (brother of George Coote, CCF MP from Alberta), and me. We had reason to believe that this also attracted the attention of the police, who probably eventually had a considerable file on that organization. It was organized by a group of United Church ministers, including several professors (King Gordon, Professor of Christian Ethics, United Theological College, Montreal; Professor R.B.Y. Scott, a noted Old Testament scholar at the same College; Professor Gregory Vlastos, Queen's University; Professor John Line, University of Toronto; Professor Martyn Estall, Queen's University; Professor Jarvis McCurdy, University of Toronto), and such full-time ministers as David MacLennan, Emmanuel Church, Montreal; Philip Mathams of a church in the Montreal region, I have forgotten just where; and that saintly old veteran of the Social Gospel, Salem Bland. Eventually it included also laymen, of whom I was one. (It was thanks to my membership in the FCSO that I was elected a delegate to the Montreal Presbytery of the United Church – if I remember correctly as an alternate to a very right-wing businessman named Murphy. It is the only time I have ever been elected to any United Church official body outside my own congregation.)

Phil Mathams was a particularly interesting character. At the age of eleven ('I was a big overgrown boy') he had enlisted in the British Army in the First World War. He was then an agnostic. He came out of the war a socialist, and, contrary to a more usual pattern, socialism made him a Christian and a pacifist. He had a lively wit, which he used with great effect in conjunction with a pronounced stammer. When the FCSO was considering the admission of laymen, Phil asked: 'W-w-what about the w-w-w-omen? Shall I call them "l-l-layettes"?' In another discussion he happened to refer to a former Roman Catholic priest who had become an Anglican, a Father Rahard. Phil could not for the moment remember his name: 'W-w-what's that ex-p-p-priest, Father, Father ——?' I said,

'Rahard.' 'That's it! Rah-rah-rah-Rahard! I knew it was something like a college yell.' Another time he was denouncing the church's failure to go thoroughly pacifist: 'The attitude of the church has too often been [in a tone of infinite scorn and disgust] w-w-w-wishy-w-w-w-washy.' He had not only wit but an excellent mind and a fine spirit. He died comparatively young.

The FCSO in its turn produced a book, *Towards the Christian Revolution* (1936), to which I contributed a chapter. Those were the days of the Left Book Club in England, of *Christianity and Communism* by John Macmurray, who had been one of my tutors at Balliol. At that time he was an ardent Kantian. By the 1930s he was discovering common ground between Christianity and Communism. He had a great influence over a number of us, especially Gregory Vlastos and me. Our book reflected this. It received an enthusiastic review from John Strachey in the Left Book Club's organ. Strachey said we were what Lenin would have called 'hards'. Some of what we said, and especially of what I said, I now consider very foolish, or worse. We were all horrified by Fascism; the Communists were then running very hard their theme of a united front against Fascism; the socialists in Germany had proved miserably broken reeds; the Western powers, by their 'non-intervention', had let the Germans and Italians carry Franco to victory in Spain; the crimes of Stalin were as yet little understood. I never became a member of the Communist-inspired League Against War and Fascism (some CCFers—including, I think, Tommy Douglas—did). But I was in favour of a united front with the Communists, until the Molotov-Ribbentrop Pact stunned the world. After arguing about this with a Communist friend (whom I suspected of being behind the invitation I received from no less a person than Tim Buck, leader of the Canadian Communist Party, to join it, an invitation I need hardly say I firmly refused), I decided I could have nothing further to do with these people.

After the Soviet Union entered the war and the Party turned its back somersault, the Communists made a determined effort to penetrate the FCSO. In due course they succeeded, and of course killed it. They began by getting one of their supporters (whether he was a Party member I never knew; he certainly acted like one) elected secretary of the organization. He was a Presbyterian minister. His wife was as devoted to the Party line as he, or more so. (In my experience the female Communist was much more deadly than the male. Several CCF MLAs were led into the Communist orbit by their wives. I once said to David Lewis that the CCF should have a constitutional rule debarring any member who had a Communist wife from being a candidate.) Between them they filled the FCSO's paper with standard Communist clichés. The executive (I had been unavoidably absent from the meeting that elected it) was completely bamboozled. I warned its members in detailed and trenchant letters that they were being led up the garden path. They were shocked by my narrowness and intolerance. They went so far as to deny my right to protest or criticize, on the ground that I could have been at the meeting that had elected these people, and that as I wasn't I had to accept whatever they did till the next annual meeting!

I had one astonishing and utterly futile meeting with these good people — for they *were* good people, admirable characters, but innocent, even more innocent than I had been; and they were determined to see the best in everyone. The immediate occasion of this encounter was a 'joint' meeting that had been held in Toronto some weeks earlier by the FCSO and the Labour-Progressive Party, the alias under which the still-illegal Communist Party was then operating, at which the chief speaker had been Mrs Dorise Neilsen MP, elected as a 'Unity' candidate. She was undoubtedly a Communist (she ended up in China). The FCSO paper had called her 'the focal point of democracy in Canada', which was patently absurd; she was the sole 'Unity' MP. I insisted on asking the executive, who had all been enchanted with her and by her, some very pointed questions. Had there been joint chairmen? No. Had there been a collection? Yes. Were there any net proceeds? Yes. Had the FCSO got any part of them? No. Who had got them? The Labour-Progressive Party.

I said: 'I have no objections to Communists being members of the FCSO. That is a matter for them and their consciences. But I do not want to see this organization controlled by any party, Liberal, Conservative, CCF, or Communist.' The response, from one dear lady, a university graduate, was: 'I am shocked to hear you advocating the suppression of the Communist Party.' I said: 'I did not advocate the suppression of *any* party. I said I did not want to see this organization *controlled* by any party, Liberal, Conservative, CFF, or Communist.' 'Well, it amounts to the same thing.' 'Excuse me. The English dictionary still has some meaning. On your showing I was advocating the suppression of *all* parties, including my own!' But I got absolutely nowhere. Several years later more than one member of the executive spontaneously confessed to me that my warnings had proved true. By that time the FCSO was dead. If the Communists had been content with influence, they might have used it to gain entry to various religious organizations. But they had to have control, so they lost everything. I believe the full record of these transactions is in the United Church archives.

During my undergraduate years at McGill I had done a good deal of public speaking. In my first year I had won the Talbot-Papineau Memorial Cup for Impromptu Speaking. (I have occasionally wondered whether I owed my success to a ferocious throat cold, which gave my voice a depth it does not ordinarily possess; the first time I heard my voice played back to me from a record I was appalled by the sound.) After that I was on the university debating team (we lost), and often took part (ingloriously) in the Mock Parliaments. When I came back from Oxford I was in some demand by various organizations—invariably, I think, of no importance. In some cases they merely wanted a speaker, it didn't in the least matter who he was or what he talked about. (I have experienced this often later, even fairly recently.) Sometimes it was an organization that was genuinely interested in a subject I really knew something about. Sometimes, of course, it was a CCF organization. Among the very few specific recollections I have of my effusions, two are frivolous.

One invitation I received was from a suburban body that held regular meetings. The man on the telephone gave me a list of the speakers they had had—including, I remember, Professor Frank Scott. It was an impressive list and I was beginning to feel rather uplifted, till the gentleman said: 'They've all been rather intellectual, we thought we'd like a change.' I accepted; but they must have had second thoughts, for the meeting was cancelled.

The other memorable incident took place at a CCF youth meeting. In the audience was a thoughtful-looking man of middle age. When the time came for questions, he rose to ask for the CCF policy on vegetarianism. Thoroughly unnerved, I replied that as far as I knew it had none. He was horrified. Vegetarianism, he told us, was the solution to the problem of war. The production of meat involved enormous quantities of land. He had been told that if England went vegetarian, it would not need to import any food at all. If every nation went vegetarian they could all be self-sufficient in food and would have no reason to covet other countries' land or try to grab it. He was glad to add that the vegetarian cause was making progress: he had just been to Brazil, and in that country everyone was eating nuts. 'Everywhere I went I found nuts: nuts in the presidential palace, nuts in the Congress, nuts in the universities, nuts in private homes.' He was clearly startled, and hurt, by the unseemly mirth that followed.

It was in these years also that I began my long and often turbulent career of writing letters to newspapers. This moved my family in Montreal, and many friends, to anguished appeals to stop: 'Everybody knows that people who write letters to the papers are crazy!' But I persisted, provoked by a steady series of pseudonymous letters from a right-wing extremist who, I eventually discovered, was the 'economic adviser' of Sir Edward Beatty, President of the CPR and of the McGill University Board of Governors—one P.C. Armstrong. His favourite pseudonym was 'Student', but he had a multitude of others, including 'Soyons Sages' and 'Soyons Justes'. I counted seventeen, and said so. He indignantly told a mutual friend that he had used only thirteen—my critical sense was evidently at fault! He explained, to someone who repeated it to me, that he never signed his name because CPR policy forbade him to. Judging by the letters I should say he was an ardent admirer of General Franco and of Salazar, the Portuguese dictator, both of whom also enjoyed the esteem of the local Roman Catholic hierarchy. He was in fact a Montreal Blimp, who if anything out-Blimped even Low's famous Colonel; the Czars would have liked him.

I saw no reason why his venom should go unchallenged, so I went after him full tilt. Fresh from England, where letters to *The Times* on every subject under heaven, and from citizens of all descriptions, were an institution, I was deaf to the pleadings of my relatives and friends. The matters in dispute all concerned the Depression and its helpless victims.

(In this they differed from some of the letters in *The Times*. I recall two series that appeared there in 1926 or 1927. One had to do with the colour of Mary Queen of Scots' eyes, the other with whether George III, opening Parliament at the onset of one of his periods of mental disturbance, had said, 'My Lords and Peacocks' or 'My Lords and Turkey-cocks'. Both series came from correspondents who were unimpeachably upper-class and who drew upon ancestral memories, advantages I did not possess.)

In 1940, when I was Quebec provincial president of the CCF (a Mexican army, all generals and few privates), a new charter divided Montreal into 'districts', each of which was to elect three Councillors representing the property owners and three representing tenants. We had one Labour-CCF sitting alderman. We decided we must nominate three tenants' candidates in the district he represented, which was, ethnically and religiously, highly varied. About 45 per cent of the people were Jewish. A large number were garment-workers and their families, with a strong socialist tradition. (David Lewis came from this district, the federal riding of Cartier. So did Fred Rose, the one Communist MP in our history.)

Choosing two of the candidates was easy: Mike Rubinstein, a labour lawyer, and Albert Eaton, an official of the International Ladies Garment Workers Union. Choosing the third was a problem. The alderman, Joseph Schubert, might have seemed the obvious choice. He had a large body of devoted followers; unfortunately he had an equally large body of devoted enemies. We dared not choose him, and we dared not choose one of his enemies. As provincial president I was tranquilly watching the nominating convention when suddenly the chairman's voice rang out: 'You!' (pointing straight at me). I said: 'Ridiculous! I don't live in the district and I'm a Gentile.' 'Sure, that's just it. Nobody very much wants you, but nobody very much doesn't want you.' I found myself in the same position as Sir John Abbott when he was chosen Prime Minister in 1891.

I had a wonderful time. All the local CCFers were more than generous to me. The only drawback was that they had no idea of time. If a meeting was called for 8:00 p.m., only by being very disagreeable could I get it started by 9:30 or even later. (When I told this to a Jewish friend from the West End, he laughed: 'Don't you know our saying: "7:30, Jewish time; that means be on hand at 9:00 sharp."' When I repeated this to a Viennese Jewish friend, he was incensed: 'It is not Jewish at all, it's Russian and Polish!')

I listened to a steady round of Yiddish speeches, most of which were superb. Men who had toiled all day in a garment factory would come in and deliver eloquent and learned dissertations on Marx and Hegel. In those days I could speak fluent, though ungrammatical, German; so once I got used to the accent I had no trouble understanding what was said, jokes and all, except of course for the occasional Hebrew word. Albert Eaton's speeches presented even less difficulty, for he spoke what his friends called 'fifty-fifty Yiddish'. His first speech began: 'Bruder chairman und freunde: Mr Rubinstein hat explained the issues of the campaign. Wir haben plenty Talenten in the members of the unions.'

The campaign had its tragi-comic moments. One black December night we were distributing leaflets. A small group of French-Canadian children passed us, shouting 'Sales Juifs!' I immediately shouted back: 'Oui. Tout à fait come la Sainte Vierge, Saint-Joseph et les douze Apôtres!' Dead silence fell. I don't suppose anyone had ever told them that all these holy personages were Jews.

My two colleagues were elected. It was a good job I wasn't as I had to leave Montreal by the summer of 1941 on my Guggenheim Fellowship.

I did not, however, spend all my spare time in controversy and turmoil. I had a lot of fun, and a great deal of what I may describe as private happiness. I did a great deal of skiing, sometimes with colleagues, notably King Gordon, sometimes with students.

My mother had a large number of cousins in Montreal who were very good to me. Some were on my grandfather's side, north-of-Ireland people who were as much at home in London as in Montreal. Some were on my grandmother's side, children and grandchildren of a great-aunt in Gaspé who had married a Jersey sea-captain, John Vibert, who had sailed all over the world. I remember him well, though by the time I got to McGill he was dead. One of his daughters lived to 103, enjoying life thoroughly till within weeks of the end, in spite of the fact that a broken hip obliged her to use a walker or a cane for the last nine years. (I had the good fortune, from 1935 on, to know well another centenarian, my mother-in-law, who was always considered rather 'delicate' but who lived to $106^1/_2$. At 103 she quoted to my wife, from memory, the whole of Browning's 'Hervé Riel', and on her 104th birthday appeared, with aplomb, on TV.)

A north-of-Ireland cousin, Charlotte, was one of two people I have known who grew steadily more radical as they grew older. Both of them, amazingly, belonged to wealthy Montreal families. Cousin Charlotte began her radicalism early, when Mr Gladstone was still alive. Her family, of course, were dead against Home Rule for Ireland. Her cook, also from Ulster, was, if anything, more so. One day, as the cook was preparing dinner, Cousin Charlotte made a favourable comment about Mr Gladstone. Sarah rolled down her sleeves: 'Mrs Porter, you will accept my notice.' 'But Sarah, why? You have been with me for twenty years!' 'I will not stay another day in a house where Mr Gladstone is spoken of favourably.' Cousin Charlotte had to recant.

Another well-to-do elderly radical was Arthur Birks, a younger brother of Henry, founder of the jewellery firm (with which Arthur had no connection). I often had Sunday dinner, or tea, or both, at his home. (His only daughter had married Henry Latter, a brother of Ernest Latter, my uncle by marriage.) Once, when he was 85, I found him sitting up in bed after a heart attack reading, with strong approval, G.D.H. Cole's *Essentials of Socialist Propaganda*. 'Eugene,' he said, 'a society divided like this into rich and poor can't last.' One of Arthur Birks' most interesting recollections was of the burial of the famous Joseph Guibord, who had been a member of the Institut Canadien. Nowadays it would be considered a very mild liberal body, but not then. It incurred the wrath of the Roman Catholic hierarchy and its members were excommunicated. When Guibord died in 1869 he was still under the ban. His wife wanted to bury him in consecrated ground. The Church refused. Madame Guibord thereupon took the matter to the courts, clear to the Judicial Committee of the Imperial Privy Council, then the highest court of appeal for Canada, which found in her favour, and the funeral took place in 1875. But feelings ran so high that the civil authorities had to call out a regiment of militia, the Victoria Rifles, to guard the cortège as it made its way through the streets to the Roman Catholic cemetery. Arthur Birks was a member of the Victoria Rifles. As there were not enough of them to form a continuous line all the way, they, like a stage army, formed a guard for a certain distance, then doubled round to the next part of the route! Guibord was safely buried, as the Privy Council judgement had said he had a right to be. But the Church had the last word: it deconsecrated his plot.

When I entered McGill in 1922 my aunt and uncle, Sybil and Ernest Latter, who were like parents to me, had sold their beautiful house behind the Little Mountain and rented one for a year in Montreal West, where I lived with them. It was the coldest house I ever was in till I went to England. You could (and we did, to test it) leave an icicle on the inside diningroom window-sill at night, and in the morning it was still there, absolutely intact.

We began to notice that the house, though new and by no means cheap, seemed to be teetering to one side. Things on tables and in cupboards toppled over without being touched. Walking from room to room, we experienced a weird sensation of walking slightly up or down hill. My uncle rang the landlord: 'Your house is falling down.' Laughter. My uncle described the symptoms and the landlord, still understandably skeptical, said he would send some workmen to look at it. They arrived, all jovial nonchalance, and went to the cellar. The next moment, with shouts of 'Sapristi!' they came leaping up the stairs, ashen white. The main beam supporting the whole house had slipped out of its niche in the foundation and was resting on a water pipe!

That autumn the Latters moved to Richelieu, seventeen miles or so south of Montreal, on the bank of the Richelieu River opposite Chambly. They had bought a superb old stone house, built by one of the British officers in the Chambly garrison in 1820. A few years before my uncle bought it, a somewhat eccentric owner had purchased the knotless pine panelling from an old convent on St Lawrence Main Street in Montreal, which was being torn down, and installed this on the walls of the whole ground floor. So the interior walls were a century or so older than the house itself.

Whenever I was in Richelieu for the weekend I went on Sunday to the old garrison parish church, with its box pews (I believe it once had a three-decker pulpit). I got to know all the regular services — Matins, Evensong, and Holy Communion — pretty well by heart. This is no doubt the reason for my devotion to the Prayer Book, and of my revulsion at the Book of Alternative Services, so called; in a good many parishes in the Ottawa diocese it is not easy to find a Prayer Book service, and in one, I am reliably informed, the Prayer Book has actually been locked up. I know of one cathedral elsewhere where it lies in a heap on the floor, under a table. At this point I am tempted to launch into a denunciation of many of the features of the Alternative Services, but I am not competent to do so. The Prayer Book Society, of which I am a member, and indeed a Patron, is doing that job professionally and eloquently.

Uncle Ernest had a large collection of paintings by well-known Canadian artists (*not* the Group of Seven, of whom he was not enamoured), many of whom he knew personally at the Montreal Arts Club. One of them, Maurice Cullen, had a house and studio on the river bank at Chambly. He and his lovely wife were among our closest friends. Both were Newfoundlanders. Mrs Cullen's son, Robert Pilot, also a fine artist, was another close friend. Mrs Cullen gave my wife and me his painting of St John's harbour as a wedding present.

The days I spent at Richelieu were among the happiest of my life. I think my wife could have said the same: a golden time.

For the first half of my twelve years teaching at McGill I was a bachelor. This was not altogether by choice. Indeed, I might have seemed marked out, like P.G. Wodehouse's Bertie Wooster, as 'one of nature's bach-elors'. When an English girl I had known well at Oxford, visiting for a weekend with my mother and me, greeted me at breakfast one morning with, 'You'd better ask the first half-dozen girls you meet to marry you, because you'll have to ask at least that number before you'll find one who'll have you,' I replied instantly with: 'Oh, do you think it would be only half-a-dozen? I'd have said at least a dozen.' I never did get as far as the half-dozen. But I did ask two, both charmers, who, fortunately for me and for them, had enough sense to turn me down. By the spring of 1935 I had completely abandoned any expectation of finding anyone who would even consider me.

Then in May I went to a Student Christian Movement camp in the Laurentians for a few days, and everything changed. One of the girls attending was Harriet Roberts, a YWCA secretary and former teacher from Saint John. She seemed to me everything that heart and mind could desire. I made an inauspicious beginning, about which she often joked in later years. During a service of worship we were sitting on the same bench. When we got up to sing, my end of the bench tipped up, depositing Miss Roberts abruptly on the floor! This might well have put an end to my hopes. But, with characteristic generosity and good humour, Harriet picked herself up (never in her life would she let anyone else pick her up if she fell), and the acquaintance blossomed.

It turned out we had a good deal in common. We both had done well at university, she at Dalhousie. We both had United Empire Loyalist ancestors, she a whole string of them, I a few. We both also had Ulster ancestors — Fergusons, Kerrs, Faulkners, Cochranes. We both loved languages. Harriet was a specialist in French, German, and Spanish (she spoke French much better than I); we both had had Latin at school, and she at university. We both prized and venerated the English language. We had similar religious backgrounds: hers Anglican and Baptist, mine Anglican, Baptist, Quaker, and Methodist. She was much more athletic than I: she had played on the Dalhousie University Women's Basketball team and was an excellent swimmer and diver. She was also, as I was to discover, far my superior both in intellect and character: she could understand Jung, who to this day baffles and frightens me.

The conference over, she went back to Montreal, I to Ottawa to spend the summer with my mother and aunt. We wrote to each other (she in one of the most perfect hands I have ever seen). I soon arrived at the conclusion, 'Nothing venture, nothing win.' She had gone to a Student Christian Movement Bible Study Seminar, held every year by Dr Sharman at Minnesing in Algonquin Park. To Minnesing, accordingly, I went, and rather to my surprise she said yes.

The Anglican Prayer Book says marriage 'is not by any to be entered upon, nor taken in hand, unadvisedly, lightly, or wantonly; but reverently, discreetly, advisedly, soberly, and in the fear of God.' I don't know that we quite lived up to that standard. If speed is the sole test, we certainly did not. Having met in May, we were married on 9 November 1935 in St John's ('Stone') Church, Saint John, by the rector and my friend the Reverend R.B.Y. Scott of the United Theological College, Montreal. I had to be back at McGill the day after Remembrance Day, so we had no formal honeymoon. We set up housekeeping at once in my flat on Sherbrooke Street, almost opposite the foot of Durocher Street. We had an ample supply of wedding presents, many of them suited rather to the state to which our families hoped it would please God to call us than to the one we were actually to enjoy.

We later moved to a flat in Shuter Street, equally convenient for anyone working at McGill, and close to the homes of several friends: notably the Frank Scotts, the Leonard Marshes, the Bielers, and Harriet's friend Pamela Stead.

Professor Bieler, a senior member of the faculty of the United Theological College, was from the Swiss canton of Vaud. Madame Bieler was Genevese; indeed, she was at the very centre of the Genevese aristocracy. Her father, Merle d'Aubigné, had been the historian of the French Reformation and responsible not only for the Salle de la Réformation in Geneva but also for the magnificent Monument de la Réformation. Her brother had designed the famous *jet d'eau* in the Lake of Geneva. I had known Professor and Madame Bieler's son, Étienne, a very distinguished atomic scientist who taught at McGill, and who came to an early death by illness on a trip to Australia where he was delivering a scientific paper. I got to know very well a second son, Jacques, and, slightly, a third, André, the well-known painter. Madame Bieler often took us as her guests to meetings of the very select and learned Cercle littéraire et musical, where, of course, Harriet was very much at home, and I was at least able to follow the proceedings. Madame Bieler also took Harriet to meetings of a somewhat less distinguished Société d'études et de conférences. This helped nourish our love of, and acquaintance with, other languages than English. Indeed, for most of our married life we often had a cluster of dictionaries on the table at meals: English, French, German, Spanish, Latin, and my old Liddell and Scott *Greek-English Lexicon*.

We frequently had groups of students in to tea. When we were by ourselves we almost always had afternoon tea—for two memorable years with our cat Wink, a superb red Angora, whose early death in an accident still wrings my heart. I had had very little to do with cats; ours was a dog family. Wink made up his mind to flatter me into loving him. He would gaze at me with an expression of adoration, then jump on to my knee and kiss me ardently. He had four ways of kissing: with the tip of his nose, with the tip of his tongue, with his lips (a thing I didn't know an animal could do), and with his whole tongue. He gave the lie to the theory that cats love us only for the sake of food and comforts: he was as affectionate as any dog. When we'd be sitting in the livingroom in the evening, reading, he would lie in the middle of the floor, sleeping; but every now and then he'd get up and jump on each of us, kiss us, and then go back to lie down and sleep again. He didn't want anything. He just wanted to tell us how much he loved us. He was also as intelligent as any dog (and I have known some dog geniuses). He knew everything we said to him. We taught him to sit up and beg, and to shake hands. He lapped up tea, and condescended to cookies if they had enough shortening in them. When we took him for the summer to an island in the Bolton Pass, in the Eastern Townships, his great delight was to go out in the boat. At the words 'Wink, would you like to go out in the boat?' he'd race down the hill and leap in, waiting for us to push off. Even when he once fell overboard, it did not lessen his ardour for nautical diversion.

Though very affectionate, Wink had his dignity. Once when he lay close to my typewriter while I was writing an article, he got rather in the way of the carriage and I said, rather impatiently: 'Oh, Wink. Go away!' He withdrew to the farthest corner of the room, to the window-sill, and turned his back. Almost at once, of course, I was remorseful. In honeyed tones I called to him. He remained absolutely aloof. Then I said: 'Wink, I ought not to have spoken like that. I'm sorry.' Back he came, and kissed me. But he had to have the formal apology.

During our summers in the Bolton Pass we did a great deal of bicycling and visiting — among other places a tiny hamlet of four or five houses where a hand-lettered sign had been set up on a straight branch of a tree: 'Ici St-Etienne de Bolton. This is it.' Later Harriet taught me to drive a car. I took my share of driving around the Townships, and later down to Cambridge, Massachusetts, by way of Gaspé, Saint John, and Halifax. I never drove but one day in Ottawa when we came to live there. Almost at once we had to give up the car. On the salary I was getting from the Canadian Congress of Labour we could not afford a baby, a house, and a car. Some twenty-five years later we got another car. But by that time I had forgotten everything I had ever learned, and scarcely knew one end of the thing from the other. I took one look at the traffic and decided that, with my nervousness, my total lack of mechanical aptitude, and my absent-mindedness, I'd be a menace to everyone on the road. So I thankfully resigned in Harriet's favour and she drove till she found it made her too nervous. From then on we relied on what I called 'Charlotte's taxis' (Charlotte Whitton was then mayor), otherwise known as the Ottawa Transport Commission. Fortunately the bus stopped almost at our door.

In Montreal of the twenties and thirties it was part of the received wisdom that private corporations were impeccably efficient, and publicly owned enterprises inevitably the opposite. My wife and I had experience of several eminent private enterprises that left us somewhat skeptical.

One was the Bell Telephone Company. In those days, when leaving for the summer, it was possible to put the telephone on half-service till the fall, which we always did. But there was usually some hitch in having the service restored. After several of these, when I had just arranged to have the instrument put back on full service, I said to my wife: 'Well, this time I suppose Bell will get it right.' When the serviceman arrived he promptly began to disconnect the whole thing. I could scarcely believe my eyes. I asked him what he was doing. 'Taking the phone out.' 'Why?' 'Well, it's the rule that when a phone has been on half-service for a certain length of time, it must go out.' 'But I've just arranged to have it put back on full service.' 'Oh! Perhaps I'd better phone the office.' He did and all was well. Apparently the reconnecting and disconnecting divisions were like the Jews and the Samaritans: they had no dealing with each other.

But the CPR bore away the palm uncontested. My wife's family in Saint John had a very fine, very large mirror that reached almost to the ceiling. They asked us if we'd like to have it. When we said yes, they had it packed by the best packing firm in Saint John. Harriet had a telephone call from the railway asking where they were to send it. '424 Sherbrooke Street West, Apartment 36.'

Weeks passed and nothing happened. Harriet called the CPR. 'Oh, it's gone to Fredericton.' 'Fredericton! Why on earth did you send it there?' 'The back of the way-bill said "Edgecombe & Co., Fredericton", and it's the rule that we must send any shipment to the address on the back of the way-bill.' 'Then why, when you asked me where to deliver it, did you send it to Fredericton?' 'Well, that's the rule.' 'Did it not occur to you that sending a thing from Saint John to Fredericton via Montreal was peculiar?' 'Well . . . the back of the way-bill . . . that's the rule.' I came in the door just in time to hear my wife say: 'I think the CPR has been most inefficient.' I reeled against the door-jamb, because to my Montreal ears this was almost blasphemy. I don't suppose in the whole history of the city since 1881 anyone had ever uttered such words before. However, the CPR graciously agreed to bring the mirror back from Fredericton and to deliver it—this time to us. Less graciously, they refused to bring it in the door till we had paid the full freight from Saint John to Montreal to Fredericton and back to Montreal.

We paid. But the story does not end there. I said to my uncle, a Montreal businessman and a devout worshipper of the CPR: 'Uncle Ernest, you always tell me the CPR never makes a mistake.' 'That's right. Not like that damn government railway.' 'Well, listen to this.' My uncle went through the roof. 'Just wait till I tell So-and-So' (a friend who was a high CPR official). I can imagine the scene: 'I keep telling my damn socialist nephew the CPR never makes a mistake. And now you go and do this!' We got an apology and a cheque.

All this, of course, was long before the days of computers. The mind boggles at the variations *they* could have played on these themes. One friend of mine repeatedly got, from a large department store, a bill for

$0.00, followed by a series of increasingly threatening letters about his failure to pay, and finally announcing that collection would be put in the hands of a lawyer. My friend knew a vice-president of the store, who said: 'Alan, there's only one thing to do: send a cheque for $0.00.' He did and received thanks and a receipt. Another friend got results by writing a letter to the computer, beginning, 'Dear Sir (or Madam)'.

During my years in Montreal I did a good deal of miscellaneous writing, nearly all of it ephemeral. For some time I wrote about 5,000 words a month for the *Canadian Forum*. Not everything was published by any means, but a good deal was and I had a lot of fun. What I enjoyed most was ridiculing anti-CCF propagandists. They were usually sitting ducks; often they lent themselves to replies in nonsense verse. I remember particularly one orator who toured the country on behalf of the Canadian Chamber of Commerce. I actually met him, probably because he had seen something I had written. He was kind enough to assure me that he did not think me 'a bad actor'. In the circles in which this gentleman moved, 'bad actor' was not only the cant phrase for a person of dubious (or worse) sexual behaviour, but was also a convenient label to stick on people of radical opinions. A businessman once told me that J.S. Woodsworth (of all people) had been thrown out of the Methodist ministry because he was 'a bad actor'!

The Chamber of Commerce public relations expert had an astonishing talent for giving his message in phrases that needed scarcely a word changed to become exquisitely absurd, and could rhyme and scan into the bargain. I turned one of these into

> Some people actually think
> Big business is as black as ink.
> They think because it's big, it's bad.
> When this I hear, it makes me sad.

This is almost exactly what he said, word for word (as I could easily prove if I had the time and energy to hunt up the clippings). As I read his utterances I could hardly believe my eyes. In Jimmy Durante's immortal phrase, they were 'All ersters, and every one woid a poil.'

His masterpiece, in the depths of the Depression, was: 'Our system [capitalism] gives everyone just what he deserves.' I wrote:

> To each our splendid system serves
> Out just whatever he deserves.
> I tell this to the unemployed,
> And they are simply overjoyed.

My later, fairly numerous, attempts at nonsense verse have been mainly for my daughters, Margaret and Helen, when they were small. Each girl had a special set of verses of her own with a tune, with which

I sometimes used to summon one or another from a distance. One of these verses justly celebrated a cocker spaniel whom an irate motorist accused of having dented the hood of his car by running into it full tilt. The complainant wanted $15 in damages (this was about forty years ago). As the dog had got off without a scratch from his alleged attack on the Volkswagen, his owner, and his friends and admirers (among whom we were conspicuous), were somewhat skeptical. Another canine tribute was to a dog who played the piano. I regret that I have not been able to tune my harp to a dog belonging to a friend of Margaret's who regularly rings the doorbell to be let into the house, and has taught his dog friends to do the same.

In the many years of our marriage—which exceeded our golden wedding anniversary, and happily produced two daughters and two grandsons—Harriet and I were never apart for longer than a few days, or occasionally weeks. Sadly, at the end of her life she experienced eighteen years of Parkinson's disease, with incomparable courage and cheerfulness (where I'd have crumpled at the outset). Even when she had to go into a chronic-care hospital I saw her every day, until my own worsening health reduced my visits to alternate, then fewer, days—though in her last year Harriet kept track of my early progress on this book by telephone. She died in November 1988.

5

The Labour Congresses

Harriet and I had a delightful year in Cambridge in 1941-2 while I worked at Harvard. I collected an enormous amount of information on my chosen subject, Canadian Cabinet government, but I got nothing written. (In 1962, when I had the Skelton-Clark Fellowship at Queen's University, I actually wrote four chapters. But a violent attack of kidney stone and an operation laid me flat for some months. I have the chapters still and think they are good; but they are now hopelessly out of date.) When the Guggenhein Fellowship ended in the summer of 1942 I had no prospect of a return to university teaching. I was eager to work for the labour and socialist movements. Charlie Millard — who was an executive of the Canadian Congress of Labour (CCL), and of the Canadian Committee of the Congress of Industrial Organizations (CIO) and the United Steelworkers of America — and David Lewis, national secretary of the CCF, wanted me there and took steps accordingly. While I was still at Harvard, Charlie arranged for me to visit the United Steelworkers' headquarters in Pittsburgh to learn, and I dare say to be looked over. After travelling by coach to Pittsburgh and staying at the YMCA, I returned the balance of the Steelworkers' cheque — creating, so Charlie told me, a sensation. I duly learned that my short visit, and looking-over, produced a favourable verdict. Anyhow in August 1942 I joined the Canadian Congress of Labour as Director of Research.

The CCL was a newly created central labour organization formed by a merger of the purely national All-Canadian Congress of Labour (ACCL) and the Canadian sections of the international CIO unions, which had been expelled from the Trades and Labor Congress of Canada (TLC) in 1939. The ACCL and the CIO were both dedicated to organizing the mass-production workers on an industrial basis, in contrast to the craft basis of most TLC unions. The ACCL insisted that the merged organizations should be absolutely free of control by the CIO, and the CIO unions accepted this. The Trades and Labor Congress constitution had barred any union that was 'dual' to (a rival of) any union affiliated with the American Federation of Labor. This had kept the Trades and Labor Congress on a short leash, and the CCL wanted none of that.

The new Congress had one big national union, the Canadian Brotherhood of Railway Employees, a variety of small national and local unions, and the Canadian branches of such CIO unions as the Steelworkers, the Automobile Workers, the Packinghouse Workers, and the Mine, Mill, and Smelter Workers. Some of these last were big; some had only a handful of members. The CCL headquarters had a few rooms in the Ottawa headquarters of the Canadian Brotherhood of Railway Employees. I shared a room with the Executive Secretary, and my salary, as nearly as I can remember, was $2,600, a few hundred dollars more than I had received at McGill. (By 1956 it had reached the dizzy height of $6,500 or thereabouts.) So the CCL was scarcely 'Big Labour'.

My title may give an impression that is not altogether warranted by the facts. 'General Handyman' might have been more accurate. With the superb help of my staff (an Assistant Director and a secretary), I provided our affiliated and chartered unions with information they needed for collective bargaining. This involved, in due course, building up a considerable bundle of collective agreements, appearing before a large number of parliamentary committees and a few Royal Commissions, drafting briefs for unions, appearing before Conciliation Boards, representing unions on Conciliation Boards, and making so many speeches and writing so many articles that I bade fair to become, even then, what I now call myself: Canada's leading chatterbox. Very early on I was a special messenger from the Congress officers to the CCF National Council. The officers had decided to recommend to the 1943 Congress Convention its formal endorsation of the CCF as 'the political arm of Labour'. I carried the good news not from Ghent to Aix but from Ottawa to Calgary.

I can remember only one case in which I was engaged in actual collective-bargaining negotiations. It was in a Hamilton glass plant. Two unions had tried to organize the plant and failed. A third had succeeded and was very much cock-o'-the hoop. The plant's general manager had come up from the ranks, hated unions, was very proud of having knocked out two of them, furious that the third had knocked him out—so far—in the election under the Labour Relations Act, determined that it would get no concessions from him without a stand-up fight. His attitude was that he had risen—from labourer to general manager, from a pittance to a good salary, from long hours to short—by his own ability and energy. These fellows didn't need a union. Any of them who were any good could do what he had done; the rest could lump it. The union leader was determined to show this old buster that he could no longer get away with dictatorship. Neither side could utter a word without a denial from the other.

The plant workers, flushed with victory, had voted for a list of demands far beyond the company's ability to pay. Each particular item was usually reasonable enough; but the grand total was staggering. I explained this to the union committee and got nowhere. I went to union meetings and heard the leader make a roaring militant speech, to thunders of applause. I was nearly scared stiff. One demand was for an increase of 30 cents an hour. I knew that the workers would be lucky if they got 15 cents. But even if they got this, wouldn't they want the blood of the leaders who had sworn it would be 30 cents?

I went to the bargaining table with misgivings. I was not, of course, the chief negotiator. My main contribution was to try to get the two sides to agree on a reasonable compromise, especially on union security, on which they were far apart. Plainly there was no chance of the union's getting all it wanted, as there was no chance of the general manager's being able to get away with conceding nothing. I suggested a formula I thought both could live with. Both replied by talking about their 'principles'. I got exasperated: 'Look! I'm for principles as much as anyone else. But can you *live* with what I'm suggesting? It doesn't give either of you what you really want. But can you *live* with it?' Finally they agreed that they could.

The settlement gave the workers a 15-cent increase (along, of course, with much else, but all far short of that staggering list of demands); and they were delighted! All that fiery rhetoric, in the Irish phrase, had been 'big offers and small blows'.

I once took a modest part in negotiations when the Canadian Brotherhood of Railway Employees was seeking a new agreement with the Canadian National Railways covering clerks and other classes. For years the Brotherhood had been trying to get, for a group of workers known as 'classified labourers', a premium of 10 cents an hour over labourers. It had never got one copper. This time round it tried again. The dispute went to a Conciliation Board, for which I had helped draft the union brief. Suddenly, just as the Board was about to sit, the company offered to give the classified labourers a premium of five cents and take this item right out of the proceedings before the Board. The Brotherhood's negotiators said they would have to submit this to their National Protective Board, all of whose members were present. They proceeded to an adjoining room. I sat still. At once, the members started urging me to come too: 'Come on, Eugene!' 'That's right, we want Brother Forsey!' 'Yes, yes, come on, Eugene!' I jibbed: 'I'm not a member of the Board or even of the Brotherhood and this is a matter of policy, in which I can have no part.' But they insisted. So in I went, determined to keep mum.

The Chairman, who rejoiced in the name of Stanley H. Eighteen, opened the proceedings by asking Bill Smith (later President of the Brotherhood) to give his opinion. Bill made a rip-roaring militant speech: Ten cents or nothing! To hell with the company's offer! Stan went round the table. All the other members endorsed Bill's stand, though in muted tones that roused my suspicions. Then Stan looked at me. 'What do you think, Eugene?' 'Oh, no. This is a policy matter. I have no right to speak.' Chorus of protest: 'No, no! We want to know what you think.' 'That's right. Come on, Eugene. We want Brother Forsey's opinion.' I kept refusing, adding that if I did give my opinion and they didn't like it, there'd be all kinds of reproaches and recriminations: '*He* had no right to speak, the blankety-blank what-not!' Renewed protests: 'No, no! None of us would say anything like that.' Finally I said: 'All right, but on one condition: that if you *don't* like what I say, there'll be no recriminations; that you'll agree that I spoke only because you insisted, and only on that condition.' This they accepted.

Then I said: 'Well, I think you should accept the five cents. These boys have got *nothing*, for *years*. I'll bet they'll be delighted to get the five cents. If you accept, they get it, no matter what happens to the rest of the demands. If you say no, the demand for ten cents goes back into the pot and may get lost, traded off for something else you want. And it's only for one year. Next year you can come back and try for the other five cents. Meanwhile these boys will have trousered their five cents.'

Stan went round the table in reverse order, and every member but Bill Smith emphatically agreed with me. When they adjourned, Stan said to me: 'My God, Eugene, I'm glad you spoke. We all knew Bill was crazy, but none of us wanted to say so.'

Stan Eighteen's name later gave rise to a rather comic event. The Brotherhood's Maritime Provinces regional director, Frank Gillespie—a most sober-sided, cautious, scrupulously correct official—found himself, at the height of the war, in Halifax. He was roused in the small hours by sharp raps on the door. Considerably surprised, he asked who was there. 'RCMP. Open up!' Frank opened up. 'Now Mr Gillespie, why are you sending cypher telegrams? Don't you know there's a war on and this is a serious offence?' 'Cypher telegrams! I never sent one in my life. I wouldn't know how.' 'Come, come, Mr Gillespie! Don't give us that line. We have proof. Come clean. Tell us what you've been up to and why.' Frank, totally mystified, kept protesting his innocence. The officer ripped out of his pocket a telegram and plunked it down before the alleged culprit. It read: 'Meet eighteen in Montreal Friday.' 'Who's eighteen and what meeting?' 'Oh, that's Stanley H. Eighteen, the chairman of our Protective Board.' 'Mr Gillespie, you can't expect us to swallow that. Come on, now, confess.' Poor Frank had to root out of bed half-a-dozen Halifax union officials to swear that Stanley H. Eighteen was a real person, an important union official of the highest respectability, whom they knew well and had known for years.

Most of my Conciliation Boards were of small importance. My last was not. I was appointed union representative of a Board for the International Woodworkers of America, British Columbia District—a large, powerful, very militant union. Its demands were numerous and formidable. We heard the parties, and the Chairman, D.R. Blair, then locked the three members in a hotel room and said we'd stay there till we agreed on a report. The report we agreed on did not satisfy the union, which denounced it—and me. We had made a minor error of fact, relating to one employee. Otherwise our report, in my opinion, was reasonable and gave the union substantial gains. But such was the uproar that I decided I'd sit on no more Conciliation Boards; the risks for the Congress were too great.

This was not a happy ending, but there was a happy sequel. A year or so later I was in Vancouver on other Congress business. I got a telephone call from the District President of the Woodworkers, saying they had changed their minds about my work 'on that Board' and wanted me to come to lunch: 'As a result of that report you signed, we got the best contract we'd ever got, and it's been the basis for all we've gained since.'

My first and biggest experience of helping unions prepare for negotiations was with District 26 (Nova Scotia and New Brunswick) of the United Mine Workers of America with the Dominion Coal Company. This was very much to my taste, with my family roots in Nova Scotia and having written an MA thesis on this very industry. I had a burning desire to be of use to workers who, in my judgement, had long been oppressed, exploited, and swindled. There had even been some talk of my becoming Research Director for District 26—one of the very few unions that had affiliated with the CCF.

The District had just emerged from an internal revolution that had produced a new, militant executive. The old one had been in for years and in the opinion of many members had gone stale. It had been turfed out, a new crowd was in control, and the pent-up frustrations of many years were bursting forth. Everybody who had a grievance had a 'demand' to remedy it, ready to be put into the list to be presented to the Dominion Coal Company. The result was a document both large and complex. My job was to estimate how much it would cost, what might have to be dropped or modified, and what arguments could be presented to support the final package.

This was no small task. None of the demands was in itself impractical or unreasonable, though some were so technical that I had difficulty making out just what they meant. But when I added them all together it soon became clear that the cost would be utterly beyond the industry's ability to pay, even though we suspected that its real ability was appreciably greater than its published figures suggested. When I had made the best estimates I could, the total was something like at least twice the highest figure the company could afford. I managed to get the list slimmed. But when I returned to Ottawa, Pat Conroy, the Congress's chief executive officer and a former official of the United Mine Workers, chided me for not persuading the District 26 officers to make it slimmer still.

Part of the trouble, of course, was that the new officers were inexperienced, jubilant over their victory in the union elections, and apprehensively conscious of the members' great expectations. Part of it also was the disorganization, the physical chaos, in the District office. I spent days and days literally cleaning up the disorder, and wishing I had brought my overalls. Grime was everywhere. Papers and correspondence (much of it of ancient vintage, and some of it unopened) were strewn over the floor. Records, especially parts of the proceedings of the 1925 Royal Commission on the industry, were gone. When I left I had at least the satisfaction of knowing that such books, papers, records, and correspondence as existed were in bookcases, filing cabinets, or on shelves, not on the floor, and were arranged in some kind of order.

A second of my early tasks was to help the Steel Workers in their 1943 strike against Algoma Steel and Dosco (the Dominion Steel and Coal Corporation in Sydney, Nova Scotia). I cannot recall doing anything of any consequence. But I did visit Sault Ste Marie and Sydney, and provide such information and advice as I was capable of giving. My chief recollection is of the contrast between the Soo and Sydney. The local unions were of about the same size, some 3,000 members. At the Soo there was a large and lively meeting of the members, to which I was invited and at which I even spoke briefly. At Sydney also there was a meeting, to which I was not invited. I was a little surprised, but of course said nothing. A day or so later the local leader, mentioning that I had perhaps wondered why I had not been included, said: 'The truth is, Eugene, we were afraid the attendance would be so small that we'd be ashamed to have you see it. And it was.' Only a couple of dozen members attended.

Apathy among union members was nothing new. When I set to work on my history of Canadian unions in 1963 I soon discovered that this had been a problem from the very beginning, more than a century earlier. But that a mere handful would turn out for that meeting in 1943, in the midst of a national strike that threatened the very existence of their union, still surprises me.

The apathy of union members was a serious problem for the CCL throughout the long struggle with the Communists, and sometimes led to bizarre results. The Communists, though usually a small minority in most of the unions, always turned up at meetings and always worked hard, with a precise idea of what they wanted. This was not always true of their opponents. Once, when the Steelworkers called a National Policy Conference, the Trenton (Nova Scotia) Steel Workers local sent a solid Communist delegation, though Charlie Millard told me there were not more than a dozen or so Communists in the whole local. Its 1,000 members, most of whom he knew personally, had just not bothered to turn out for the meeting that elected the delegation.

I was sent to a number of international gatherings. Two I remember particularly. The first was a meeting of the International Labour Organization (ILO), which was then in Montreal. The CCL could not send a delegate; that right belonged to the Trades and Labor Congress. But we could send two 'workers' advisers', and we did. Mosher explained to me that all the officers would be busy on other and more urgent matters at the date set, 'so I don't see what we can do except send you and Andy' (Andy Andras, then Assistant Director of Research) — this in a tone almost of consternation. He added hastily: 'Not that you wouldn't be excellent representatives!'

We found ourselves in distinguished company, among many veterans of the international labour movement and representatives of the leading employers, as well as the very able and experienced officers and staff of the ILO.

One of the union leaders was Léon Jouhaux of France. I met him almost at once, and on learning that I had spent some time in England, he asked for information of the doings of 'le baron de Vombley'. This turned out to be Sir Walter Citrine, former Secretary of the British Trades Union Congress, who had recently been created Lord Citrine of Wembley! Jouhaux then commented on what he called 'la conférence de Seetle' (a single syllable for Seattle). Then it was time to go into a meeting of workers' delegates and advisers, where Jouhaux opened the proceedings with a notable speech.

He began by urging us, in quiet and mellifluous tones, to remember that we were all workers' representatives; that there was therefore no need for controversy; that we could all speak in a calm and reasonable manner, with no need to raise our voices. We all nodded respectful agreement. But the very next moment the walls rang and the ceiling seemed to rise about six feet in the air: Jouhaux was denouncing the employers! It was a superb piece of invective that could have been heard halfway across the city.

One of the subjects on the agenda was a revision of the ILO constitution. A passage in it led to a prolonged wrangle between the British and French delegates. In those days there was no simultaneous translation, but we had the two texts before us. As I listened it was borne in upon me that the two delegations in fact wanted exactly the same thing, but the particular word at issue had not been properly translated. The ILO translators were what would now be called 'world class'; but even so, with expressions of the greatest diffidence and respect I ventured to suggest an alternative word (I think in French). The two delegations looked at each other: 'Oh, if that's what it means we can accept that!' The word was changed.

I had one other minor achievement at this meeting. The International Labour Office proposed something that seemed to me very dubious. I said so, in French. The very eminent official responsible offered a justification for his proposal; but my amendment carried.

I think it was at this meeting that I met Ad Stael, the Office's senior official assigned to relations with the union movements. Stael was a Dutch-Jewish agnostic (or atheist) assigned to the ordinary orthodox unions. The 'Christian' (Roman Catholic) unions had another official assigned to them, Father Roy, a French Jesuit priest. Father Roy had had some difficulty evading the Germans in order to get to Montreal. Till he arrived, Stael had to represent the ILO at conventions of the Canadian and Catholic Confederation of Workers, which was then a collection of tame cats, completely dominated by the clergy, and proclaiming what Pierre Trudeau was later to call 'our "social doctrine of the Church"'. Stael got on famously with the Catholic unions. But of course when Father Roy arrived he handed the job over to him. Not for long: Roy went to a CCCW convention and came back frothing at the mouth: 'Never seen such a collection of reactionaries in my life! I absolutely refuse to have anything further to do with them. You'll have to do it, Stael.' And Stael did!

Later the CCL sent me as an adviser to a convention of the International Confederation of Free Trade Unions in Vienna. As far as I can recall I made no contribution whatever, except to listen.

By this time there was simultaneous translation, and all of us were provided with walkie-talkies. The delegate from the Cyprus unions was delivering a philippic against everything British—not merely the British government, but the British Trades Union Congress; everything. When he had finished, the TUC delegate rose to reply. His speech was a model of moderation, restraint, understatement: 'Mr Chairman: The delegate from Cyprus has, in my opinion—and I trust I shall not be considered to be using too strong language—somewhat overstated certain aspects of the situation in his country, and,—again, I hope I shall not be thought to be guilty of immoderate terms—minimized certain others'; and so on, all with glacial calm. Something made me wonder what the French interpreter was making of this. I twiddled the button and was rewarded by a speech of passionate eloquence. I turned to look at the interpreter's booth. He was purple in the face; shouting at the top of his voice; waving clenched fists. I said to myself: 'Hello! The Englishman must have changed his tune!' Not a bit of it: there he was, still with his 'I trust I may not be considered abusive if I say . . . '; still with his impassive countenance; still with his hands moving not a half-an-inch! It was a vivid example of what l'esprit de la langue can do even to the best of interpreters.

At Vienna the CCL and the Trades and Labor Congress both had del-egates. The TLC's method of choosing them was very simple: it rotated the appointments among its affiliated unions. This time their delegate was to go on to the ILO conference in Geneva, where he would, of course, be the sole representative of Canadian unions (though with Stuart Hodgson, of the CCL, as an adviser). Unfortunately he was not quite sure which conference was which, or exactly what his own status was. He sought enlightenment from Donald MacDonald: 'Brother MacDonald, who's the workers' representative here at Vienna?' 'Well, this is a meeting of the International Confederation of Free Trade Unions. We're all workers' representatives here.' 'What about Geneva?' 'That is the International Labour Organization conference, made up of workers' representatives, Governments' representatives, and employers' representatives.'

This innocent abroad duly went on to Geneva, where he distinguished himself after a fashion. The Canadian Government had been accustomed to delegates from the Trades and Labor Congress at ILO meetings saying nothing in particular and saying it very well, like the House of Peers in *Iolanthe*. To be more precise, it had been used to their singing a seemly chorus of satisfaction when the Government representatives reported the Government's policies and achievements. This time, to their amazement and consternation, the delegate delivered a very critical speech. The explanation was that he had asked Stu Hodgson to write the speech. Stu gave him the CCL's highly critical view of the Government's actions, or inaction. The voice was the voice of Jacob, but the hand was the hand of Esau. As P.G. Wodehouse would have put it, 'It was a nasty jar for the poor perishers' in Ottawa.

I was almost invariably fortunate in the people I worked for. Aaron Mosher, President of the CCL, was always very kind to me, though his position was largely honorary. He was a sitting duck for funny-money cranks. He could not rid himself of the feeling that somewhere there lurked a simple solution for all our economic ills, and that it probably lay in some change in the monetary system. The cranks somehow found this out and descended on him, usually at weekends, like birds of prey. He listened, then sent them to me on the Monday.

They were an extraordinary collection of eccentrics. Their notions were weird and complex, and their self-confidence was boundless. My method for dealing with them was to listen; then to explain that my mind worked slowly, and that I could not make any useful comments on their very important and far-reaching proposals until I saw them in writing. They were always eager to respond, and within days I'd get voluminous manuscripts. Then I'd make a meticulous examination of the first page or two, pointing out that this detail seemed to be capable of two interpretations, one obviously impracticable, the other perplexingly vague; that the next sentence raised similar problems, etc., etc. This usually ended the thing, though in one case it produced a splenetic letter stating the writer's surprise that a union official should turn out to be a mouthpiece for

Wall Street bankers. The author of this diatribe, I may add, had assured me that Stalin would certainly adopt his proposals (of which I expressed some mild doubts), and he insisted that the Congress should approve them forthwith. He rejected at once my statement that they would have to go before a Congress Convention before they could be approved. No, no: they must be accepted immediately *in toto*.

In due course my methods worked. The cranks ceased to darken my door. It is said that in the old days hoboes left a sign on certain householders' doors signifying to the brethren, 'This one's no good.' I think the funny-money merchants must have done something similar. At any rate they came no more. Whether Mosher knew this I have no idea.

Pat Conroy, the Secretary-Treasurer of the CCL, was the chief executive officer, and throughout his time in office (1941-51) I worked under his direction. He was a remarkable man, possessing one of the profoundest and most original minds I have ever encountered. One example of his brilliance stands out in my memory. Before Czechoslovakia fell to the Communists, a group of Czech journalists visited the United States and Canada. When they came to Ottawa, Conroy invited them to lunch, and me with them. Towards the end of the meal he asked them what they thought of 'the spiritual condition of the United States'. I recall nothing of their reply; but I sat spellbound as Conroy set forth *his* idea of that condition.

Pat was far from being an uncritical admirer of the United States. His wife, to whom he was devoted, was a former American, but that did not prevent him from saying, on his return from an American union convention: 'Individually Americans are perfectly charming; collectively they are completely lunatic', a judgement that often came back to my mind during the reign of Reagan.

Though Conroy was an old friend of Philip Murray, President of the CIO (they came from the same place in Scotland), he fought an unremitting and unrelenting battle for the independence of the CCL from the CIO—which, though enshrined in the CCL Constitution, was often forgotten or ignored by the CIO. He was a superb orator who always had a mastery of his subject. His style was crisp and clear; his voice carried to the farthest reaches of any hall. He invariably spoke from strong conviction, solidly based. I have never known any speeches that packed more emotional wallop than his to CCL conventions. Though he faced formidable opponents, he was more than a match for them all.

Pat Conroy not only had one of the best minds but was also one of the most moral men I have known. I always felt that he never, even in the smallest things, acted except for reasons rooted in what the Scots Presbyterians used to call 'the eternal verities'. His moral certitude was admirable, and of course one of his great strengths. But it had one drawback: it made it hard for him to change his mind, hard to admit that he might have made a mistake, hard to accept that a decision he had made had perhaps been not the wisest. I think it was this aspect of his character that robbed the Canadian labour movement of one of its greatest leaders. Conroy, in a dispute with international union leaders, had good reasons for resigning his leadership of the CCL in 1951. But I, and many others, felt that they were not good enough—certainly not good enough to warrant his refusal to come back, as he was urged to do when the CCL and the TLC merged in 1956.

In 1952 Pat was appointed Labour Attaché to the Canadian Embassy in Washington. I never, of course, saw any of the dispatches he sent home, but people who did see them have told me they were gems: lucid, lively, original, incisive, pungent. I can well believe it. When they become available to the public, historians, especially of the labour movement, will have a treasure.

Conroy was a devout Roman Catholic. Charlie Millard, the Canadian head of the Steelworkers—and as such a towering figure in the CCL—was a devout United Churchman. Both carried their religion into their union (and in Millard's case his political) work. Both were social Christians, strong characters and great leaders, and firmly anti-Communist. It was a tragedy that they so often failed to see eye to eye, partly because Millard was an unswerving believer in international unionism, while Conroy was a convinced Canadian nationalist.

Millard I knew well. His background and mine, very different in many respects, were also somewhat alike. Both our families were Methodist and Conservative. (Though he was always rather secretive and apologetic about this, Charlie had been named after Sir Charles Hibbert Tupper, one of the great warriors of the Conservative Party from 1882 to 1904.) This meant that both of us grew up with strong religious convictions and a belief in their social application. It meant also that we were totally free from traditional Liberal laissez-faire 'free enterprise' prejudices, which were wholly foreign to English and Canadian Conservatism alike, and particularly to the Ontario Conservatism that gave us Ontario Hydro and the pioneer Ontario Workmen's Compensation Act (which was for many years the model for the British Labour Party's draft bill on the subject). Accordingly with the Depression we were both able to take to socialism like ducks to water. This, however, was emphatically not Marxist revolutionary socialism. It was grounded in the British, not the continental European, socialist tradition: it was evolutionary, parliamentary, pragmatic, and closely linked with the trade unions. British socialist tradition took much of its inspiration from Christian socialism (which was not the 'Christian democrat' or 'Christian socialist' creed of Europe or Latin America). Christian socialism was strong both in the Church of England and in the Free Churches—names like Frederick Maurice, Scott Holland, Bishop Gore, Keir Hardie, and Arthur Henderson spring to mind.

As the leader of the Canadian CIO unions Millard played a decisive part in the establishment of the CCL. In the unity movement that produced the present Canadian Labour Congress he was equally potent; in his own union he was a giant. But all Canadian workers owe him an immeasurable debt for what he did in the wider field of labour unity and union commitment to political action. 'If you would see his monument, look about you.'

Donald MacDonald, who succeeded Conroy, was I think the closest friend I had among the leaders. He had come up the hard way, having been blacklisted, after a strike, both by the Dominion Coal Company and his own union, the United Mine Workers, of which he was president of Local 4560. Like Conroy, he was a devout Roman Catholic who carried his religion into his union, co-operative, and political work. He became leader of the CCF in the Nova Scotia Legislature and was a friend and co-worker of those two great saints of the St Francis Xavier University co-operative movement, Father Moses Coady and Father Jimmy Tomkins. A brilliant local union president, he once got for his members exactly twice what they had demanded, to the surprise of his District officers.

His ethnic background was multicultural. He was a Clanranald MacDonald, but his mother was a French woman from Newfoundland, and one of his grandmothers was Irish. (His pride in being a Clanranald MacDonald did not prevent him from marrying a Campbell, and from naming his son Donald Campbell MacDonald.) He had only one fault. His experience had driven into him the ineradicable feeling that the employer was always wrong, and when he became Secretary-Treasurer of the CCL and later of the CLC he carried this feeling with him. So when members of the staff turned up for work at whatever hour suited their fancy, he could not bring himself to impose discipline. He raged, he fumed, he grew purple, but he did nothing. The employer was still wrong, even when he was himself the employer!

Very early in his career as Chief Executive Officer of the CCL, when the big international unions wanted one of their own men, MacDonald had to face a major campaign to throw him out. It was a near thing, but MacDonald won, partly because the Nova Scotia Steel Workers refused to follow the leaders of their own union. They knew Donald's quality and they reacted against orders from 'Upper Canadians'. An appreciable number of other international union members also bolted.

MacDonald did a splendid job, first as Secretary-Treasurer of the CCL, then in the same office with the CLC, then as President of the CLC, then as the first non-European President of the International Confederation of Free Trade Unions.

He and I had a lot of fun together. One example occurred when the two Congresses merged. The Unity Committee had set up a sub-committee to produce a statement of the political aims of the new Congress. For some reason or other the sub-committee did not meet; or if it did, produced nothing. The time for a report was close at hand when MacDonald called me in and told me to do the job, using the TLC's 'Platform of Principles' and our own 'Political Action Programme'. This might have proved difficult because officially the TLC had been resolutely non-partisan for most of its career (though in fact it was very close to the Liberal Party), while the CCL, ever since 1943, had steadily endorsed the CCF. But the 'Platform' and the 'Programme' were not really very dissimilar. The TLC had, in its earlier, salad days, adopted a series of rather radical proposals; and once they were embodied in the Platform of Principles in 1898, there they stayed (with the exception of compulsory arbitration of labour disputes, hastily expunged in horror in 1902 when the Government proposed compulsory arbitration for the railways). So all I had to do, in fact, was to rearrange the order of the Principles and in some cases slightly modernize the wording.

MacDonald took my draft to the Unity Committee. It was received with consternation by the TLC members: 'public ownership' of this, 'public ownership' of that. 'Of course we know you people are socialists, but we can't take this.' MacDonald asked them to look at their own Platform, number—, number—. There it was! 'Oh!' This was repeated several times. Finally they gave up.

It was during MacDonald's time as Chief Executive Officer of the CCL that the two Congresses presented to the Royal Commission on Canada's Economic Prospects (1955-7), chaired by Walter Gordon, a joint brief, a document of many pages. I wrote about ninety per cent of it, my Assistant Director about five per cent, my research assistant about 2 $1/2$ per cent. The TLC contributed the rest. The brief went in, with of course no indication of who had done what, or how much. Not long afterwards, after another couple of joint actions where again the CCL produced most of the brief, the TLC announced that it would engage in no more, as it had done most of the work and we took most of the credit!

Bill Dodge, of the Canadian Brotherhood of Railway Employees, who succeeded MacDonald as Secretary-Treasurer of the new Canadian Labour Congress, was an old friend and fellow CCFer from Montreal days. He soon put a stop to the free-and-easy habits of some of the staff in arriving for work when it pleased them. He was also a notably sensible man, except in his zeal to appease Quebec nationalists. Naturally, therefore, he did not like my 1962 presidential address to the Canadian Political Science Association, 'Canada: Two Nations or One?' This did not surprise me. A year before he had brought me a speech he had made on the same general subject. In it he said that 'English-speaking Canadians still only grudgingly concede the rights granted to the French-Canadians by the Treaty of 1763.' This was rather too much for me to swallow.

I said: 'Bill, do you know what those rights were? Let's look at the list in Dr Maurice Ollivier's *British North America Acts and Selected Statutes*. The Treaty granted to the French-Canadians exactly two things. First, the right to practise the Roman Catholic religion "so far as the laws of Great Britain permit"; second, the right to depart to France, if they wished, within eighteen months, with their movable goods and the proceeds of the sale of their immovables. Are you telling me that English-speaking Canadians, almost exactly two hundred years later, "still only grudgingly concede" the right of Claude Jodoin [the CLC President] to go to Mass? Are you telling me that English-speaking Canadians still only grudgingly concede the right of people, the last of whom must have departed this life almost two centuries ago, to leave Canada in 1764?'

Bill's reply was a triumph of irrelevance. 'Oh, so you think French Canadians should have only the rights given them by the Treaty of 1763!' 'I don't think anything of the sort. They already have far more, and I think, and have often said in speech and writing, that they should have more still. But that is a very different thing from saying that English-speaking Canadians still only grudgingly concede the rights granted in 1763.' I still wonder who had fed Bill this preposterous nonsense. But the gullibility of many English-speaking Canadians, especially academics, for Quebec nationalist fairy-tales is the eighth wonder of the world.

I encountered it again at Queen's University during these years, when some dogmatic ignoramus asserted flatly that in the Manitoba Schools Question of the 1890s the Government of Canada did 'nothing'. I had literally to shout him down, at two o'clock in the morning, with a recital of the facts. 'Did the government of Sir Mackenzie Bowell, on 21 March 1895, pass a Remedial Order-in-Council ordering Manitoba to restore the Roman Catholic Separate Schools? It did. I have read it; P.C. 834. When Manitoba refused, did the government of Sir Mackenzie Bowell introduce into the House of Commons, 11 February 1896, a Remedial Bill to restore the Separate Schools? It did. I have read it [this was a slight embroidery; I have never read the whole enormous document]. Did Sir Charles Tupper keep the House of Commons sitting for nine solid days and nights trying to get it passed? He did. What stopped him? The obstruction of the Liberal Opposition, led by a French-Canadian Roman Catholic from Quebec by the name of Wilfrid Laurier, helped by some extreme Protestant English-speaking Conservatives; that and the fact that Parliament was within a week of the end of its maximum legal five years when Sir Charles threw in the towel because there was not the faintest hope of getting the bill out of committee.' (Bowell, incidentally, was a Past Grand Master of the Orange Order. He detested Separate Schools. But he thought the Manitoba Roman Catholics were constitutionally entitled to them, and that settled it.)

Claude Jodoin, President of the TLC and the first President of the CLC, did an outstanding job of getting the merger off the ground in 1956 and helping the two staffs to work together. I cannot recall any friction. Jodoin was always ready to listen, and he had abundant common sense. His appalling stroke and premature death in 1975 robbed us of a wise leader.

Jodoin, a French-Canadian Roman Catholic, was in several ways a contrast to the President of the CCL. Aaron Mosher, a Nova Scotian, belonged to the United Church of Canada. Jodoin's union experience had been in the women's garment industry, Mosher's in the Intercolonial and Canadian National Railways. Jodoin's union was international, Mosher's was purely Canadian. Jodoin came of a very well-to-do Montreal family; as a boy he had been driven to school in a chauffeured car; then the family lost its money in the Depression. Mosher came from Cow Bay, and had begun his career as a freight pusher in the Halifax station.

Mosher had come up the hard way. He had organized workers on the Intercolonial from absolutely nothing and in the teeth of a hostile management. The general manager of the railway threw him out of his office. Mosher promptly took the train to Ottawa and tackled Sir Robert Borden, and won. Mosher was an avid poker player, and was capable of playing literally all night and then presiding at a CCL convention at nine in the morning, fresh as a daisy. I know, because at one convention I had the room next to his in the hotel, separated only by a folding door; and I sat in the convention and witnessed his virtuoso performance as chairman. He was always in complete control, of himself and of the delegates. He knew the rules thoroughly and applied them with a firm and impartial hand. In this last respect he was, so I was told by colleagues who had attended CIO conventions in the United States, very different from his American counterparts. Both organizations imposed a time limit on all speeches. But in the CIO, high officials of the Congress or its unions were allowed to speak substantially longer. Not in the CCL: high official, rank-and-filer, friend and foe all toed the line. 'I'm sorry, Brother So-and-so, your time is up.' 'But Brother President, I just wanted to . . .' 'Your time is up!' And that was final. Brother So-and-so might be a giant or a pigmy; he might be the director of a large and powerful union, or an obscure delegate from a small local. He got his five minutes, or whatever the limit was, and not one second more.

When the staff at CCL headquarters decided to form a union, and did, they ran up against heavy weather in Mosher. 'What do you want a union for? Aren't we all just good friends here?' Whether the staff's negotiators burst into laughter at this standard employer formula I do not know. Conroy told me, with a chuckle, that he had to do the bargaining with Mosher! 'A.R.', as we all called him, finally grunted a reluctant, 'Well, I suppose you wouldn't want a union unless you needed it', and the negotiations proceeded to a successful conclusion.

I was also exceptionally fortunate in the people I had working with me. First and foremost was Abraham Andras—known, revered, and loved by a generation of union people as 'Andy'. A man of extraordinary ability and versatility, he was superbly good at a host of subjects. He was widely and deeply read, notably in comparative religion and the poetry and art of William Blake. He came of a Montreal Jewish working-class family (he was David Lewis's brother-in-law) and graduated from high school in the depths of the Depression, with of course not the slightest chance of getting to university. He got a job in a laundry, at 30 cents an hour, working in water halfway up to his knees. He eventually found his way to the CCL, where he became Assistant Director of Research, then later Director of Legislation for the CLC. During the time he was my assistant he was responsible for almost every initiative the department took. He started the collecting and indexing of union agreements. He suggested establishing the library. He became our expert on pensions, and Canada's leading authority on unemployment insurance. He wrote a booklet on the subject that was adopted by the Department of Labour for its own use; and he handled with outstanding success countless cases before the unemployment insurance umpire. His knowledge of the system was encyclopaedic and unrivalled.

Andy had just one fault: he was too modest. His lack of a university degree had given him a profound (alas, too often undeserved) respect, even veneration, for those who had one. He had some disillusioning experiences, including one with a school inspector who had never heard of William Blake. These did not altogether cure him, and I spent a good ten years boosting his ego (one of my few good deeds). I used to say to him: 'Andy, you're worth a shipload of most of the Ph.D.s I know', and so he was. While remaining modest, he did arrive at a reasonable appreciation of his own powers and became a deservedly respected figure far beyond the confines of the labour movement. His early death was a stupendous loss. He is commemorated by a scholarship at Carleton University and a co-operative home for senior citizens in Ottawa.

Soon after the CLC was formed the Liberal government was defeated and John Diefenbaker took office. I was the only person at CLC headquarters who knew a Conservative from a hole in the ground, and I had several friends in the new Cabinet: the Prime Minister himself, J.M. Macdonnell, Davie Fulton, Donald Fleming, and George Nowlan. When the Congress officers wanted to convey something to the Prime Minister unofficially, they sometimes asked me to see him. He had said his door was always open to me, and it was (I was careful to appear at it as rarely as possible). As a result I was in a position to give our officers some warnings, but I seldom did so. If I had not adhered so faithfully to my role as a trade-union civil servant I might have prevented some difficulties. I have often been sorry I kept so uncharacteristically quiet.

The CCL officers, or some of them, seem to have proceeded on certain assumptions that are well illustrated by what happened when the position of CLC Director of Legislation fell vacant. The obvious man for the job was Andy Andras. But I discovered that some of the top brass were contemplating the appointment of a veteran former TLC official who had just been dropped from a lesser position where he had been a conspicuous failure. One of the officers, who regarded this possibility with acute alarm, and who knew that if this appointment took place my department would have to do the work, urged me to speak to Jodoin. I did. Innocent as the cat with the cream on its whiskers, I began my brief by saying that what I was about to bring up was not properly my business, but that if the problem was not effectively dealt with it would seriously affect my work. The position of Director of Legislation was obviously a most important one, and must be filled by someone thoroughly competent. If it were not, most of the work would fall on me and my staff and we simply could not do it. We already had our hands full with our own jobs — more than full. In the emergency caused by the vacancy I had drafted the annual submission to the new Government, and gladly. All of us were ready and willing to pinch-hit in an emergency. But we could not operate on an emergency basis for 365 days a year.

Jodoin took this with perfect amiability, then asked: 'Whom do you suggest?' I said: 'Andy. I'd hate to lose him, but he is precisely the person for the job.' 'Well,' said the President, 'of course he would be excellent. But we have a number of positions coming up now — for instance, Assistant Deputy Minister of Labour, Labour Attaché in Brussels, Unemployment Insurance Commissioner, and this one.' He implied, if he did not say, that the officers might want Andy for one of the other jobs, probably Unemployment Insurance Commissioner. As they were all Government, not Congress, appointments, I was startled to hear them spoken of as if they were in the gift of the CLC. The conclusion I drew was that the TLC had been on such cosy terms with Liberal governments that it had been in the habit of saying to Ministers: 'You know old So-and-so, of such-and-such a union. Well, he's got rather past his best. Couldn't you make him Commissioner of What-Not?' and the Liberal Government had usually obliged. It seemed clear that at least some of the officers thought this relationship would still prevail with the new government. I knew it wouldn't. John Diefenbaker as a yesman or nodder for the CLC I could not envisage.

Andy *was* appointed Director of Legislation. Though Gordon Cushing, the CLC's first Secretary-Treasurer, was appointed Assistant Deputy Minister of Labour, the Congress's nominations for the other government positions were firmly, even acrimoniously, rejected.

Ruth Marlyn, first my secretary, then my research assistant, was invaluable, having an excellent and highly cultivated mind. She was stimulating and delightful. I was fortunate also in most of my other secretaries. Joyce Jones I enjoyed only till she went on to higher things as secretary to one of the executive officers. Helen McComb had a photographic memory, also a pointed wit that came out in crisp phrases, uttered in a deceptive drawl. Dawn Dobson, like Andy, had one fault: she was too modest. Excellent at her job, she was also very gifted musically and at home in all the arts and letters. With her too I put in a good deal of work boosting an ego. Betty Eligh, the last of my secretaries, had the appalling job of seeing me through a large part of writing my history of the Canadian labour movement, 1812-1902, which she did well, bearing it all with exemplary patience, cheerfulness, and good humour. She had her reward, though not of my making, when she became secretary to John Diefenbaker.

One of our greatest and most beloved characters in the CCL was Silby Barrett, a leading member of the United Mine Workers of America's District 26. Silby was an east-coast Newfoundlander who had gone to work in the Nova Scotia mines at the age of sixteen. He had little formal education but was extraordinarily able, a tough negotiator, above all a man of his word. His favourite expression was 'Leave us be honest'. He lived up to it, and saw that union and employer alike adhered to any agreement they signed. Long after he died I kept meeting industrialists he had fought with and negotiated agreements with who spoke of him with respect and even affection. He was a doughty leader of the CCL in its earliest and most daunting years and ended up as a Vice-President.

Silby had a photographic memory and a language — and occasionally an arithmetic — all his own. The tales of his sayings are legion. Many of them I have put on tape for the United Steel Workers and the history department of the University of Toronto. Here are a few.

'John Buckley [Secretary-Treasurer of the TLC] tells me 'ow 'e come h'up to h'Ottawa wid a delegation from de Trades and Labor Congress to meet de Cabinet and Mackenzie King, and 'ow Mackenzie King slaps 'im on de back and talks to 'im in private for twenty minutes. "John", says h'I, "when dem fellas starts to slap me on de back, den I knows it's time for de workers to kick me in de pants. Leave us be honest! Mackenzie King is de fadder of company unionism on dis continent, and it's de h'only t'ing 'e ever did fadder. H'I faddered nine children, and h'all 'e ever done was fadder company unions to take de bread out of deir mouths."'

Silby was an ardent, though not uncritical, member of the CCF. During the 1948 Ontario election campaign he visited one of his chemical unions in Sarnia. (John L. Lewis had put him in charge of the Canadian section of the United Mine Workers' grab-bag of miscellaneous unions.) He found it being addressed by the local CCF candidate, a retired teacher named Humphries. Mr Humphries was an ex-Liberal, and the burden of his speech was that the Liberal Party of old had had a glorious record, but that it had fallen from grace, and the CCF was now carrying on the tradition of the old Liberal Party. 'H'I could see dat dis wasn't gettin' nowhere wid de byes,' Silby said to me, and proceeded to quote his response.

'Brudders, Mr 'Umphries 'as given us a very fine 'istory of de h'old Liberal Party. But h'I h'aint much h'interested in de h'old Liberal Party, nor de h'old Tory Party eider. When h'I gets up to de pearly gates and meets St Peter, d'ere's lots of t'ings h'I'll 'ave to confess. But d'ere's one t'ing h'Ill not 'ave to confess: h'I never cast a Liberal nor a Tory vote. No! Dat's one t'ing h'I never done.

'Now den, h'I h'aint a church-goin' man. But h'I reads de Good Book sometimes. And what does de Good Book say about de Liberals and de Tories? H'it says: "H'it's h'easier for a camel to go t'rough de h'eye of a needle dan for a rich man to h'enter de Kingdom of 'Eaven." T'ieves, dat's what de Good Book says about de Liberals and de Tories: t'ieves! And den you goes out and votes for dem!

'Now den, you sees me, 'ump-backed de way h'I am [Silby was somewhat stooped, though it did not prevent him from going back into the mine when he was defeated for union office in his late middle-age and out-producing everybody else]. H'I suppose you t'ink h'I was born dat way. No. I got dat way working 'ard for me living all me life, wid a lot of bastards of millionaires on me back. But when de CCF gets in, den h'I won't 'ave no more bastards of millionaires on me back. Den h'I'll straighten up [suiting the action to the words]; den h'I'll be free!

'And d'ere's anudder t'ing de Good Book says about de Liberals and de Tories. H'it says: "H'every man shall sit under 'is own vine and fig-tree, and h'eat de fruits d'ereof." But de Liberals and de Tories, dey 'as a better plan: dey'll divide dem up and 'eat dem for ye!'

'And when h'I'd finished dat speech, Eugene, de byes 'ad some enthusiasm.'

In Nova Scotia in the 1920s Silby had to compete with a noted Communist orator, J.B. McLachlan. He spared no effort. On one occasion he wound up with: 'What dis country needs is more machine-guns!' 'And when h'I says dat, Eugene, all de newspaper byes couldn't get out fast enough to put it on de wires. Dey didn't wait to 'ear me finish. When dey's gone, h'I says: "And when h'I says machine-guns, h'I means ballot-boxes."' (Donald MacDonald always said that the 'finish' was a later addition.)

District 26 bought the *Glace Bay Gazette* and appointed Nathan Cohen editor. The enterprise was not altogether successful. Silby's verdict was: "'E's a nice fella: 'e's a 'ell of a nice fella. But 'e knows as much about conductin' a newspaper as h'I knows about conductin' de moon across de world.'

Before the Duncan Royal Commission, in 1925-6, Silby concluded his evidence with a list of measures that must be taken, winding up with:

'And if dem t'ing's is not done, Mr Chairman, not a wheel will turn in District 26.' Sir Andrew Rae Duncan was deeply shocked: 'Mr Barrett! Are you presuming to threaten this Royal Commission?' 'Dat's not a t'reat. Dat's a promise.'

When Joseph E. Atkinson, proprietor of the *Toronto Star*, died in 1946, the *Star* called Silby for a statement. They got it: 'Dis man h'Atkinson was a millionaire, wasn't 'e?' 'Yes, Mr Barrett, Mr Atkinson was a very wealthy man.' 'Den 'e 'ad a million dollars. H'in my book, no man can make a million dollars honest. So if 'e was a millionaire, 'e was a t'ief. Now 'e's a dead t'ief.'

At the start of collective bargaining negotiations, it was Silby's habit to say: 'Now, den, leave us take up dis agreement claw by claw.' There is a story, perhaps apocryphal, that someone remonstrated: 'Silby, it's clause by clause', and that Silby replied: 'D'ere's some people dat doesn't know de singular from de pluraler.'

One employer urged Silby not to insist on a particular clause: 'Surely, Mr Barrett, on this point a verbal agreement would be sufficient?' 'No. Dem verbal agreements, dey h'aint wort' de paper dey're writ on.'

On a notably untruthful man in Glace Bay: ''E's a liar, Eugene. 'E's a turrible liar. 'E's such a liar ye can't believe 'im even when 'e's lyin'.' I often thought of this when some of President Reagan's advisers were testifying in the Iran-contra affair.

Silby was very close to John L. Lewis, who once sent him to investigate a strike in Harlan, Kentucky, where the miners and the sheriff's deputies were shooting each other every hour on the hour. 'De first t'ing h'I done', said Silby, 'was to call a meetin' of de local union. H'I goes h'early, to see 'ow dey does t'ings. First, de white men comes in, and dey files up de right 'and side of de h'aisle and sits down, and pulls out deir shooters and deir six-guns, and lays dem on deir knees. Den de black men comes in, and dey files up de left side of de h'aisle, and sits down, and pulls out deir knives and deir razors, and lays dem on deir knees. Den de president comes in, and 'e lays down 'is six-gun on de table, and raps wid it for h'order. "Brudders", 'e says, "we 'ave wid us to-night Brudder Silby Barrett, a h'international commissioner sent by our h'International President to investigate dis situation. H'I will now h'ask Brudder Barrett to say a few words." So h'I says: "Brudder president and brudders, h'I've seen 'ow dis meetin's been conducted up to de present. First de white men comes in, and sits down on de right 'and side of de h'aisle, and pulls out deir shooters and deir six-guns and lays dem on deir knees. Den de black men comes in, and sits down on de left 'and side of de h'aisle, and pulls out deir knives and deir razors and lays dem on deir knees. Den de president, 'ere, 'e pulls out 'is six-gun, and lays it on de table, and raps wid it for h'order. Well, if dat's your God-damned h'American unionism, you can 'ave it." and h'I walks out.'

It's a wonder he wasn't lynched. I suppose they were all too paralysed with astonishment. Of course he had hit the nail on the head. As long as the white miners and the black miners were at odds, the employers and the sheriff's deputies were in clover.

Silby did not usually have difficulty getting a hearing. But there was a shipyard local union in Halifax that prided itself on being thoroughly 'democratic'. No leader, however exalted, was allowed to speak from a platform; everyone spoke from the floor. The meetings were held in a beer hall. When a meeting began, the bar closed. But as each member always took care to provide himself beforehand with two *quarts* of beer, this did not notably interfere with the liveliness of the proceedings. Silby at this time was Regional Director of the Congress. But that made no difference. He spoke from the floor, like everyone else, and like everyone else he was well heckled, till the uproar stopped him completely. His silence momentarily silenced the rest. Then Silby's voice rang out: 'Now, den, de're's lots of t'ings h'I doesn't know. But de're's one t'ing h'I does know, and dat's parliamentary procedure. In District 26, we goes by parliamentary procedure. We goes by Bourinot. And Bourinot says: "D'ere's only one God-damned fool can 'ave de floor at a time"; and h'I got it first.' There were no more interruptions.

I have said Silby sometimes had an arithmetic all his own. Once, when he was on a Pullman with some commercial travellers who got boasting about the wonders of nature they had seen, Silby could stand no more: 'All dem t'ings is nutting. H'I comes from Newfoundland. In de h'early days, when h'I was a by, h'I went out wid de fishin' fleet, down to Labrador. Now dat's where you see somet'ing: h'icebergs! And dem h'icebergs is really somet'ing. Dey's 'uge. Dey's h'immense. Dey rises 'undreds of feet in de h'air. And de t'ing you've got to remember about dem h'icebergs is dis: t'ree-t'irds of dem is h'under water!'

Again, on which union should have jurisdiction over a particular plant: 'Well, now, dat's a 'ard one, because de product is one-'alf textiles, one-t'ird rubber, and one-quarter chemicals.'

When Silby was National Director of the CCL, the Automobile Workers in Oshawa were in the throes of one of their struggles with General Motors. They relied heavily on the advice of J.L. Cohen, the most prominent labour lawyer of his day. J.L., a man of great ability and genuine devotion to the labour movement, did not think of himself as a mere adviser but rather as a force, a guru, a leader, though perhaps leading from behind the scenes. He threw his weight around in a manner that irritated some of the union clients whom he thought of rather as followers and pupils. They resolved to appeal to Caesar, in this case Silby.

Accordingly when he came to Oshawa they asked for his opinion on the role of lawyers in the labour movement. Cohen was sitting in the front row of the meeting. Silby did not hesitate a moment: 'L'yers in de Labour movement? H'I'll tell ye. In District 26 we 'as our 'eadquarters in a building at Senator's Corner. All day long de byes comes in wid deir problems and deir troubles, and we does what we can to 'elp dem. Dey comes in from de mines and from de street, and dey brings a lot of mud and dirt, and by de h'end of de day de place needs cleaning. So den we brings in de scrub-women, and dey brings deir mops and deir brooms and deir brushes and deir pails, and dey cleans de place, and we pays dem, and dey go 'ome. L'yers in de Labour movement? Dey's like de scrub-women.'

I was very rarely admitted to meetings of the Congress Executive Council. I never wanted to be, except when it was discussing some proposal that would involve work for the Research Department so that I could tell them just what would have to be done, how feasible it was, what it would cost, and how long it would take. The officers were very reluctant to let me in the door. I think they were afraid I'd try to influence policy, a task for which I had neither appetite nor aptitude. But I was present once in 1948 when the Council discussed the Marshall Plan and I witnessed a remarkable performance. C.S. Jackson, the Communist leader of the United Electrical Workers, delivered a detailed philippic against the Plan. He damned it with bell, book, and candle: it was bad for the workers of Canada, bad for the workers of the United States, bad for the workers of Britain, bad for the workers of Europe. When he had finished, Sol Spivak, of the Amalgamated Clothing Workers, a staunch anti-Communist, took the floor: 'Brother Jackson is right. I agree with Brother Jackson.' Astonishment and consternation reigned. If the Pope had announced the beatification of Martin Luther, we could hardly have been more thunderstruck. But the astonishment gave way to bewilderment as Sol continued: 'Brother Jackson's first point was that the Marshall Plan would be a wonderful thing for the workers of Canada. I agree with Brother Jackson. Brother Jackson's second point was that the Marshall Plan would be a wonderful thing for the workers of the United States. I agree with Brother Jackson. Brother Jackson is right'; and so on for every one of Jackson's specific points. I never saw anyone more nonplussed than Jackson. He made not the faintest attempt to reply. I suppose the Party had given him no 'line' to take on anything like this. The rest of us could never make up our minds whether Sol had simply misunderstood Jackson (English was not his mother-tongue), or whether he had deliberately chosen this method of spiking the Communist guns. In any event it spiked them.

Two other recollections of my twenty-seven years with the Congresses stand out in my memory. One has to do with the Locomotive Firemen's strike in 1957; the other with a major dispute between the Canadian

Brotherhood of Railway Employees and the Canadian National Railways.

For most of their existence the four Railway Operating Brotherhoods — the Conductors, the Trainmen, the Locomotive Engineers, and the Locomotive Firemen — had held aloof from the rest of the labour movement. They were the 'aristocrats of labour', skilled, indispensable workers in an indispensable industry with a virtual monopoly of long-distance transportation. But technological change hit them hard. Even then, for a time, the Firemen not only maintained their position but even improved it, against the Engineers, because many of the Firemen went on to become engineers but kept their membership in the Firemen, with the benefits they had built up there. Then the diesel engine threatened to knock the ground out from under the Firemen, and at long last, just before their strike, they affiliated with the Canadian Labour Congress. They needed its help.

But the Firemen were so used to doing everything on their own that, though their offices were directly above the office of the CLC President, in the CLC building, the day their strike broke out they had not informed him of it! Indeed, they had gone home for the day. I shall never forget the look on Jodoin's face as he told me this. They soon had to change their independent attitude, and it was thanks to the Congress that they came out of the strike as well as they did.

The Conciliation Board in one major CBRE-CNR dispute produced a bizarre situation. For years the Canadian Brotherhood of Railway Employees had relied on two McGill professors, Jack Weldon and Burton Keirstead, to draw up its briefs for Conciliation Boards, which they had done with notable success. This time, however, an Austrian spellbinder had got the ear of the Brotherhood's officers and had mesmerized them into entrusting the task to him. Weldon and Keirstead had charged the Brotherhood $6,000 for their work. The spellbinder said he wouldn't look at it for less than $17,000. I suppose this convinced the officers that he must be a veritable wizard, so they took him on.

I had already had experience of his bumptious incompetence. When Weldon and Keirstead rang me, in horror and alarm, begging me to warn the Brotherhood officers, I promptly did, but to no effect. They went ahead with the spellbinder and he produced a huge document, with a vast bundle of appendices.

The Board met. David Lewis was the Brotherhood's nominee. He took one look at the brief and appendices and had to ask his colleagues on the Board to disregard the whole thing and delay the proceedings till he could get something reasonable to put before them. He called me. I told him I was not in the least surprised. It was just what I had expected.

He sent me the documents and they were appallingly bad. The spellbinder could not even add, subtract, multiply, or divide correctly, nor even copy correctly his own results in the appendices into the brief.

If the typescripts still exist they would bear out what I have said, and more. There were something like twenty appendices, of which, if memory serves, fourteen or fifteen were totally worthless and the rest very seriously defective. In the appendices the culprit in effect had added oranges to apples, divided by plums, got the sum wrong, and the percentages, and then miscopied the results. The whole thing was a mass of junk, and the Congress Research Department had to do it all over again.

My work had its comic moments. Once, in the course of a couple of weeks, I had made two speeches in two different places on two different subjects. I almost never spoke from a text, rarely from even brief headings, and on both these occasions I said things that I afterwards thought might not be altogether to the taste of some of our unions. My apprehension proved well founded. A fortnight or so after the second speech I got a letter, unsigned and undated, from a United Automobile Workers local union: 'Dear Sir and Brother, In a recent speech you made statements which have bewildered and disturbed our members. We want an undertaking from you to refrain from such statements in future. Yours fraternally', and a typed name.

I replied: 'Dear Sir and Brother, I have your unsigned, undated letter complaining of unspecified statements, in unspecified speeches, on unspecified subjects, in unspecified places. The Canadian Congress of Labour has some 250,000 members in its affiliated and chartered unions. I am sorry that I cannot give you any undertaking to refrain from saying anything that may bewilder or disturb one or more of these members. If you will tell me just what statements of mine you object to, I shall be glad to deal with the matter. Yours fraternally.' I heard nothing more.

My last big project for the CLC was my *History of Canadian Trade Unionism, 1812-1902*. On my return to the Congress in 1963 from a year at Queen's University as Skelton-Clark Fellow I found the officers contemplating a Centennial Project, a history of Canadian trade unionism. There had already been several attempts at a history, but the best of them were sketchy, most of them were full of factual mistakes and badly written. We all agreed that a decent piece of work was sorely needed. Clearly it should be done by a reputable professional historian. But labour history was not then the 'in' thing it has since become. Few, if any, professional historians had any knowledge of the labour movement or its history and all the good historians we knew of were neck-deep in major projects of their own.

So there seemed no help for it: I must undertake the job. How long would it take? Three years at least (this proved to be the understatement of all time; what I came to call my 'infernal book' was a millstone round my neck for eighteen years). Very well. I'd be relieved of all other work for that time. Russell Bell, my Assistant Director and a very able economist, would take on the Research Department, and Mrs Dobson and I would devote ourselves to the book.

It soon became plain that to cover the whole tale of Canadian trade unionism, from its earliest years to 1967, was utterly beyond my capacity and resources, even with a big extension of time and the help of about a dozen graduate students several Canada Council grants provided. By July 1969, when the age limit superannuated me, I had managed to complete a draft bringing the story down to 1902. This, fortunately, was a logical stopping place, as it was the year of the Great Schism, when the Trades and Labor Congress of Canada threw out all the organizations that were 'dual' to unions of the American Federation of Labor.

Then I stepped on the treadmill.

We had arranged with a publisher. I sent off the draft. After enormous delays came the reply: the firm had been taken over by an American publisher who declined to proceed.

I sent it to a second publisher, who turned out to be an expert procrastinator. Sometimes my letters, asking for instructions on cutting or other changes, went unanswered for months — except, occasionally, for a note saying that Mr —— was on holiday in Europe.

At length came definite word: the draft must be drastically shortened. Four scholars had read it. One said it was just too bad to publish at all. The other three reluctantly concluded that it must be published, with many changes; I was obviously too old to do it over again. So I set to work. I cut the text by more than a third, and the footnotes from 5,200 to 1,800, and included a good deal of fresh information published since 1969 by the numerous labour historians who had sprouted all across the country.

The publisher sent the revised version to scholars. I got back a fresh bundle of opinions, most of which struck me as fat-headed, or written from ignorance of the difficulties of the task. One critic, who had previously said that certain passages needed drastic cutting, now lamented that I had cut them! Another said: 'The nature of the sources peers forth unashamedly.' My comment was: 'I had no idea my footnotes were so indelicate.' After some further delay, this publisher said it could not publish the thing at all: too expensive.

All this performance, or want of it, had taken years. Finally I almost gave up. But the Labour History Committee of the Canadian Historical Association did not. After some further delays, mostly unavoidable, they winkled extra grants out of the Social Sciences Federation and got the University of Toronto Press to take on publication.

The Press appointed as editor a young man just about to enter his first year of law school. He did an excellent job of rearranging the chapters but a poor one of the footnotes and a very poor one of the bibliography, which I had to do over again. He also undertook to correct and improve my English, mainly by substituting long words for short and changing the word order so as to take the stuffing out of what I was trying to say. I fought him for six weeks, in incandescent fury. Unluckily for him

I had the *Oxford Dictionary*, Fowler's *Modern English Usage*, the Bible, Shakespeare, and a few minor authors on my side. On the foul doctrine that it is improper to end a sentence with a preposition, I fired at him not only Churchill's 'Up with which I will not put', but a whole page of Dorothy Sayers' scathing indictment of the 'pedants, God mend their ears', who preach it. Not for the wealth of the Indies would I go through this experience again.

The book is, on the whole, dull—though whenever I turn to it to refresh my memory I am astonished to find it less dull than I had thought. I wanted to include in the Preface an account of the difficulties I had faced in writing it and my lively reply to the scholars' criticisms. But the University of Toronto Press would not let me.

6

Of Politics and Politicians

Brought up as I was, I could scarcely fail to become a political animal. Politics, long before I achieved even a minor position in it, has been a central interest of my life.

In 1940 I had been a substitute candidate in Montreal because the party couldn't get the person it wanted. I was also a substitute candidate when I ran for the Ontario legislature in 1945 and for the House of Commons in 1948 and 1949.

In 1945 Mackenzie King and George Drew, the Premier of Ontario, called elections within a week of each other. The Ottawa CCF had already chosen Walter Mann, a local teacher of high renown, to run for both the Ontario legislature and the House of Commons. But obviously this was now impossible, legally and physically: there had to be a second candidate, for one job or the other. I had told the CCF provincial election committee that if they were stuck for a candidate anywhere I'd be available. So it was decided that Walter should run for the one job, and I for the other. But who for which? Ted Jolliffe, the Ontario CCF leader, had high hopes of winning the provincial election (in 1943 the CCF had come within a few hundred votes of getting as many seats as the Conservatives). He said he wanted me for his Cabinet. So I ran provincially. Both Walter's constituency and mine were hopeless; the CCF was almost wiped out in the Ontario election and fared little better in the Dominion. Walter and I were ignominiously defeated.

In 1948 the Dominion Conservative Party elected Mr Drew as its leader. He had to get a seat in the House of Commons. Russell Boucher, MP for Carleton County (Ottawa's county), resigned to open that seat for him. Carleton was then almost wholly rural, and full to the brim of Ulster Protestants. It had never, provincially or federally, elected anyone but a Conservative except provincially in 1919, when it had returned a United Farmer. That was the sole blot on its escutcheon.

The CCF felt it had to put up a candidate. There was one young man who had almost everything: he was a veteran, a student, highly intelligent, most personable. But there was one gap in his qualifications: he was not a Protestant. A group of us mulled the thing over. No one wanted to be accused of being anti-Catholic. We looked at each other uneasily. Then Pat Conroy, Chief Executive Officer of the Canadian Congress of Labour, spoke: 'If you nominate a Dogan like me in Carleton County you're licked from the start.' Pat was a devout and active Roman Catholic. No one could accuse him of being anti-Catholic. So the rest of us nodded gloomily and tried to think of an alternative. What we wanted, of course, was a farmer and a Past Grand Master of the Orange Order. Finally we decided I was the nearest available thing to that: I had, in my time, milked cows and pitched hay and I was unquestionably a Protestant. So I was it.

Our campaign was pathetic. Of course we had to run it on a shoe-string. The Canadian Congress of Labour gave us a cheque for $350. None of us had ever seen such a thing before and we passed it around almost with reverence. How much else we got I cannot remember; but it cannot have been much because in those days I was a financial 'big interest' among CCF supporters: I gave it $50 a year! The Liberals did not nominate a candidate. So we picked up a few Liberal votes (we won the only French-Canadian poll in the county). Mr Drew got 12,219 votes. I got 3,371.

I remember only four particulars of the whole affair. One is that Drew persistently called us the 'National Socialist Party' (the official name of Hitler's party in Germany); that at the official meeting where Drew and I were nominated, there was a high old row between Drew and Bill Temple, the CCFer who in 1943 had defeated Drew in his own provincial riding (Bill was a fiery temperance man, and we had brought him in in hopes of getting some temperance votes); that at one meeting I had an audience of four—my wife, Pat Conroy, Percy Wright, MP, and the chairman. One evening at home I had a telephone call to inform me that the speaker was coming to take me for a little ride. He came—but I had called the police and they arrived just after he drove off, apparently baffled by locked doors.

When the election results came in my committee, in my presence, was loudly unanimous that in the approaching general election we must have a different candidate. I just would not do. I heartily agreed. But when the time came there were no takers: I was nominated again. This time the Liberals also put up a man. My vote dropped to 2,155, Drew's rose to 18,141.

So I never got to the House of Commons until, as a senator, I was able to attend a joint sitting of both Houses held in honour of some visiting dignitary.

I have noted that I remember every Prime Minister who has held office since 1894 except Sir Charles Tupper, who left Canada before I was born and came back only in his coffin. Three of these thirteen I knew well: Meighen, Diefenbaker, and Trudeau — especially Meighen.

I first heard him and met him when I was in high school, the same school his two sons attended. He was incomparably the greatest parliamentarian of my time, probably the greatest Canada has ever had, and from the first I listened enthralled. Never a note, never a written word in front of him; never a hesitation; never a repetition; every name, every date, every quotation impeccable; never at a loss; invincible with interrupters and hecklers; never ruled out of order. The speeches were masterpieces, alike in matter, structure, and manner; classical in their flawless English, memorable in their phrasing.

Meighen was fond of young people and very outgoing with them. I recall particularly one late afternoon when, a teenager, I was walking up the centre walk of the Parliament Buildings. The sun was in my eyes; the gentleman coming towards me had his hat down over his forehead, shading his face. I did not recognize him. Then he said: 'Well, Eugene, not speaking to your friends?' 'Mr Meighen!' He stopped and we chatted briefly. It was the beginning of that 'fierce devotion' that his biographer, Roger Graham, says so many of his friends felt for him. When he became Prime Minister in 1920 I was swept by enthusiasm; when he was defeated in 1921 I was in the depths; when he lost the election of 1926 the bottom dropped out of my political world. Had he remained Leader I do not think I could ever have left the Conservative Party.

Meighen was perhaps the most unpretentious man I have ever known. He was utterly without 'side', totally unimpressed by age, wealth, or social position. He judged everyone solely by what seemed to him their merits. (So did Mrs Meighen.) This did not always sit well with the billowing rank and fashion of the Conservative Party. John Stevenson, then Ottawa correspondent of the London *Times* and a devoted friend of Meighen's, told me that at the Imperial Conference of 1921 Meighen would chat politely but perfunctorily with some bigwig whom he found dull, but spend an hour with an assistant private secretary he found interesting.

I had one early, notable experience of this myself. In those days the opening of Parliament was followed by an evening Drawing Room, where débutantes were 'presented' to the Governor-General and his wife. It was a great social occasion, and everybody who was anybody was expected to be there. Attendance by the Leader of the Opposition and his wife was *de rigueur*. In January 1922, when Meighen had just resumed this position, the Drawing Room fell on a day when the Meighen boys had invited a small skiing club, to which they and I belonged, to their home for the evening. The date had been fixed long before, at the opening of the skiing season. Anyone but Mr and Mrs Meighen would almost certainly have put it off. Not they. I am perfectly certain it never occurred to them. Mr Meighen did indeed go to the Drawing Room, but only after he had given all of us a most cordial and unhurried welcome. Mrs Meighen did not go at all. She stayed with us, and was the life and soul of the party.

All through the parliamentary sessions of 1921 to 1925 I haunted the reserved gallery of the House of Commons when I was in Ottawa, and read *Hansard* when I was not, following avidly every one of Meighen's speeches. I took every chance I had to go to Conservative meetings during the election of 1925. By that time I was at McGill and able to watch at close range the despicable and mendacious Liberal campaign against Meighen in Quebec. What was more, I followed with indignation and contempt the efforts of some leading Montreal English-speaking Conservatives (notably Hugh Graham, Lord Atholstan, who had extracted a knighthood from Laurier and a peerage from Borden) to drive Meighen from the leadership of the Party. They considered him dangerously progressive: after all, he had once moved to reduce the duties on agricultural implements, and he had played a leading part in the nationalization of the Grand Trunk, the Grand Trunk Pacific, and the Canadian Northern Railways. Their efforts to ditch him culminated in the putting forward of E.L. Patenaude to lead an 'Independent' Conservative movement in Quebec in the 1925 election, which succeeded in keeping Meighen out of the province. The *Star* (Atholstan's paper) and the *Gazette*, and their allies and backers, pulled out all the stops, with rhapsodical reports of Patenaude meetings and predictions of big Conservative gains in Quebec. It was widely reported, and believed, that this same crew contributed to a 'slush fund' to defeat Meighen in his own constituency of Portage la Prairie, Manitoba.

The campaign failed dismally. Outside Quebec, Meighen won 112 out of 180 seats in the House of Commons (a sufficient commentary on the oft-repeated charge that though he was a great parliamentarian, he could not win the electors). In Quebec the Party won four seats. As I remarked in a student newspaper, *The McGill Fortnightly Review*, no one who knew the intellectual calibre of the people who inspired and backed the Patenaude campaign could have been surprised at the result, and probably no one was less surprised than Meighen. That article got both me and the editors into very hot water with the university authorities. It was a paean of praise of Meighen, and I was a Conservative, having been actually vice-president of the McGill Conservative Club. The editors were Frank Scott (socialist), A.J.M. Smith (socialist), Allan Latham (who called himself a Communist), and A.P.R. Coulbourn (socialist). They were all hauled on the mat on account of *my* article! So was I. On the strength of it I was accused of being a 'Bolshevik' (that was the precise term used), and charged — by the Principal, Sir Arthur Currie, in an hour-long interview — with having attacked 'the St James Street gang'. I had used no such phrase; but Currie repeatedly insisted I had, even telling me to go back and re-read the article, where I'd find it! I sent him a copy, challenging him to show me where. I got no reply. I sent a copy also to Meighen, who wrote that he was 'unable to find in it any trace of Bolshevism' and expressed astonishment that Currie should have spent a solid hour haranguing me on it: 'He must have very little to do.'

Immediately after the general election Meighen made his famous Hamilton speech, in which he said that if another war broke out the Government, before sending any troops overseas, should place its policy before the people in a general election. This raised a storm among many Conservatives. Meighen was accused then, and has repeatedly been since (even as late as 1988), of proposing that before Canada *entered any war* the question of going in or staying out should be submitted to a referendum. This is, of course, totally false. Meighen demolished it at the Winnipeg Conservative Convention of 1927, but the fable persists.

I have special reasons to remember his speech because immediately after it was delivered Dr Hemmeon, at a meeting of the student Political Economy Club, challenged me to say what I thought of 'my Leader's' proposal. I rose at once to its defence. I was mercilessly heckled by Liberals, socialists, Communists, and dissident Conservatives. I think the general verdict was that I did not come off vanquished, but what I am very proud of to this day is that I made exactly the defence Meighen later made in Winnipeg. He spoke, of course, incomparably better. But the arguments were identical.

I was in the gallery of the House of Commons for almost every word of the debates on the Customs Scandal of 1926 and the subsequent constitutional crisis. My most vivid memory of the actual debates is Meighen's speech (on the Scandal), which lasted for hours and was as usual replete with names, dates, precise quotations, all delivered without a note of any kind. More particularly I recall one incident. Mr Boivin, the Minister of Customs, interrupted: 'Will the rt. hon. gentleman permit a question?' 'Certainly', said Meighen, and sat down, adding, *sotto voce*, 'You'll be sorry.' (*Hansard* does not record this; but Mrs Meighen and I both heard it.) Boivin was a very able man and a skilled parliamentarian, and his question, which appeared to be bolstered by precise facts, was formidable. Meighen immediately made a devastating reply, demolishing every one of Boivin's points, word by word, comma by comma.

I was also in the House when the King government was defeated in the small hours of June 26, and I was sitting behind Mrs Meighen when Meighen's confidential messenger brought the news that Mr King had asked the Governor-General, Lord Byng, to dissolve Parliament and that he had refused. King thereupon resigned and Meighen became Prime Minister. I had not, even then, the slightest doubt that Lord Byng's refusal of Mr King's request for a dissolution of Parliament was completely constitutional, and indeed essential to the preservation of parliamentary government. Nor had I the slightest doubt that Meighen's temporary government of ministers without portfolio, acting ministers of departments, was constitutional. I watched with anguish from the gallery the fumblings of the Conservative front bench in reply to Mr King's attacks on the constitutionality of the temporary government (attacks which, of course, were wholly and demonstrably without foundation). Meighen was out of the House; under the law as it then stood, with his acceptance of the Prime Ministership he automatically vacated his seat. R.B. Bennett, who could also have trounced King, was campaigning in a provincial contest in Alberta. Most of the Progressives were swept off their feet by King's rhodomontade, and the persuasions of the great Grit constitutional 'authority', J.S. Ewart; and when Mr Bird, a Progressive, broke his pair and voted with the Liberals in the crucial division, the Conservative government was defeated by one vote. I saw and heard the dénouement.

I lost touch with Meighen till 1932, when I had a meal with him on one of my visits to Toronto in connection with the League for Social Reconstruction. I did not hear from him again, or he from me, till late in 1940 or early in 1941; hardly surprisingly, for I was then deep in the CCF, and Meighen, if he thought of me at all, probably thought I had lost my wits.

Throughout the years from 1926, however, I had never changed my opinion that the constitutional crisis of that year was profoundly important; that Meighen's course, all the way through, had been absolutely right; that he had been the victim of fraud, humbug, demagogy, and gross ignorance. The more I read about it and thought about it the angrier I got, and the more determined that something must be done about it.

I had already made one small attempt in 1930, at a meeting of the Canadian Political Science Association. When I had finished reading my short paper a distinguished-looking elderly gentleman at the back of the room rose and set to work to refute what I had said. In fact what he refuted were things I had not said, nor even thought. My paper had contained one small error of fact but he hadn't spotted it. When he sat down I replied. I said I was sorry that I had so signally failed to make myself clear, which was no doubt the reason why 'the gentleman at the back of the room' (I had no idea who he was) had, if I might say so 'with all the respect due from a young man to an older man', so completely misunderstood me. I then proceeded to restate my case in words of one syllable for children of three. I sat down.

My mother and aunt were shaking with laughter. My aunt said later: 'Do you know who that was?' 'No, but obviously some nice old Grit backwoods farmer who knows nothing of constitutional law or practice.' 'That was J.S. Ewart, KC.' I was thunderstruck, but not in the least repentant or cowed.

There was a sequel. Ewart was evidently furious that I had not realized who he was ('Not to know me argues yourselves unknown'). The result, a few weeks later, was a telephone call from the Secretary-Treasurer of the Association, Dr Sedley Cudmore. Would I come to his office? There was something he wanted to speak to me about. I went, wondering what it could be. I could never have guessed.

Mr Ewart wanted him to ask me if I would consent to the paper's not being printed! I said: 'Dr Cudmore, if you and the other officers of the Association consider that it is not worth printing, that is your judgement, which I should not for a moment question. But that I should consent to its not being printed because Mr Ewart does not like it is a very different thing. The answer is "No"; and I must add that I am astonished that you would transmit such a request.'

'Well, would you object to Mr Ewart's caveat being printed with it?' 'Certainly not. He wants to suppress me; I have not the slightest wish to suppress him. Let him print all the caveats he pleases. He has no case and he knows it.'

John Stevenson told me Ewart was going around town breathing forth threatenings and slaughters and vowing to write a pamphlet that would silence me forever. No caveat or pamphlet ever appeared. To the best of my knowledge Ewart never again uttered one syllable on the subject.

But 'the Authorized Version of Canadian history' continued to denounce Meighen and Lord Byng for 1926, and in the summer of 1940 I decided to do a thorough job on the subject, a long article that might be definitive. It blossomed; it expanded; till my wife said, 'Why not make it into a Ph.D. thesis on the royal power of dissolution of Parliament?' That did it.

I soon decided to send the two chapters on 1926 to Meighen so that he could warn me of any howlers, historical or legal. I wrote and asked if I might. He at once said yes. He then proceeded to send me voluminous comments, not challenging or questioning anything I had written, but remonstrating with me for being too mealy-mouthed. I was delighted with this criticism, for my wife had felt I had been just the opposite. I was triumphant, and proceeded to follow Meighen's exhortations to 'tell forth thy tale, and spare it not at all.'

There was a sequel to this also. Meighen wrote that he wanted to see the whole thesis. Of course nothing could have pleased me more. So off it went, and there descended on me, for months, a flood of detailed comments; some pencilled in the margin of the typescript, some in long typewritten letters. (They are now all in the National Archives.) One comment reveals Meighen's self-deprecating humour. I had quoted a statement of his. In the margin he wrote: 'I was just going to write on this, "Excellent", when I looked at the footnote and saw where it came from.'

Meighen loved jokes on himself. I remember three such stories. The first took place after Meighen had left politics when J.W. Dafoe, editor-in-chief of the *Winnipeg Free Press* and one of the Solons of the Liberal Party, came to Toronto to speak to the Canadian Club, or the Empire Club—I have forgotten which. It was, of course, to be a purely non-partisan affair, and the people in charge asked Meighen if he would move the vote of thanks. He said he would. Dafoe, being Dafoe, took the occasion to deliver a blistering attack on the tariff policy of the Conservative Party. Of course Meighen could not let him get away with that. So his vote of thanks took Dafoe to the cleaners. As he was leaving the hall he heard three newspapermen discussing the vote of thanks. One said: 'Well, Tom, what did you think of Arthur's speech?' 'Oh, it was all right, I suppose; but I hope to God no one ever asks him to move a vote of thanks to me!' After Meighen had published his collection of speeches in 1940, his small grandson saw it on a table and laboriously spelled out the title, 'U-n-r-e-v-i-s-e-d a-n-d U-n-r-e-p-e-n-t-e-d', adding, in a weary tone: 'And uninteresting'.

The third story involved me. Before going to the United States for my Guggenheim Fellowship I had to get a visa. The official at the American Embassy asked me for two references. Not without pride I offered, as the first, 'the Rt. Hon. Arthur Meighen.' 'Who's he?' 'The former Prime Minister of Canada.' 'Do you know a banker?' I told Meighen the story. He laughed and laughed.

I finished my thesis with literally nine minutes to spare. My wife and I sat up the whole night before the deadline, I two-finger-typing the rough, she typing the fair copy. The deadline was noon. I reached the office of the Dean of Graduate Studies at 11.51. Fortunately we lived very near.

Then came the business of publication. I submitted it to the Canadian Branch of the Oxford University Press. Unknown to me, Meighen wrote a strong letter of recommendation to W.H. Clarke, the manager. The reply was favourable, but it came with the edict, 'It must be cut in half.' I was in despair. But Meighen wrote me such a letter as the wisest and kindest of fathers might have written to a son: 'Eugene, for me as for you, there is not one superfluous word. But it must be cut. You can do it.' I did. *The Royal Power of Dissolution of Parliament in the British Commonwealth* appeared early in 1943 (it was reissued in 1968).

The result was mildly sensational. MacGregor Dawson, soon to be King's biographer, wrote a review less notable for logic than might have been expected from such a scholar. He did not question a single one of my statements of fact. He did not accuse, let alone convict, me of any material omissions. He did not attempt to refute any of my arguments, but he merely regretted that I had allowed myself 'to become the critic of Mackenzie King on the one hand, and the apologist for Lord Byng and Mr Arthur Meighen on the other' — without showing that any of my statements of fact were inaccurate, or any of my argument flawed.

It remained for the formidable J.W. Dafoe to take up the torch that had fallen from J.S. Ewart's hand thirteen years before. In two successive two-column articles, unsigned but unmistakably his, he reviewed my work. The articles were nicely compounded of outright mendacity, gross distortion, and sheer Billingsgate. Experience of newspaper editors told me that a full answer would almost certainly never see the light of day, so I wrote the *Free Press* only a very short letter, picking out four or five of Dafoe's most glaring misrepresentations and giving chapter and verse. This appeared, with a 'Note' that I had 'ducked all his most serious criticisms'.

My visits to Toronto had become more frequent, and I always looked in on Meighen. He was incensed by Dafoe's 'reviews' of my book and even more so by his 'Note'. 'What are you going to do about Dafoe?' 'You saw what I wrote.' 'Yes. Is that all you intend to do?' 'Yes.' 'Why?' 'Because controversy with a reviewer, especially if he's an editor, is a mug's game. He always has the last word, and the author is dismissed as a bear with a sore head, or a cry-baby who can't take his medicine.' 'You're wrong. You should let him have it both barrels.' I shook my head.

Back in Ottawa I ran into Tommy Douglas. 'Eugene, what are you doing about Dafoe?' 'Well, you saw what I wrote.' 'Is that all you're going to do?' 'Yes.' 'Why?' I repeated what I had said to Meighen. 'You're wrong. You should let him have it both barrels.' I said: 'Tommy, if you and Arthur Meighen give me the same advice, in the same words, you must be right. I will.'

I did, starting with a 3,000-word letter in which I dealt with seventeen of Dafoe's criticisms with a trenchancy that I think even Meighen himself could hardly have bettered; and, what is more important, in each case I had the facts, and logic, on my side. To each letter Dafoe attached a fresh 'Note', with a fresh misrepresentation.

Part way through this performance Meighen met at some social affair Victor Sifton, publisher of the *Free Press*. Sifton said: 'Dafoe himself is writing those criticisms of Forsey's book. And he'll go on as long as Forsey will.' 'No, he won't.' 'Why, what will he do?' 'He'll print a certain number of Forsey's letters, each with a fresh lie appended; and then he'll say: "Mr Forsey has now had ample space to state his case. We shall print no more from him." And then he'll add a fresh lie.' 'What makes you say that?' 'He did it to me.'

And this is precisely what Dafoe did. His final effort was a gargantuan whopper. He accused me of having quoted at some length from a speech of Burke's in the House of Commons without a word of Pitt's reply in the same debate.

I read this, as may be imagined, with more than uneasiness. Had I really been guilty of so outrageous an omission? Had I been careless, or worse? I immediately hunted up the *Parliamentary Register*, the *Hansard* of those days. There was Burke's speech. It was followed by: 'Mr William Wyndham seconded the motion, which was negatived without a division.' There was no record of any speech by Pitt on the subject. However, the *Parliamentary Register* did not claim to be a verbatim report. Perhaps Pitt *had* made a speech in this debate, or at some other time and in some other place. So I searched every collection of Pitt's speeches that I could find, and every *Life* of Pitt. Not so much as one syllable could I discover. I had quoted in my book from statements of Pitt's followers and disciples on the subject of dissolution of Parliament. All of them supported what I had said. Not one of them gave the faintest ground for believing that Pitt had said anything to the contrary.

I wrote Dafoe a letter setting out all this and challenging him to produce his evidence. I added: 'I know you won't print this. But I hope you'll read it.'

He did. But he ignored the challenge. Instead he sent me a letter calling me 'a left-wing mudslinger and character-assassin'. As his first article had accused me of being a Tory conspirator, I felt this rather evened things up. (I have known only one parallel. Many years later, at Couchiching, at the height of the Quebec separatists rumpus, I made a speech on 'French' and 'English', Quebec, and the rest of us. Two people came up to remonstrate. One said: 'You have sold out to the French Canadians.' The other: 'You are inspired by hatred of Quebec.') I sent Dafoe's letter to Meighen, writing on the back of it: 'I am tempted to reply as Lord Sandwich, one of Wilkes' boon-companions, did to a similar letter: "Sir, Your letter is before me. It will soon be behind me."'

Dafoe was a very able, very learned, very eminent man, and a great journalist. Between elections he could be very independent. But, at least in his later years, once the trumpets sounded he could bang the Grit drum as hard as any man, and a great deal more effectively than most. Some years later an American professor wrote a history of the Canadian Conservative Party during Meighen's years. He sent me the manuscript asking me to pass it on to Meighen, with the warning that it 'did not purport to be written from the inner circle of the Conservative Party.' A great deal of it was based on the Dafoe Papers in the Public Archives. Meighen's comment was: 'The book is not written from even the circumference of the Conservative Party, but from the confines of chaos. In that dark monarchy, Professor —— has been provided with a chair, a table and a telephone connected with a lot of noisy and mendacious Grits.'

All my correspondence with Dafoe is in the Archives, with contributions from various others, including B.K. Sandwell of *Saturday Night*, who wrote that he was 'proud to hold a towel in my corner.' My own parting shot was to ask Dafoe if it would not have saved time, energy, ink, and paper simply to have stated at the outset that the editor of the *Winnipeg Free Press*, speaking *ex cathedra* on a matter of constitutional law and practice, was infallible.

From then on Meighen was perhaps my closest friend. We wrote each other constantly. After dinner one evening on one of my visits to Toronto we got discussing the fire that destroyed the old Centre Block of the Parliament Buildings in 1916. Mrs Meighen suddenly said: 'Eugene, you know it was Arthur who saved the Library.' I was thunderstruck. 'No, I never heard that.' 'Yes, when the alarm was sounded, Arthur, being Arthur, thought at once of the Library, rushed over, and shut the iron doors.' I looked at Meighen in astonishment. He said: 'Oh, yes. Did I never tell you that?' (I recalled this too late to get it into Roger Graham's biography of Meighen.) I may add that this story has been strongly contradicted by people who say it was Mr McCormac, of the Library staff, who shut the doors. All I can say is that the Meighens certainly told me what I have just recounted.

When I was in Toronto he always took me to lunch at the Albany Club, and often home to supper. The members of the Club to whom I was introduced usually received me with polite dismay, not to say horror, and at first tried to carry it off with 'Glad to see you're in good company for once', or some such phrase; at which Meighen always bridled: 'You mean I'm in good company.' Eventually they gave up; but their faces said plainly: 'Of course, everyone knows Arthur has the queerest friends.'

The fact was that Meighen's friendships knew no bounds of creed, class, or party. He was a cordial admirer and friend of one of King's Ministers, T.A. Crerar, and, more surprisingly, of Bill Irvine, the CCF firebrand. He was absolutely loyal to his friends, come what might. One, a municipal official, went to jail for some official misconduct. Meighen of course thoroughly disapproved of what the man had done, but he visited him in jail.

In the summer of 1953, when I was in India, he had an illness that may have been a stroke. The symptoms were peculiar: for eleven days he hiccoughed incessantly. He was sure he was going to die and sent for his son Max. When he arrived, Meighen told him he was near his end and when he died he wanted only three people to say anything about him: Grattan O'Leary, Max Freedman, and Eugene Forsey. Max, who was sure his father was recovering, started to laugh. 'What are you laughing at?' 'Well, Dad, do you realize what you have just said?' 'Of course I do. What do you mean?' 'Well, you're a Conservative and a Protestant. Grattan is a Conservative and a Roman Catholic. Max Freedman is a Liberal and a Jew. Eugene is a Protestant and a CCFer.' 'I never thought of that.' 'No, you wouldn't. But it's the first thing anybody else would notice.'

One of the guests at an Albany Club lunch was the Honourable Wesley Gordon, one of R.B. Bennett's ministers, who had been Chairman of the House of Commons Committee on the Beauharnois scandal of 1931-2. Gordon said that the Committee had the goods on Mackenzie King and had drafted a strong report accordingly. Before it could be presented, however, King got wind of it and went to Bennett with an *ad misericordiam* appeal. Bennett capitulated and went to Gordon, insisting that the report be watered down: 'The honour of the Prime Minister of Canada must not be besmirched.' Gordon said the original wording would have finished King.

Another frequent guest at the Albany Club was Hugh Clark, Joe's great-uncle, a very close friend of Meighen's who had been Parliamentary Under-Secretary for External Affairs in Borden's Union Government. He was a most entertaining person, with a delightful turn of phrase and a pungent wit. His one-liners for his brother's paper, the *High River Times*, were famous. (Joe has told me that deciphering Uncle Hugh's handwriting in these contributions was his first job.) Hugh once tried to get Meighen to read some recent statement of King's. Meighen pushed it away. 'No, Hugh, no. I have suffered enough in my life. I will read nothing more by or about Mackenzie King as long as I live.' Hugh Clark lived to a great age, and 'his eye was not dim, nor his natural force abated.' He paid me two of the highest compliments I ever had. Once, on reading something I had written: 'You're just like Arthur. You never spatter the target.' The other followed the CBC-TV interview Meighen had with me.

That was an occasion. Meighen disliked the CBC and disliked television. But the CBC was understandably anxious to get him on the air. Very reluctantly he agreed, on one condition: that I should be the interviewer. So the CBC summoned me to Toronto. Meighen took me to the Albany Club as usual. During lunch he laid it down that he would talk about nothing but the Salvation Army (of which he was a great benefactor). My heart sank. But of course I could say only that that was a matter for him alone to decide.

As we walked back to his office he said he had never felt so tired in his life. As he was then over 80 and had had some minor strokes, my heart sank again. I suggested he should go home at once and rest, but he firmly refused. I then ventured to say that I had been hoping he might feel able to say something about Sir Robert Borden. 'You have given me the beginnings of the germ of an idea.' My heart rose a little.

At the office I left him, promising to call for him at his house about 6:00 that evening. I arrived to find that he had completely forgotten about the engagement. My dismay must have been clear in my face, for he said at once: 'It's all right, Eugene. I'll be ready in a few moments.' He was, and we went downstairs. There a fresh difficulty presented itself. I said we'd get a taxi. 'No. [He had a rooted objection to taxis. Why, I have no idea.] Nan [Mrs Meighen] will drive us.' 'But Nan's not here.' Still a firm refusal. I sneaked off to the telephone and called a mutual and devoted friend who lived nearby. By the time we left, Mrs Meighen had returned, but the friend drove us.

We went on the air. I introduced Meighen and he started in. To my inexpressible relief there was not one syllable about the Salvation Army, nor even a word about Borden. Instead he gave us a scintillating account of various incidents in his political career. Greatly daring, I supplied one word, part-way through, when he hesitated for an instant. After the broadcast ended he said to me, rather reproachfully: 'You never asked me about Borden.' I said: 'No. Not for the world would I have interrupted you for that or any other purpose.'

The interview brought Meighen a flood of fan mail, which delighted him, the more because he had felt he was going downhill. The letter he liked best, and sent on to me with great glee, was from Hugh Clark: 'Dear Arthur, You were magnificent. You never were better. And thank goodness Eugene had enough sense to stay in the background and keep quiet.' I wrote Hugh: 'The finest compliment I ever had.'

The record of that interview was lost. The CBC arranged to another, but on the date set Meighen and I were both ill and the whole thing fell through.

Meighen spent his Sunday afternoons walking around Toronto, calling on the aged and infirm, who ranged from retired carpenters to millionaire widows of Cabinet Ministers. I know, because I took one of those walks with him. I wish I had been present when, on another of these rounds, just after the death of Sir William Mulock, he called on Professor George Wrong. Of course Mulock's name came up; and Professor Wrong gave a very candid, and very derogatory, account of certain aspects of Mulock's career, notably his fondness for the other sex. He wound up, however, with this: 'But, Arthur, I am not an impartial witness. There was always bad blood between the Blakes and the Cawthras. [Mrs Wrong was a Blake, Mulock's mother was a Cawthra.] And, in fairness to Mulock, in justice to Mulock, I must add that I understand that in the last ten years of his life his behaviour was very much better.' Meighen's comment to me was: 'Think of it, Eugene. From 92 to 102 he was fairly respectable!'

Meighen has been painted as an arch-reactionary. This is a caricature. When the question of jurisdiction over unemployment insurance was under discussion, it was argued that the matter fell within 'property and civil rights in the province', an exclusive provincial jurisdiction; that to transfer it to the Dominion would require a constitutional amendment; that this would need the unanimous consent of the provinces; and that Quebec would never consent. Meighen was not prepared to let it go at that. He pointed out that Section 94 of the British North America Act,

1867, gave the Dominion power to take over all or any part of property and civil rights in Ontario, Nova Scotia, and New Brunswick, provided the legislatures of those provinces agreed. He argued that, by necessary intendment, this must apply to all the Common Law provinces (that is, every province but Quebec). So, if all the provinces except Quebec wanted a single unemployment insurance system, they could have it, by using Section 94. Quebec would not want to be left out, deprived of benefits that all the rest of the country enjoyed, and a fully national system would eventually evolve. Professor Frank Scott made the same argument. Nothing came of it. But it was scarcely the argument of an arch-reactionary. (Incidentally, Meighen is often also accused of being anti-French Canadian, but he was the first Prime Minister to appoint a French-Canadian minister from outside Quebec, Dr Raymond Morand of Windsor.)

Nor is this all. When Mr Bennett introduced his New Deal legislation in 1935, Meighen, leading the Government in the Senate, fully supported it, and did a thorough redrafting job to make it more effective. At the farewell dinner to Bennett in 1939, he said of the legislation: 'In all its important features it was sound and timely. The Statutes, indeed, received almost unanimous approval from both Houses of Parliament. This is not the time to impeach the wisdom of their being submitted, as they were, to the Privy Council on a question of constitutional jurisdiction. Personally I do not think they should have been so submitted, and personally I think that in respect particularly of those Statutes which implemented treaties already made by this country, such as the Hours of Labour Act and the Day of Rest Act, the Chief Justice of Canada was right, and the negative verdict of the Privy Council was wrong. I not only think, but know, that that verdict has precipitated our Dominion into a constitutional chaos from which we cannot emerge for years. . . . I lament a decision which maims and paralyzes our country's powers as a nation, and condemns us to a perpetual incapacity in the making of proper and necessary arrangements with other countries on subjects which are usefully dealt with by Treaties and by Treaties alone. Anyway, this legislation of 1935 is a credit to the Prime Minister of that time and will be a beacon light to guide our footsteps in years to come after we emerge, if we ever emerge, into that state of constitutional regeneration which we are groping for today.'

Meighen reiterated this opinion to me many years later. Here, as on unemployment insurance, he and Frank Scott sang to one clear harp.

It has been alleged that Bennett himself did not believe in his New Deal. I am convinced that this is wrong, and for a very simple reason: Bennett was a Methodist. He had been brought up, as I was and as all Methodists were, to believe in conversion. On the subject of the New Deal he was converted. His sister Mildred, and her husband Bill Herridge, the

Canadian Minister in Washington, who had seen Roosevelt's New Deal at close quarters and been captivated by it, were the evangelists.

The fact is that both Meighen and Bennett were in the authentic tradition of Canadian Conservatism. Borden, in 1908, had proposed nationalization of the telephone system. Sir Rodmond Roblin gave Manitoba its provincially owned system. Sir James Whitney and Sir Adam Beck established the Ontario Hydro. Whitney passed the Ontario Workmen's Compensation Act, which became the basis for all the other provincial Acts and for the British Labour Party's proposals on the subject. (The Act was based on a report by Sir William Meredith, a former leader of the Ontario Conservative Party.) Borden nationalized the Canadian Northern (which he had called Sir William Mackenzie's 'infernal railway'), the Grand Trunk, and the Grand Trunk Pacific. Meighen vigorously defended his action, not only in the House of Commons but in Montreal itself, the very citadel of the CPR. No wonder the Montreal tycoons distrusted him, and did their best to drive him out of the leadership. In those days most Canadian Conservatives did not burn incense before the American idol of 'free enterprise'.

I think Meighen never quite gave up hope that some day I'd come back to the Conservative Party, where he felt I belonged. But he never pressed me. Oddly enough I have voted Conservative oftener than I have voted anything else. During my twenty-nine years in the CCF I was almost always in a constituency where there was no CCF candidate; in Montreal I was in the constituency of C.H. Cahan, for whom I had no hesitation in voting.

Now comes the sad, and for me discreditable, part of the story of my relationship with Meighen.

It begins with his return to the Leadership and his candidature for the House of Commons in a by-election in South York in 1942. He was opposed by the CCF. The Liberals stayed out officially, though I believe they supplied the CCF with a lot of ward-heelers. The CCF campaign against Meighen was a disgrace. Two articles in the party paper drew a parallel between Pétain and Meighen with Pétain's picture at the top of one and Meighen's at the top of the other. This was only one example of many. The article went so far as to print what purported to be an extract from a speech of Meighen's in the Senate that inserted a word, and a significant word, Meighen had never uttered. I protested privately to an influenctial CCF colleague, who replied that the offending matter came from 'a historian whom we both know.' I said nothing publicly. Naturally I was reluctant to speak out against my own party. Also, I felt that if any man was capable of demolishing this kind of garbage, that man was Meighen; he would need no help from me. So I kept quiet (I was down at Harvard, on my Guggenheim Fellowship) and stayed put. But Meighen scorned to answer the attacks: he concentrated on the real issue, the conduct of Canada's war effort. It was a typical example of his reliance on reason, and on the good judgement of the electors if they had the facts and logical arguments presented to them. I should have left Cambridge and come up to Toronto to take the stump in Meighen's defence. It is a lasting grief and reproach to me that I did not.

Worse was to follow. During Meighen's last few years I very seldom got to Toronto, and I very rarely wrote to him. Indeed, I cannot remember having done so at all (though I believe there are letters extant which show that I did, occasionally). Anyhow, I feel that I failed him, failed the friend to whom I owed so much, the one person above all others that I should have cherished with unceasing gratitude and delight as long as he drew breath.

I did of course pay tribute to him when he died in 1960. I was an honorary pall-bearer at his funeral; and when Mrs Meighen died (at 102) in 1985, I represented the Prime Minister at her funeral. I was not worthy.

My first encounter with John Diefenbaker was, I think, in 1948, just after my inglorious performance in the Carleton by-election. I was hunting up something in the Parliamentary Library when he advanced across the room, saying in a loud voice: 'I want to congratulate you on the fight you put up in that by-election.' As the man I had been fighting was the leader of Diefenbaker's own party, I was considerably taken aback. I nevertheless managed to summon up some appropriate words of thanks. After that I saw something of Diefenbaker from time to time at the few social functions I attended. Then came the Pipeline Debate of 1956, when the Conservatives and the CCF drew together over the procedural issue of closure, and in defence of the rights of Parliament. I bore, from outside the House, a modest share in the battle. I watched the Conservative convention that made Diefenbaker Leader and hailed the result of the 1957 election as 'our great deliverance'.

Well before the election, however, in February 1957, I received a telephone call from the new Leader. He rang me at the CLC office. 'Eugene, we're on a private line. No one can overhear us. I want you in the House of Commons. I'm not offering you a nomination, I'm offering you a seat.' This, I have always thought, was one of the most striking manifestations of Diefenbaker's self-confidence (Meighen said he had never heard anything like it). I never found out what seat he had in mind because, after I had deprecated any usefulness I might have, Diefenbaker asked me to come to see him to discuss the matter. I agreed to that. But when I told my wife, she said: 'You know you can't do this. You must not waste his time by going.' She was, of course, right. So I wrote him: 'Principle, health, and livelihood alike forbid.' That ended it.

After the election Diefenbaker assured me that his 'door would always be open' to me, and it was. I rarely troubled him. I have always felt that when any of my friends were in high office they had problems enough without my adding to them. On my first visit the Prime Minister said: 'I never was more disappointed than when I got your note. If you'd done what I wanted you to do you'd be a Minister of the Crown.' I replied: 'I'd have been a millstone round your neck.'

The friendly relationship came a cropper after the CLC had its first full-dress meeting with the new Cabinet. I had prepared the Congress memorandum. (The officers struck out one passage. Apropos some attack that had been made on the compulsory check-off of union dues, I had written: 'I have never heard of any workers who protest against this, refusing to take the higher wages, shorter hours, longer vacations, more statutory holidays, or better pensions the union won for them. If there is any such worker, his body should be stuffed after his death and put on exhibition, with a charge for admission. We could pay off the national debt.') Michael Starr, Minister of Labour, replied. He took up each of our proposals *seriatim*. This one the Government had already accepted: he would be introducing the bill next week. That one also it had accepted: administrative action had been taken. So on through the list. Almost all we had asked for was granted at least in part, and specifically. Mike's only slip was to mix up rationalization of a certain industry, which we had proposed, with nationalization! I felt that the occasion had been a success, not least because the Minister's performance gave the lie to the notion that the Government was a one-man affair.

But the euphoria did not last. President Jodoin followed Starr, in a short speech that said nothing in particular. Then Diefenbaker spoke: 'I have nothing to add to what the Minister has said.' And for the space of ten minutes or so he proceeded to prove it. It was rather like one of Ramsay MacDonald's later speeches: loud detonations in a dense fog. But through the fog came, repeatedly, phrases like 'free enterprise', 'the principles of free enterprise'. It left the impression that for Diefenbaker, pure nineteenth-century Manchestertum liberalism was right up at the top of the list, and the unemployed and workers generally were right at the bottom. He had indeed nothing to add; but he had subtracted a great deal.

That this was a ludicrously false picture of the Government's policy was evident to anyone who had listened to the Minister's speech. In effect it contradicted almost everything Starr had said. I was appalled, and felt I had to do something about it. So I wrote the Prime Minister what I thought was a very carefully phrased letter, saying that I thought his speech had done him and his government an injustice. Every one of the things Starr had said involved an interference with free enterprise. The Government had come out for them presumably for good reasons. They were in tune with the Prime Minister's own attitude throughout his career. It seemed a pity not to take credit for them, especially before such an audience. I cannot remember exactly what words I used, but that was the general tenor. I showed a copy of the letter to the Honourable J.M. Macdonnell, who said he did not see how it could be taken amiss.

But it was. I got no reply, and for a long time aftwards, whenever the Prime Minister and I happened to see each other, all I got was a curt nod. I was in the dog-house.

But I got out! In 1963 Peter Newman published his book, *Renegade in Power: The Diefenbaker Years*. I reviewed it on the air, unfavourably. A telephone call followed, this time from Ken Binks, National Director of the Conservative Party, a long-time fervent supporter of Diefenbaker and an old friend of mine. 'We want you to run. This has the authority of the Chief.' This time I said no at once.

For the next few years I found myself on the same side as Diefenbaker in a number of controversies: the battle against the elimination of 'Dominion' and 'Royal Mail'; the battle for a flag that would not deny our history (when the new flag was first hoisted, a cousin in Newfoundland always crossed the street to avoid walking under it).

So from 1963 to 1968 my friendship with Diefenbaker was restored. During most of those years also my fringe contact with the Conservative Party was resumed. I attended a Fredericton Thinkers' Conference in 1964. I was invited to but did not attend the similar Montmorency Conference in 1967.

After Diefenbaker was thrown out of the leadership I met him only occasionally, briefly and casually. He usually asked why I did not come to see him. The only reason was that I was too busy, notably on my history of trade unionism. However, one day when I had been looking up something in the Parliamentary Library, it got too late to go back to my office and I said to myself, 'I wonder if John's around.' I went up to his office. There he was, with the door open. I said: 'John, have you a moment to spare?' 'I have all the time there is. Come in. Sit down.' For the next half-hour or so I was regaled with a Cook's Tour of Canadian politics. I was sorry I did not have a tape recorder.

Two items remain in my memory. At one point some topic of the moment came up. 'Now, Eugene, this is a subject on which Stanfield ought to be making a statement. Instead of that, he's taking a two-week immersion course in French.' Then John's eyes started to shoot sparks and I said to myself: 'Here comes one of his best.' Sure enough, out it came: 'Eugene, we Baptists know all about immersion [pause], but we don't stay under for two weeks!'

The other highlight was on the subject of the financier Mr Marcel Faribault. 'They tell me, Eugene, that I don't pronounce it properly. But I call him "Ferryboat", ferryboat to disaster.

'In 1962 the great *experts* on Quebec, who know *everything*, said to me: "Get Faribault. All your troubles will be over." I said: "Send him up." He arrived, and we sat down to talk. "Mr Diefenbaker, it has always been my dearest wish to represent my country in Parliament." And when a man talks like that to me, Eugene, I have my suspicions. However, I said, "That's fine. Where do you propose to run?" "Sherbrooke." "That's fine." "Now, Mr Diefenbaker, there is an indispensable condition. I am not a rich man—" "Just a moment, Mr Faribault. You are worth between seven hundred and fifty thousand and one million dollars." "Where did you get that?" "From a source which I think you would recognize as reliable." "Well, be that as it may, I have five children. I shall require from you a bond, accepted by my company, for five hundred thousand dollars, payable in ten equal annual instalments." And not one word, Eugene, about how long he'd stay: one day, one week, one year! I said: "Mr Faribault: if that's the indispensable condition, good afternoon!"

'In 1965 the same great *experts* on Quebec, who know *everything*, said again: "Get Faribault. All your troubles will be over." I said: "Send him up." He arrived and we went into the library. I said: "Mr Faribault, before we say anything else, that five hundred thousand dollar nonsense is *out*." "Oh, you misunderstood me completely. That was not a fixed sum. That was just this and that, this and that."' John provided not only a superb imitation of Faribault's voice and manner, but of his explanatory gestures. I gasped. 'He wanted you to bargain with him!' 'Exactly; and he seemed to think that made it better!' 'Whereas,' I said, 'it made it —' 'Ten thousand times worse.' We put that aside. 'Then Faribault said: "Mr Diefenbaker, do you know who is the man in this country who knows more about external affairs than any other man in this country?" I said: "Well, I thought Paul Martin thought he did, though Pearson seems sometimes to kind of pull the rug from under him." "*I* am the man who knows more about external affairs than any other man in this country. I shall require from you a pledge that I am to be Secretary of State for External Affairs." I said: "Mr Faribault, no Leader can give you that pledge. He can promise you a seat in the Cabinet. But the minute he promises you a particular portfolio, he makes *enemies* of every one of the seven or eight other men who want that portfolio." "Well, be that as it may, there is a minimum condition: every policy decision in every Department must be shown to me before it goes into effect." "Mr Faribault: if that is the minimum condition, good afternoon."'

I told this story to Pierre Trudeau. He said: 'Well, you and I both know Faribault. It all rings true, except for one thing: the five hundred thousand dollars. That surprises me.' I said it surprised me too, and that the late Bob McKeown had told me that when Diefenbaker had told the tale to him, it had been one hundred thousand.

It always amazes me that the Conservative Party took Faribault seriously as a candidate (he was not successful), and in a working-class constituency; and that so many people took him seriously as a constitutional expert. When I was on the Joint Committee on the Constitution, in 1971-2, Faribault was on the list of witnesses. He was to appear on a certain date. The day before, we received his brief: 168 foolscap pages! I was in despair. How on earth could I read this by next morning? But Providence intervened with a blizzard, and Faribault could not come till a fortnight later. By that time I had read the brief. It was full of howlers, specific statements purporting to be statements of fact that were simply not so: 'The British North America Act says . . .' and it didn't. 'On this, the British North America Act is silent' and it wasn't—a specific section or sections dealt with the matter concerned. If Faribault had been a student in one of my Canadian Government courses, I'd have ploughed him without an instant's hesitation. His economic and social ideas were pure eighteenth-century. Why on earth any party would have put him up in a working-class constituency was, to quote Meighen again, 'one of the mysteries which are really quite insoluble.'

In my more jaundiced moments I have often said that Canada is a paradise for humbugs. If you have enough nerve, gall, rind, crust, you can palm yourself off on most of the population as a reincarnation of Socrates, Caruso, or Pope Innocent III. No one who knows anything about philosophy, or music, or the Catholic Church will be taken in, but the generality of people may be. So-called, usually self-so-called, constitutional experts are a case in point. They are 'thick as autumnal leaves in Vallombrosa', and often of as much value. That is one reason why I have always jibbed at being called a 'constitutional expert', the more so because the fact is that while I know a great deal about a very few rather minor and obscure points of Canadian constitutional law and practice—a good amount about some others, a fair amount about still others, a little about a few more—I know absolutely nothing about a very large part of the subject.

I got into Diefenbaker's dog-house a second time when I took my seat in the Senate as a Liberal. I saw him in the Parliamentary Restaurant a day or two later, and he fixed me with a basilisk glare: 'When I heard you were going to sit as a Liberal I was *shocked*. I was *shocked*, and I don't care who knows it.' I said: 'Oh, John! You'll come to my funeral just for the fun of making faces at me.' He was so amused that I got out of the dog-house again. He could not resist an occasional dig, as when he saw me lunching with Colin Gibson, Liberal MP, and, passing our table, leaned over and said: 'You're both in very bad company.' But about a year later his secretary, Mrs Eligh, telephoned to invite me to come up to the Chief's birthday party. I went and was warmly received. As I left, Diefenbaker turned to his wife and said: 'Olive, Eugene says I'll go to his funeral just for the purpose of making faces at him.'

I have often been asked what I consider my 'greatest achievement'. Till a year or so ago I always replied, 'None.' But then I reflected: I had got into John Diefenbaker's dog-house twice, and *out* twice! I doubt if many people could match this.

Pierre Trudeau I think I have now known for nearly forty years. We met, if my memory serves, in 1952 at the first meeting of the Institut Canadien des Affaires Publiques, a French-language version of the Couchiching Conferences. I was, again if my memory serves, one of its founding members and attended most of its early sessions up in the Laurentians. Trudeau was of course one of the leaders. I was also a member of the Rassemblement (not to be confused with the separatist Rassemblement pour l'Indépendance Nationale), a mixed bag of opponents of the Duplessis regime, of which, again, Trudeau was one of the leaders. Besides, he did a great deal of work for the Quebec unions of the CCL, and we exchanged notes on various proposals they presented to the Congress headquarters.

In 1964 I attended a conference at Banff on Canadian unity, where the French-speaking delegates were almost all separatist or hemi-demi-semi-separatists, and where a great many of the English-speaking delegates were so anxious to show themselves kind, conciliatory, broad-minded, and penitent that they were prepared to agree to almost anything, however impracticable, absurd, or destructive. I felt obliged to point out some of the impracticabilities, absurdities, and destructiveness; and found myself looked at askance as a result. I came back, not repentant but disturbed, even shattered in mind; so much so that I wrote Pierre, saying I was to be in Montreal on a certain day and should like to see him. I explained that I had been at this Banff conference and had found myself regarded as an Anglo-Saxon bigot. I did not think the description was warranted; but if it was, I wanted to do something about it. He wrote back, inviting me to lunch. There I recounted what had happened at Banff, and my part in it. Pierre was not greatly surprised. He had been invited to the conference himself but had declined, as he knew what most of the French-speaking delegates were likely to say, was tired of hearing it, and didn't think his presence would have any effect. On my own contributions to the proceedings he was reassuring.

When he came to Ottawa as one of the 'three wise men' from Quebec, he rang me up and invited me to lunch in the Parliamentary Restaurant. I think he wondered what I, as a long-time CCFer, would think of his joining the Liberals. He raised the question rather tentatively. I immediately said: 'Pierre, if I had been in your position, I'd have done exactly what you did, and for the same reasons.' In 1968, when the Pearson government was defeated on the Finance Bill, he consulted me on the constitutional issues it raised and I was able to offer some opinions that I think he found helpful.

When Mr Pearson announced his retirement, and the Liberal Leadership was opened up, Professor William Kilbourn came to see me. He said a group of academics was proposing to issue a letter advocating

Pierre Trudeau for the job. Would I sign it? I said yes, instantly—'On one condition, that Pierre doesn't turn thumbs down. He may feel that my support would do him more harm than good.' 'If he becomes Leader, would you run?' 'Yes, but on the same condition.' That was the last I heard of this suggestion, so I presumed Pierre had recoiled, as I suspected he might. Years afterwards I asked him. He said he knew nothing of the matter.

When Trudeau's leadership campaign began, I offered his staff any help I could give. No one took the slightest notice. Then my younger daughter, an enthusiastic Trudeau supporter, wanted to get into the game. I took her around to headquarters and she was signed up. I said: 'I'm ready to help in any way I can, but nobody seems to want me.' 'Would you write something for our campaign leaflet?' 'Yes. How much, and when do you want it?' 'Five hundred words, for Monday.' I promptly produced the five hundred words. The French translation appeared under the heading, 'Le Canada a besoin de Pierre Trudeau.' The English original contained, I remember, the sentence: 'He is as tough and flexible as steel.' I was careful to say that I was not a member of the Liberal Party, but—since whoever became Leader would become Prime Minister—I ventured, even as a rank outsider, to say I thought Trudeau was the man. National unity was in peril: only he could preserve it. When Trudeau made his first big speech on national unity I wrote him, in French: 'This is magnificent. This is what I have been waiting for. I shall support you by any means in my power, even to the point of total silence' (which I thought might be the best gift I could give him).

After he became Prime Minister I was working in my CLC office one Saturday morning when Mitchell Sharp, Secretary of State for External Affairs, rang me with an incredible message: 'Pierre wants to appoint you Ambassador to the Vatican.' I said: 'Mitchell, are you pulling my leg?' 'No, I'm serious.' 'But it's preposterous. My great-grandmother was a Belfast Protestant, and the last thing I'm fitted for is diplomacy. Besides, I am a teetotaller and I'd refuse to serve alcohol to guests.' I thought that would clinch it. But to my astonishment it didn't. Mitchell said I was a second choice—Frank Scott had turned it down. But Trudeau wanted me to accept.

I agreed to discuss it with two high officials of the Department of External Affairs. They must have been horrified at the idea, but were too polite to show it. I then asked Trudeau to spare me five minutes to tell me why he thought I should accept. He invited me to lunch. I remained unconvinced, and the country was spared an appointment that would have appeared ludicrous, and might have been disastrous.

Later I was invited to become Indian Claims Commissioner. This I did not consider for a moment. It would have required profound knowledge of a very large and intricate subject of which I knew nothing, and which

I was too old to learn. It would also have called for all those qualities I'd have needed for the ambassadorship that I conspicuously lacked.

When, in October 1970, Trudeau asked me if I'd accept appointment to the Senate, I at once said yes. 'You wouldn't do those other two things I wanted you to do.' 'No, because I'd have been a disaster. But I think I can be useful in the Senate, especially on the Constitution Committee.' He then told me he had asked Frank Scott, who was considering it, and Thérèse Casgrain, who had accepted. I said: 'Splendid! I suppose Thérèse will sit as an NDP Senator' (I didn't know she was browned off). 'I don't know where she'll sit. I never thought of asking her. I don't give a damn where any of you sit. By the way, you might tell Frank that. I didn't think of mentioning it to him.' I replied: 'Well, I shall sit as a supporter of your Government. I am a Pierre Elliott Trudeau man from the crown of my head to the soles of my feet.' He laughed. I added: 'I don't guarantee always to agree with you.' Carl Goldenberg, when I told him this, said: 'You didn't need to add that. Pierre hasn't known you for fifteen years for nothing.'

Once Pierre became Prime Minister I seldom saw him until I became a Senator, and even then usually only at caucuses. Fairly often, however, I offered memoranda to his staff on constitutional points, which they could transmit to him if they saw fit.

When the election of 1972 came on, I said I'd do anything I could to help. There was no reply. I said to my wife: 'Well, I told Pierre I'd do anything I could. Apparently there is nothing. So my conscience is clear and I don't have to do any work!' I spoke too soon. A few days later Trudeau's office rang me: 'The Prime Minister has to be here in Ottawa for four days on official business. His campaign plane will be idle unless we can get up a scratch team to use it while he is tied up. Will you be part of that team?' Of course I said yes, and for four days I careered across the continent, speaking here and there, from Winnipeg to Comox and the Yukon. On this and other forays I spoke in ten ridings. We lost every one of them, though in fairness I must add that several of them were already Opposition seats.

In the process my ego got a small dividend. Our steward and stewardess were both French-speaking (so were a good many of the people on the scratch team). Naturally I spoke French to them. Evidently I was on my day and in luck, for the last evening, when we stopped in Toronto, I chatted in English at the plane's door with the chairman of the Prime Minister's Youth Committee (a young man from the Eastern Townships of Quebec, English-speaking but bilingual). The stewardess came up to us, looking reproachful. I wondered why. Then she said, in English: 'You two ought to be ashamed of yourselves: both of you French, and speaking to each other in English!' I said, in French: 'But Mademoiselle, I have the right to use my mother tongue!' 'Of course. But that's French.' 'No,

Mademoiselle, it's English!' 'What! I thought you were French.' Then, to the steward at the other end of the plane, she said: 'Monsieur Forsey est Anglais.' 'Quoi! Je croyais qu'il était Français.' I rose onto cloud nine.

I think I was a major trouble to Pierre only once: on Bill C-60 of 1978, his Constitutional Amendment Bill. I was firmly and undeviatingly with him in his opposition to separatism and all its works. I also supported him completely on his handling of the Quebec October Crisis of 1970. I thought, and still think, he was right. I said so then. I have said so many times since, publicly and privately. Frank Scott and Thérèse Casgrain, with far greater knowledge than I, and with an unequalled record on civil liberties, took the same line. Undoubtedly the Quebec provincial police took the opportunity to pay off old scores by picking up people who ought not to have been picked up. But that was not Trudeau's doing.

One thing the critics of 'Just watch me' and what followed forget, or ignore, is that the Government of Canada acted at the request of the Government of Quebec and of the Administration of the City of Montreal. It was they who asked for the troops, not some Anglo-Saxon, bloodthirsty, 'anti-French' reactionaries. In my judgement Pierre Trudeau kept Quebec in Canada when no one else could have done it. In my judgement also, he saved us from Baader-Meinhof gangs and Red Brigades.

What he did to the parliamentary system and to the public service is another matter. The remark about Members of Parliament being just 'nobodies' once they were off Parliament Hill did not betray much respect for the House of Commons; and there were other statements which suggested a belief that once a government had won an election it could do pretty much what it pleased until the next election.

As for Trudeau's treatment of the public service: the system of musical chairs in which senior officials were shifted from department to department at such a speed that the quickness of the hand almost deceived the eye has had results that, to say the least, are highly questionable. I had tales of this from a wide variety of senior public servants: a Prince Edward Islander, a French Canadian from Quebec, an Indian nuclear physicist; an English-born and -educated friend in the National Research Council; an ex-Hungarian in the Department of Health and Welfare. All of them I knew well. If I had got the story from only one of them—or if any of them had been incompetent, foolish, or hypersensitive—I might have discounted it. But all were highly able and experienced. They were unanimous that knowledge and experience were being subordinated to the possession of a degree in Public Administration. The theory apparently was that proficiency in the art of 'management' covered everything. Anyone who could 'manage' anything, from a department store or a supermarket to a bank or a railway, could 'manage' anything else: the Departments of Labour, Transport, Immigration, Health and Welfare, Agriculture.

In a speech in the Senate I commented on this with some asperity. A few days later I got a letter from a French-Canadian official in one of the departments enclosing an article he had written on the subject for the Department's own paper. It painted a picture even more lurid than the one I had sketched.

The author, speaking from his own experience, said what happened was that a new Deputy Minister—fresh from, let us say, the Harvard Business School—arrived. He surveyed the department and pronounced it all wrong. It had to be reorganized from top to bottom. This took about two years, during which chaos reigned. Then the Deputy Minister moved on to another department. His replacement, also a 'management' wallah, fresh from another business school, surveyed the reorganized department and found it all wrong. It had to be reorganized from top to bottom. This took another two years, at the end of which the second monarch of all he surveyed also departed, and a third took his place and repeated the performance.

I suspect that before he entered politics Trudeau, looking at Quebec, decided that some of its troubles came from a lack of knowing how to handle business, private or public—a lack of knowledge of management. In this there was probably much truth. Traditional Quebec education had produced excellent theologians, lawyers, doctors, but not too many first-class businessmen or administrators. The solution was obvious. But was it? Has the application of it to the Public Service of Canada given us a better public service?

I am told that one Minister in the Trudeau Cabinet who had been accustomed to having at his elbow a Deputy Minister with long experience in his Department, and vast knowledge of its problems, supported by a corps of lesser officials with long experience and intimate knowledge of particular parts of the Department and their problems, suddenly found himself bereft. His new Deputy Minister and his subordinates knew all about management. But they knew little or nothing about the specific problems of the Department or their history, even less about the regional or local aspects of those problems. I am told also that the Minister concerned grew exasperated when he found that the Deputy Minister, asked for information or advice on a specific matter, could only reply that he didn't know and didn't know any lesser official who did.

In short, Trudeau was not omniscient or infallible; and he sometimes let his tongue run away with him. But his two major achievements are to my mind unquestionable, and if Canada survives as a united and 'peaceable kingdom', future generations will rise up and call him blessed.

Looking at his successors brings to my mind the old rhyme on two successive English Prime Ministers:

Myself, aged 10.

Mother, Florence Bowles Forsey, in the Geological Survey Library in the 1930s.

ABOVE: *A studio portrait taken in Vienna in 1955 when I was attending the conference of the International Confederation of Free Trade Unions. (Copyright Fayer-Wien, I.)*

LEFT: *A family portrait taken in 1948 for the CCF by-election: my wife Harriet and our daughters Margaret and Helen.*

ABOVE: *With Governor-General Jeanne Sauvé and Prime Minister Brian Mulroney after being sworn in as a Privy Councillor, 10 June 1985.*

LEFT: *During the Convocaton at Trent University, Peterborough, when I received the honorary degree of Doctor of Letters, 26 May 1978.*

Our Golden Wedding anniversary, 9 November 1985.

At the dinner for Pierre Elliott Trudeau, 6 April 1988, to mark the twentieth anniversary of his election to the Liberal leadership. The former Minister of Finance, Marc Lalonde, is in the background. (Courtesy the Ottawa Citizen.)

Pitt is to Addington
As London is to Paddington.

And there is a quotation from Charles James Fox on the same pair that is even unkinder.

Mackenzie King I met once. His then secretary, Howard Henry, was a friend of my family, and of mine, and took me to a reception at Laurier House. This was of course long before I had written anything much about Mr King. Afterwards I could not have got inside the door, nor perhaps even have been dragged there. I shall not even try to summarize here what I said about King in *The Royal Power of Dissolution of Parliament* or *Freedom and Order*, or in numerous articles in the *Canadian Forum*. It would be tedious.

I have said elsewhere that 'even on his loftiest oratorical flights, King always took along a verbal parachute with which he could bail out if things got too hot.' Mr Pickersgill has celebrated King's 'passion for accuracy'. Anyone who wants to see how erratically this operated can find details, with chapter and verse, in my article 'Mr King and Parliamentary Government' in *Freedom and Order*.

King's ego was of massive proportions. I have one story that illustrates this superbly. During the Second World War a delegation of United Church ministers, including the Reverend Dr John Coburn, called on King to urge him to impose restrictions on the liquor traffic. He listened in silence. Then he said: 'That is all very well, gentlemen. But do you know what is going on, right inside your own church?' The delegation, somewhat apprehensively, said no, wondering what tales of clerical debauchery were about to be unfolded. 'Well,' said Mr King, 'only last week, in Winnipeg, in —— United Church, they had a special service of prayer. And they prayed for Churchill, and they prayed for Roosevelt, and they prayed for Stalin; but they never prayed for me. And that is just an example of the kind of campaign that has been carried on against me right from the beginning of the war, in an effort to undermine my position.' This story I got in identical words from my colleague at the Canadian Congress of Labour, Norman Dowd (who had it from Dr Coburn himself), and from Dr Coburn's own son.

Meighen told me the story of Mackenzie King and the ringing of the first bell in the Peace Tower of the new Centre Block of the Parliament Buildings. (He had it from the architect of the building, J.A. Pearson.) Determined to ring the first bell in the tower, King could only reach it, at the then stage of construction, by going up in the exterior construction elevator, but he had no stomach for this. It seemed a complete impasse. Then someone had a brilliant idea. Let one of the construction workers, high up in the tower, have two ropes, one leading to the bell, the other to Mr King safely on *terra firma*. When King pulled his rope the construction worker would pull the bell rope, the bell would ring, and everyone would be satisfied. So it proved. King had a section of his rope cut off and mounted upon it a brass plate saying that this was the rope with which the Rt. Hon. W.L. Mackenzie King rang the first bell in the Peace Tower.

Another illustration of the same egoism came to me from a lady who was employed in King's office during the war. Shortly before Christmas one year, when battles were raging on sea and land, Mr King was preparing to send out Christmas cards. They were to bear his own signature. He wanted it to be his best signature. This lady was set, for days, the task of looking through documents the Prime Minister had signed to pick *the* signature.

King was a slave-driver to his employees. One of his secretaries told me that once when he was about to leave Ottawa for his statutory vacation, he handed King a file of papers. King promptly gave him a fresh assignment, to be undertaken forthwith. He submitted; the vacation was off. This secretary once attended a public lecture of mine at Carleton University on the 1926 constitutional crisis. I did not mince words and rather expected this gentleman to light into me. To my immense surprise, he said: 'I do not think Mr King ever really understood parliamentary government.' I said: 'Well, Arthur Meighen and I long ago reached that conclusion. But of course we're a pair of irreclaimable old Tories. To have our opinion confirmed by a dyed-in-the-wool Grit like you, who knew Mr King intimately, is really breathtaking.'

Meighen once said to me: 'Eugene, I think you're the only man in Canada except myself who fully realizes the moral turpitude of Mackenzie King' (and he was not referring to his private life, of which he knew nothing and cared less). I had, and have, what it would be wholly inadequate to call a very poor opinion of King's mind, character, and career. But I have never been among those who damned everything he said or did, just because he said it or did it. On the contrary, whenever I thought he was right I said so; for instance, in his disallowance of the Alberta Acts in 1937; and in his dispute with Duplessis over the position of Lieutenant-Governors. I have also always said that he did a great deal to build up an excellent civil service (it was still civil, in those days), and that he was a good judge of men: he picked good people to be Ministers, and, though he was always the master of his Cabinet (as any Prime Minister should be), he gave them their heads; he didn't breathe down the back of their necks. Though he was a slave-driver to his staff, he was capable of very kind acts. One example of this I got from a retired Public Works electrician who was once summoned to Kingsmere to do a rather complicated repair. It involved crawling under the house, and the job needed a flashlight. The electrician crawled under, and King crawled after him and held the flashlight.

John Stevenson's detestation of King persuaded him to buy, and circulate widely, a furious pamphlet attack on King by a very elderly retired civil servant who had rendered great service to various civil servants' organizations and had become a sort of home-grown Communist. The pamphlet was about as scurrilous as it is possible to be and was not remarkable for accuracy. John sent copies to Meighen and to me. Meighen, reading it, was thoroughly alarmed. He told me to get rid of mine at once; it was dangerous; if the RCMP found it I could be in serious trouble. He also insisted that when I got back to Ottawa I should call Stevenson and tell him, in the strongest terms, that it just would not do, and should not be circulated at all. I duly delivered the warning. John simply chuckled and said: 'Well, it may not be entirely accurate, but it certainly gives the old boy what for.'

This destructive approach to politics, which has surfaced again over the Meech Lake Accord, is one I have never been able to understand. I know of at least two people who ought to have known better whose attitude on that document is: 'If Trudeau's against it, I'm for it.' I know one very able journalist whose attitude towards the Senate is that whatever the Senate does or says is *ipso facto* wrong. This seems to me the ultimate *trahison des clercs*. I have always tried to make up my mind on public issues by looking at the facts and the arguments, regardless of whether they came from people I approved of or people I disliked. 'Has he got his facts right? Is his argument logical?' Those are the questions I have always asked myself;not, 'Is this what King says? Is this what Joey Smallwood says?' Or, for that matter, 'Is this what Meighen says? Is this what Trudeau says?' People I dislike can be right. People I admire and respect can be wrong.

Of the many other politicians I have known or observed, there are a dozen of whom I have special memories.

One is C.H. Cahan, who was a candidate for the leadership of the Conservative Party at the Winnipeg convention of 1927 and was later Secretary of State in the Bennett government (1930-5). He was a man of great ability and great breadth of mind, who suffered, and triumphed over, a great personal sorrow and never reached the position for which he felt himself (with some reason) qualified. His sorrow was the conduct of one of his sons, who used his father's power of attorney to build up a mountain of debts and was convicted after a trial in which, to the best of my recollection, his father had to take the witness stand against him. Cahan paid off every copper of his son's defalcations. He had to bear a second sorrow: the early death of a second son, whose short career in public life gave promise of great things.

One of the features of Montreal politics in Cahan's later years was what was known as 'telegraphing', a code word for impersonation of voters. (In one election, in Verdun, a man came up to George Mooney, the CCF candidate, at the end of the day and told him enthusiastically that he had been paid to vote for one of Mooney's opponents and vote often, adding:

'And I voted for you, George, seven times.') It was practised on a massive scale and was no respecter of persons. Lady Shaughnessy, presenting herself at a polling station, was informed that Lady Shaughnessy had already voted. The Anglican Bishop of Montreal, presenting himself, was informed that Dr Farthing had already voted. Cahan warned all his supporters to vote early lest a similar fate befall them. I obeyed him to the letter. I did not stop even to wash my face, let alone shave: I shot out the door the moment the polls were open and dashed at top speed for the polling booth.

Cahan liked to call himself a 'continuing Conservative', in contrast to 'Progressive Conservative'. This suggests a traditional, outmoded, Blimpish Conservatism. In fact he was what nowadays the journalists call a 'Red Tory'. He was not in the least scared by the possibility of a CCF government. He was a great admirer of J.S. Woodsworth. When he himself was defeated in 1940, he was delighted that Woodsworth had been re-elected: 'Well, I'm glad to see that Winnipeg North Centre did its duty.' He spoke eloquently at the Montreal memorial service for Woodsworth. This was hardly the behaviour of a reactionary.

A second dear friend of many years' standing was the Honourable J.M. Macdonnell. We were both Rhodes Scholars and Balliol men, which I think is how I first came to know him. He was not a gladiator in the House of Commons. He was too capable of seeing the other side of every question, too confident of the good intentions of his opponents, and of their perhaps greater knowledge of this or that particular subject under debate. He told me once that Sir Thomas White said to him: 'Put off Oxford, Jim!' He also told me that when he had drafted a speech of unusual vigour and showed it to Gordon Graydon (then the acting Leader in the House), Gordon told him not to make it. 'Why not?' 'Because it's not Jim Macdonnell.' 'The best advice I ever had' was Jim's verdict to me. He was, however, a doughty fighter for freedom of speech and academic freedom (he had had much to do with frustrating the determined attempt in 1940 to get Frank Underhill dismissed from the University of Toronto). He was a pillar of good causes. He kept the Conservative Party alive in the dark days of the 1940s when it was reduced to a corporal's guard in the House of Commons: he got financial contributions from people who would have given them to no one else, and did it by asking them if they believed in parliamentary government. Of course they all said yes. Well, they must believe in the necessity of an Opposition, and a strong one. Of course they had to agree with this. Then come across! And come across they did. The Conservative Party he fought for, and begged for, was a party with room for progressively minded people: he was one of the powers behind the Port Hope Conference. I used to call him 'the conscience of the Conservative Party'; and when, at the memorial service for him the organ played Bunyan's hymn 'To Be a

Pilgrim' ('Who would true valour see,/ Let him come hither . . .'), the tears came to my eyes.

With Robert Stanfield, whom I admire greatly, I have only a slight acquaintance. Others can tell stories of his wit (of which, alas, the general public knows little). I can speak from personal experience only of his complete honesty and self-effacingness.

While he was Premier of Nova Scotia I happened to be in Halifax. I wanted to pay my respects. I went to the Province House and reached it at the back door. There was Stanfield, in a hard hat, making a speech to what were evidently people from the construction industry. I saw his eyes light on me. When he finished and the crowd had gone, I went over to the steps and said: 'I came to pay my respects.' 'Won't you come in?' 'No, thank you. I have paid my respects. I shall not waste your time.' 'Well, goodbye. Have a good day.' Most politicians, I think, would have said I must come in (though inwardly they would have been cursing the nuisance). Not Stanfield. I would have been wasting his time; he knew it; I knew it. Why make any pretence?

When Stanfield was elected leader of the Conservative Party, J.M. Macdonnell asked me to find out what the union people in Nova Scotia thought of him. I wrote the CLC's chief official in the province. He replied: 'Of course we don't see eye to eye with him on a great many things. But we can always rely on him. We go in with a list of things we want done. He looks at it and says: "This first one is good, and practicable. I'll do it." And he does. "This second thing won't work," and he tells us why. "Part of this third is good, and it will work. I'll do it." And he does. "The other part won't work," and he tells us why. "Your fourth proposal is new to me. I'll have to think it over. Come back Thursday, and I'll give you your answer." We go back Thursday and we get our answer, yes or no; and if it's yes, he does it.'

On Stanfield's first day in the House of Commons, my New Brunswick wife and I were in the Gallery. There were graceful words of welcome. Stanfield acknowledged them, with equal grace, observing that he was a new boy in this Chamber, adding: 'Though I have had some experience in a senior Legislature.' I whispered to my wife: 'That's one for the Upper Canadians!' (The legislature of Nova Scotia was established in 1758.)

When Stanfield was still Leader I met him at some social affair in the Parliament Buildings. He told me he was going to China the next week for four days, adding: 'And I shall come back an instant expert on China.' I said, 'No, I know you better than that. People often say to me: "Mr Stanfield is too slow." My invariable reply is: "Mr Stanfield has a quaint Nova Scotian idea that we should think first and speak later. The country is full of people who do the opposite."'

Years later I was in Halifax for the centenary of the Dalhousie Law School. I was staying at the Lord Nelson Hotel; so was Stanfield. At breakfast I went across the dining-room, again to pay my respects. He invited me to bring my coffee and we had a conversation. In the course of it, I said: 'Diefenbaker was a millstone round your neck.' The reply was vintage Stanfield: 'Well, he might have been more helpful.' Until he actually resigned I was always convinced he would, one day, be Prime Minister. After he resigned I said this to a prominent Liberal friend. He said: 'Yes. So were we. And we were scared stiff because we knew that if he once got in, we'd never get him out!' He would have been a great Prime Minister. I said to him in 1983: 'If the Conservative Party had had any sense, it would have gone down on its knees to get you to stay.'

How, when, or where I met the Honourable T.A. Crerar I cannot recall, but we became very good friends, though he must often have disapproved strongly of my opinions. I saw him often in Ottawa, occasionally in Winnipeg, and, after he left the Senate, in Victoria. We always had a lively conversation. Once, the subject of rheumatism came up. I remarked sadly that I had formerly had it in my hands, and was now afraid it was going into my feet. The riposte was instantaneous: 'I hope it's not going into your head, Eugene!' 'Well, I hope so too. But when I see some of the highly intelligent and highly educated people that I do talking what seems to me arrant nonsense, I can't help asking myself whether I'm crazy or they are.' Bless his heart, Crerar came back with an emphatic, '*They* are, Eugene.' (This was when so many English-speaking people, especially academics, were genuflecting before the altar of Quebec separatism.) The last time I saw him he was, I think, 95. His mind was as sharp as ever and we had a grand afternoon recalling old times. One thing he said was that the French Canadians in Parliament generally spoke so much better than the English: 'What they said was not necessarily wiser or more sensible, but they said it better.' I agreed. He added: 'Of course, we had some good people too. Arthur [Meighen] was magnificent.' 'He was indeed. And there was another man who was pretty good too. What was his name? I have it: Crerar!' Of course he was immensely pleased, but I meant it. You have only to read his last speech in the Senate, delivered without a note and absolutely first-class alike in matter and manner. He was an old-fashioned Liberal, with a strong belief in individual character and initiative. I think it was this that led him to say: 'Eugene, if our old friend Arthur were alive now, I think he and I'd agree better than we used to.' 'I think you would.'

Then there were the CCF leaders James Woodsworth and M.J. Coldwell. I knew them both well. Their names are writ large in Canadian history, and by better hands than mine. For me to add anything on Woodsworth would be like painting the lily, gilding refined gold.

Coldwell was of English birth and upbringing: a Devon man. At the University College of Exeter he was vice-president of the Conservative

Club—which may have had something to do with his declaration to me, many years later, that he could easily have voted for John A. Macdonald. He came to Canada as a teacher and was sent first to Alberta, where he was billeted with a farmer who became a close friend. After many months the farmer one day asked him casually where he came from. Coldwell replied proudly: 'Oh, I'm English. I come from Devon.' The farmer gaped. 'Well, of course it's all right now, because I know you. But if I'd been told before you came to us that you were English, I wouldn't have had you in the house.' Those were the days of 'No English need apply' across the West. Coldwell did not have an English upper-class accent (he could easily have passed for a Nova Scotian or a New Brunswicker, or a member of one of the 'old families' of Montreal), so his speech had not given him away. He was an Anglican. But when the *Parliamentary Guide* asked him for his 'religion', he wrote 'Christian'. A journalist duly noted that so many members were Roman Catholics, so many Presbyterians, so many Baptists, and so on; and there was 'one Christian, the Member for Rosetown-Biggar, M.J. Coldwell.'

Coldwell had a story that strikingly indicated William Aberhart's ascendancy over the ordinary people of Alberta. During Aberhart's premiership one of the leading members of the Alberta CCF was speaking to a public meeting in a rural constituency. When he came to the budget that Aberhart's government had just brought down, he was of course critical of it. But before he could say more than a sentence or two, a man in the front row rose: 'Stop! We will not listen to any criticism of Mr Aberhart or his government. If you continue with this, we shall all leave.' The speaker protested that he had not said, and did not intend to say, anything derogatory of Mr Aberhart. But this was a public question and Mr Aberhart, like any other public man, must expect to have his policies discussed and criticized. The whole audience rose as one man and left. The speaker turned to other subjects, and the audience gradually drifted back. Then he came back to the budget and the performance was repeated, I think several times.

Coldwell was, in general, a mild-mannered man, not given to strong words or even gestures. But not for nothing did he hail from the West Country of England. On a platform in Wolfville, Nova Scotia, during a general election, he very nearly came to blows with George Drew; and when, on 1 June 1956, during the pipeline debate, Mr Speaker Beaudoin ruled that 'the House should be placed in exactly the same position as it was when I resumed the chair yesterday to submit the Chairman's ruling to the House'—turning what has been called Black Friday into Thursday—Coldwell marched up the centre aisle shaking his fist at the Chair.

Coldwell never forgot his origins. When I was running for the House in 1948 someone, in conversation with him, referred to me as 'that

Frenchman'. Coldwell knew my origins. He shot back: 'Frenchman nothing! He's a Devonian, like me.' Long after the NDP founding Convention of 1961, he told me he thought I had been quite right on the 'two nations' question but that he was so afraid of Hazen Argue's carrying the Convention and becoming leader that he kept quiet.

Of course I knew also the first two leaders of the NDP, Douglas and Lewis.

Tommy Douglas was a superb speaker of the homespun type. The speeches of his successor David Lewis were in the grand, classic style of English parliamentary oratory, with echoes of Gladstone, Rosebery, Asquith. Tommy, with his wit and his fund of pithy and apposite stories, perhaps got closer to his audiences; and he had what David never had, a chance to show what he could do when the electors had given him the power to do it. For one thing he laid the foundations of medicare. He also proved as Premier of Saskatchewan that a CCF government could handle the tasks of government and do it well. His works live after him.

David Lewis was one of my students at McGill. In my course on Canadian government his performance was less spectacular than might have been expected. I think he was just too busy with political work. Even then, he was a superb speaker, indefatigable, and totally self-sacrificing. As National Secretary of the CCF he had a very stiff row to hoe and he hoed it well, though the crop was disappointing. I doubt if the CCF could have survived without him. After the New Democratic Party was formed, and he had committed himself to the 'two nations', and I had left the party accordingly, I saw very little of him, though I watched from afar, with admiration, his work in the House of Commons and on the hustings. His death robbed us of a really great man.

Stanley Knowles I have known well for some forty years. We were both in the CCF, he eminently, I humbly. We were both in the Canadian Labour Congress, he as Executive Vice-President, I as a senior employee. We are both of Nova Scotia and New England ancestry; indeed, in 1988 we discovered we are tenth cousins, descended through our Nova Scotian ancestors from William Brewster, who came to America on the *Mayflower*.

Stanley succeeded J.S. Woodsworth as MP for Winnipeg North Centre. Woodsworth himself had a hand in that. When he was on his last journey west to British Columbia, the train stopped of course in Winnipeg and a group of the local CCF faithful came to say a last farewell. The old leader was very frail, but he still had fight in him. Referring to the forthcoming by-election, he told the group that 'Winnipeg North Centre must be held'. They assured him it would be. 'And the nominating proceedings must be absolutely democratic!' 'Oh, of course!' The friends said their goodbyes. As the last of them passed through the door, Woodsworth called after them: 'And it must be Stanley Knowles!'

I happened to be at CCF headquarters in 1942 when the news of Stanley's triumph arrived. It was received with pleasure, but the pleasure was muted: 'Oh, of course Stanley is a fine person. But he'll never be anything but an obscure back-bencher. What a pity they couldn't have chosen someone who'd really amount to something!' It didn't take long for everyone to discover that in fact they *had*!

Quite apart from his monumental work for pensions, Stanley stood in the front rank of the parliamentarians of his time. Among experts on procedure, a most intricate as well as vital matter, he has probably never been surpassed. J.M. Macdonnell once said to me: 'What a lawyer he'd have made!' Catching an error in Beauchesne's great text on procedure was not easy. I did it once myself (a massive set of mistakes on the subject of disallowance of provincial Acts). Stanley did it again and again.

Never in my life but once have I given anyone definite advice. Stanley was the one exception. To everyone else who ever asked me, I gave a firm refusal: too much of a responsibility. But when Stanley was defeated in the Conservative sweep of 1958 he was offered two jobs: CCF organizer and Executive Vice-President of the CLC. He came to see me and asked which he should accept. I said: 'Stanley, I've never done this before. But this time I have no doubt at all about what you should do. You are five years younger than I. But you are not in your first youth. Besides, many years ago, as you have told me yourself, you were stricken by a very serious and destructive illness. Miraculously its progress was arrested before it could do you much harm. But if you take the job of CCF organizer you'll have to travel all over the country, in all kinds of weather, with inadequate facilities, under all sorts of difficulties, and on a meagre income. It will kill you. You owe it to yourself, your family, your friends, the party, and your country to stay alive. If the alternative were to take a plush job with Standard Oil, the situation would be different. But if you come to the Congress you won't be forsaking your principles or going over to the other side. You'll be working for the same people you've been working for all your life: the ordinary working people of Canada. Take the Congress job.' He did.

Among the minor politicians I have known, one of the most interesting was Jean-François Pouliot, a member for Témiscouata from 1924 until he was made a senator in 1955. When he first sought the Liberal nomination there, the bigwigs of the party were strongly against him. They put up their own man, and brought to the nominating convention a formidable phalanx of federal and provincial ministers to back him. As one after another of the notables sang the praises of their favourite, Jean-François, who had no notabilities to support him, began to feel far from hopeful. Then suddenly he had an idea. He summoned a small boy: 'Here are the keys of my office. Here is the key to my desk. Go to my office. Open my desk. Open the top drawer on the right. Take out the large brown envelope and bring it to me.' 'Oui, m'sieu.' The bigwigs having fired their volleys, it was Jean-François's turn to speak. 'You all know me. I am just plain Jean-François Pouliot. I have not got the Minister of Justice to support me. I have not got the Attorney-General. I have not got the Minister of Roads, or the Minister of Municipal Affairs, or the Minister of Public Works. But I have something my opponent has not: I have a letter from the Pope!' He had and he waved it. Jean-François had in fact written two learned works, one on the law of the fabrique, one on the law of the parish. They had been published, with page-long Latin dedications to a Cardinal. They were *the* authorities in the whole world on the two subjects, and Jean-François had a letter of congratulation from the Pope. In the Quebec of those days, that was the end. His opponent was never heard of again.

Jean-François was incensed by the bad English translations of his French speeches in the Senate (they were very bad; I had some experience of the same thing myself); to such a point, I am told, that he finally refused to make any French speeches there at all: he did not want to have his English-speaking friends think he had lost his wits. His English was in fact excellent. He once said to me: 'I learned my English in bar-r-r-rooms. That's why I have such a strong Scotch accent.' He was enormous fun. He had also a very good mind. It is a pity that he went down in parliamentary history more for his wit than for his more solid qualities.

This is the place to say that on the whole I think the people of Canada have been well served by their Members of Parliament, in both Houses. I have known a great many of them. In my judgement almost all have been of good quality: upright, hard-working, conscientious; often of superior intelligence, generally at least above the average.

Frank Scott, one of the principal draftsmen of the Regina Manifesto, took a decisive part in its passage through the first convention in 1933 of the CCF, of which he was one of the founding fathers and the National Chairman from 1942 to 1950. I have referred elsewhere in this book to my association with him at McGill, in the League of Social Reconstruction, in writing *Social Planning for Canada*, and to his influence on the development of my knowledge of constitutional law. (Apropos McGill's view of his leftist activities, Frank once said that the Board of Governors thought a professor's place was in the home.) Our friendship extended over the half-century of his many achievements. A member of the Royal Commission on Bilingualism and Biculturalism, Frank was a champion of the rights of French Canadians long before it was popular among English-speaking Canadians to be so. But when French-Canadian nationalism threatened the constitutional rights of the Quebec English-speaking Protestant minority in education, he was one of the authors of the masterly legal report that still forms the basis of their defence. What other of our major poets has been also a great constitutional lawyer? What other of our constitutional lawyers has been even a minor poet? Behind Frank's tall, handsome, rather austere appearance there were passion and compassion, generosity and tolerance, sensitivity, a witty sense of humour that could respond to any occasion, and an enormous relish for life. All these things I appreciated and enjoyed.

Another comrade of the CCF, King Gordon, was one of the most remarkable men I have ever known. I met him first when he came to the United Theological College in Montreal as Professor of Christian Ethics. I was also his comrade in the League for Social Reconstruction and the Fellowship for a Christian Social Order (which owed its existence largely to his inspiration and hard work). He went on to the editorship of the New York *Nation*, then to the United Nations, where he played an important part in the peace-keeping work in the Sinai and the Congo. He came back to Canada to professorships at the Universities of Alberta and Ottawa and work for CIDA, and to head the Group of 78 on Canadian foreign policy. He was spared the long illness that saddened Frank Scott's last years. Till almost his last moment he looked and sounded exactly as he had forty years before, and his mind was as keen, his energy as unflagging, his sympathies as all-embracing. I have never known anyone who genuinely cared so deeply for all kinds of people, not just groups but individuals — every person he encountered.

One of the founders of the Civil Liberties Union, and one of its doughtiest warriors, was the remarkable R.L. Calder, former Crown Prosecutor of Montreal. To begin with he was trilingual: English, French, and Gaelic. His father was a Highland Scots Presbyterian from Cape Breton, his mother a French-Canadian Roman Catholic from Quebec. (It was his proud boast that he was 'descended from the first man to put a plough into the soil of New France', Louis Hébert.) Neither of his grandmothers could speak a word of English: one only Gaelic, the other only French. Calder himself was superbly eloquent, literate, and witty in both English and French, and undoubtedly in Gaelic. In the First World War he rose to be second-in-command of the Royal 22nd Regiment (the famous 'Van Doos'); then he was transferred to be second-in-command of the Canadian Black Watch. 'I knew', he told me, 'that there was muttering in the Black Watch: "What are they doing, sending this little Frenchman to be second-in-command of a Highland regiment?" I knew they were all watching to see what I'd do in the mess the first night, when the piper would present the commanding officer with a horn of whisky with a traditional Gaelic phrase, and the commanding officer would accept it with another traditional Gaelic phrase and then repeat the performance with the second-in-command.' Calder accepted the horn of whisky, gave the traditional Gaelic response, burst into the 'Skye Boat Song' in Gaelic, and sat down. Colonel McCuaig said, 'Well, Calder, that was very nice. What was it?' 'What?' said Calder. 'You, the Colonel of a Highland regiment, don't know what that was?' It turned out that Calder and the piper were the only two men in the regiment who had any Gaelic beyond the two traditional phrases. 'I heard no more about the "little Frenchman".'

Calder had a number of good stories about his experiences in Quebec courts. One was of Judge Sicotte, who, when an accused pleaded 'not guilty', always looked at him severely over his glasses, shook his head, and said sternly: 'If you were not guilty, you would not be here.' Calder said Sicotte reminded him of the Irish judge who is reputed to have said that he never listened to the defence: he found it confused him. As Crown Prosecutor Calder had one very notable case: the Frank case. Tony Frank, Montreal's first big gangster, was accused of murder. He swore he would never be convicted: 'I'm too rich.' Calder swore he would convict him and he did. Years later I was riding in a taxi in Montreal and the driver said to me: 'Do you remember Tony Frank?' 'I do indeed.' 'In those days a convicted man sentenced to hang was taken to the place of execution in a special street car. I drove the streetcar that took Tony Frank to be hanged. All the way to the place of execution he kept saying: "They'll never hang me. I'm too rich."'

Calder took several Padlock Act cases without fee, and unfortunately without success. One of them was before the then Chief Justice, Sir Matthias Tellier. The person involved was said to be a Communist and quite probably was. But that, of course, was not the question. None the less Sir Matthias saw fit to pose some question to Calder on Karl Marx. He could not have made a bigger mistake. Calder was probably the only person in Canada outside the Communist Party who had read every word Marx ever wrote. He came back in a trice with what promised to be a Ph.D. dissertation on Marx, and the Chief Justice's head was soon swimming. He interrupted the lecture: 'Mr Calder, you are wandering from the point.' Calder bowed: 'I am following Your Lordship.'

In 1926 he was appointed counsel to the Royal Commission on the Customs Scandal. This, of course, did not last long. The Conservative government later, through Sir George Perley, offered him a judgeship. But there was a string attached. 'Calder,' said Sir George, 'we want to make you a judge. But what *are* you?' 'Well, I'm a barrister of so many years' standing; I've been Crown Prosecutor of Montreal, I —' 'No, no, no. We know all that. What *are* you?' 'I'm telling you what I am.' 'Calder, we have two judgeships available. You can have one of them. But you must say whether you're English or French.' Calder drew himself up to his full height of about five feet six and said: 'I am a prefiguration of the Canadian that is to be.' 'Then we can do nothing for you.'

Calder was passionately devoted to the cause of civil liberties. He was a Liberal, and his liberalism was more than formal. The Taschereau government's interference with the prerogative writs (injunction, certiorari mandamus, quo warranto, and prohibition), which he considered bulwarks of the citizens' rights, infuriated him and produced a brilliant pamphlet, *Comment s'éteint la liberté* (How Liberty is Extinguished). He left the Liberals and sought a Conservative nomination for Parliament. It was denied him because in an 'English' constituency he was considered 'French'. That finished the Conservative party for him. Eventually his struggle for civil liberties led him into the CCF. When people asked him why he had twice changed his party, his reply always was: 'I change my party as I change my shirt, and for the same reason.'

Occasionally my marginal career has collided with public events of some importance, and may have had some effect on them.

One such case arose when the Canada Pension Plan was brought forward in 1966. While it was under discussion, and after Quebec had made plain that it intended to have its own plan, I had a sudden visit from a prominent Conservative Ottawa lawyer of my acquaintance (who later became a member of the Ontario Cabinet). I knew him moderately well, but we were not on such terms that he was in the habit of dropping in occasionally. To my astonishment he wanted to know what I thought of Ontario's also staying out of the national plan. The theory was that if both Ontario and Quebec stayed out, Quebec's doing so would not be so disruptive of national unity. Two provinces—one 'French', the other 'English', both opting out—would prevent the thing from becoming a 'French-English' division.

I said I could understand the argument and the reasons for it, but that it was too clever by half; that in my judgement, in politics, other things being equal, the simplest course was the best. There were times when one had to adopt a policy that was complicated. But in general the less elaborate it was the better people would understand it, and the more likely they would be to support it. In this case I thought that all that would get through to the public was 'Quebec is opting out, Ontario is opting out, the whole thing is dead.'

He left. I have sometimes wondered if the Premier had asked him to try out the idea on me. If so, it is conceivable that what I said may have had something to do with Ontario's decision to opt in.

In the pipeline debate of 1956 my part was at least more conspicuous. On 31 May, the day before 'Black Friday', the *Ottawa Journal* published two letters attacking Mr Speaker Beaudoin's decisions during the debate. One was from me and it was read in the House of Commons that evening. I was elsewhere. When I got home the telephone rang. It was Colin Cameron, MP: 'Well, Eugene, we've just poured you down the drain in the interests of democracy.' He then recounted with zest how he had raised a question of privilege on my attack on the Speaker's decisions; how he had read my letter into *Hansard*; how the Speaker had risen to the bait and virtually dictated Colin's motion of privilege (which, of course, took precedence over everything else, throwing the Government's whole essential time-table into disarray); how George Drew had re-read my letter to the House, with strongly favourable comments; how others had chimed in. Davie Fulton also rang me to supplement Colin's account.

The rest is history: how, next morning, the Speaker backtracked and succeeded, in effect, in turning the clock back so that Friday became Thursday; how pandemonium erupted.

I had had a brief moment of thrilling anticipation of being called to the bar of the House to withdraw what I had written, or face imprisonment in the Carleton County jail. I had even chosen my reply: 'I regret nothing that I said. I regret only the necessity of having to say it.' I had not made up my mind whether to say this in English or in French. The Speaker's change of heart, and *coup d'état*, robbed me of my one possible moment of glory. I took a mild revenge by writing a stinging 'learned' article about the pipeline affair for the British journal *Public Law*.

It is barely possible that there are two other cases, more recent, where I may have had some effect.

In the prolonged discussions leading up to the Meech Lake Accord, it seems to have been generally assumed that any reference to Quebec as a 'distinct society' would be contained in a preamble, which, of course, has no legal force. In an article some months before the Accord, I noted that Mr Bourassa had spoken of such a preamble's giving Quebec new powers over language, and I commented that it would not. Can this have had anything to do with the change from preamble to a clause making the 'distinct society' a mandatory principle of interpretation of the whole Constitution (bar multiculturalism, immigration, and the aborigenes)? The possibility, however faint, is tantalizing.

When the Meech Lake Accord appeared in 1987 I had some correspondence with one of the officials in the Privy Council Office whom I had known since he was a child. I pointed out the danger that the 'duality' clause might be used by the minorities to get the courts to force on Parliament and the provincial legislatures measures that the minorities thought the clause entitled them to; in other words, a possible major limitation on the legislative power of both Parliament and the legislature.

The official dismissed the possibility as a flight of my imagination. He called my attention to Section 36 of the Constitution Act, 1982 (the equalization section), which merely stated principles, but gave the courts no powers at all. I looked at that section, and pointed out that it began: 'Without altering the legislative authority of Parliament or of the provincial legislatures, or the rights of any of them *with respect to the exercise of their legislative authority*.' In the Meech Lake Accord there was no such saving phrase.

In the final text that emerged from the all-night session in the Langevin Block there is a 'non-derogation' clause. But it does not mention 'the exercise of their legislative authority'. So it is arguable that the final text leaves it open to the courts to say: 'We can't give you any new powers. We can't take away any of the powers you have. But you *have* certain powers. We *can* order you to use those powers to give the minorities the rights the duality principle is supposed to guarantee them. Do it.' The Supreme Court of Canada did this in the Manitoba language case.

Perhaps if I had held my tongue there would have been no non-derogation clause at all; perhaps, even, the distinct-society clause would have remained harmlessly in the preamble! Perhaps the fringe just may have touched the centre.

7

The Board of Broadcast Governors

The appointment of the Board of Broadcast Governors in 1958 opened a new chapter in Canadian broadcasting history. Till then the publicly owned Canadian Broadcasting Corporation had been both an operating and a regulating body. It had its own stations; it had a string of private affiliates across the country. Together these made up a nation-wide network. There were also a large number of privately owned stations that were unaffiliated but regulated by the CBC. They, and their allies in the Conservative Party, had objected more and more vociferously to the CBC's dual role, and the new Conservative government had decided to end it. The new Broadcasting Act left the CBC intact as an operating body, but entrusted the regulating of the whole system, public and private, to a purely regulatory body, the Board of Broadcast Governors.

It had three full-time members, twelve part-time. The full-time members were the Chairman, Dr Andrew Stewart, former President of the University of Alberta; the Vice-Chairman, Roger Duhamel, afterwards Queen's Printer; and Carlyle Allison of the *Winnipeg Tribune*. The part-time members were Robert Furlong, for Newfoundland (who left almost immediately to become Chief Justice of Newfoundland, and was succeeded by Leslie Marshall, St John's businessman); Roy Duchemin, of the *Cape Breton Post*, for Nova Scotia; David Stewart, for Prince Edward Island (he soon left to become Provincial Secretary, and was succeeded by Joseph Burge, a potato grower); Dr Colin B. Mackay, President of the University of New Brunswick, for that province; Dr Mabel Connell, dentist, for Saskatchewan; and Joseph Brown, Vancouver businessman, for British Columbia. Quebec had Dr Guy Hudon, Dean of the Faculty of Law at Laval University; Yvan Sabourin, lawyer and Leader of the Conservative Party (what there was of it) in the province; and Mrs Irene Gilbride.

Ontario had Edward Dunlop, a distinguished war veteran; the Reverend Dr Emlyn Davies; and me.

Most were patronage appointments, several were defeated Conservative candidates. I have no idea of the political opinions of Stewart or Davies. Marshall was a Past-President of the Newfoundland Conservative Association. Colin Mackay was the nephew of Hugh Mackay, Conservative Leader in New Brunswick. Dr Connell was John Diefenbaker's dentist. Mrs Gilbride had, conspicuously, 'delivered' the Conservative vote in Montreal West. Dunlop's wife was a Tupper.

This does not by any means tell the whole story, however. Three members were distinguished academics: Stewart, Hudon, and Mackay. Allison and Duchemin were journalists. Davies was the learned and eloquent minister of Yorkminster Baptist Church, Toronto. Stewart, Duhamel, Hudon, Mackay, and Davies would no doubt have been dubbed 'intellectuals'. Mrs Gilbride was an expert on slum clearance and prison reform, and had served both with unstinted devotion (she alarmed her son, a well-known insurance man, by her hospitality to ex-convicts).

I looked like a conspicuous exception to the patronage appointments. But the exception was perhaps more apparent than real. I was a well-known member of the CCF, a twice-defeated CCF candidate against George Drew, Leader of the Conservative Party, and I was also a trade union official of some standing. On the other hand I was notoriously a close friend of Arthur Meighen, I was also a friend of the Prime Minister and of J.M. Macdonnell, Davie Fulton, Minister of Justice, and George Nowlan, the minister in charge of broadcasting affairs. Moreover, the pipeline debate of 1956 had put me off the Liberals completely, and, though I had voted CCF in 1957, I greeted the Conservative victory as 'our great deliverance'. Probably the Government felt it had to have a labour representative of some sort and I looked like the least objectionable. I had also lobbied hard with Davie Fulton for the preservation of the CBC. I remember reminding him that J.H. Pope, at a critical moment in the history of the CPR, had said to Macdonald, 'John A., the day the CPR goes bust, the Conservative Party goes bust the day after', and applying this warning to the CBC.

There may have been another and more respectable reason for my appointment: I was a friend of Graham Spry. Graham, with Alan Plaunt, had been largely responsible for the creation of the Canadian Broadcasting Commission, which became the CBC. Graham knew everything about Canadian broadcasting, and, though a strong and devoted (and notably self-sacrificing) CCFer, had close friends in all parties. It may have been he who got me put on the BBG. I suspect he was not always altogether happy about my performance.

As far as I know, none of the members of the Board had any appreciable knowledge of the scientific or technical aspects of broadcasting, and we had a very small staff. I did not even have a TV set, as I told George Nowlan frankly when he appointed me. (I bought one immediately.)

I took a rather larger part in the Board's work than some of the other part-time members. This was partly because I lived in Ottawa, partly because my French was better than that of most of the English-speaking members.

Colin Mackay, as anyone who knows him will readily believe, was the wittiest member of the Board. He enjoyed teasing Mrs Gilbride, and, at least once, me. Mrs Gilbride one day was lamenting the burden of having to read the numerous and voluminous briefs submitted to us. 'Dr Mackay, how do you deal with it?' 'Mrs Gilbride, it's perfectly simple. I weigh them. Anything over a certain weight goes to the waste-basket.' 'Dr Mackay!' Colin was able to reassure her. But later, when we had been hearing applications for increases in power, Mrs Gilbride noticed that Colin's eyes were shut. At the end of the hearing she told him she was so sorry he was having eye-trouble. Colin, surprised, asked her why she thought so. 'You had your eyes closed for most of the afternoon.' 'Oh, I was asleep.' 'Dr Mackay! You are being paid public money.' 'Mrs Gilbride, I can tell you exactly what each of the applicants said,' and he did. They had all given exactly the same reasons, and Colin, after several repetitions, had just taken forty winks. Mrs Gilbride was satisfied, but baffled.

Colin was an old friend of mine. I had had an early taste of his quality at the installation of a new President of Carleton University. I said to him: 'Of course this is old stuff to you.' 'No. I never had an installation.' 'What!' 'No. I knew what people were saying, that it was just a patronage appointment, and nepotism. So I said, "Let's not have a lot of people getting up on a platform and saying things they don't mean. Let me get to work; then if I'm any good, I'll show it; and if I'm not, they can throw me out." ' He proved himself an excellent President. Lord Beaverbrook was the Chancellor, and Colin played him like a salmon. On the charge that his appointment had been mere patronage, my patrician Saint John mother-in-law had the definitive Saint John comment: 'The publicity was very badly handled. They ought to have said that his mother was a Bridges.' For the benefit of Upper Canadians, I may explain that Dr Bridges had been to New Brunswick what Egerton Ryerson had been to Ontario. When he spoke on education, no dog barked.

Colin had his own way of dealing with certain university problems. Under his predecessor, Norman MacKenzie, the university had bought a large property from Fred Neil, the university groundsman. There was just one condition attached: Mr Neil was to keep his own small house, beside a noble pine tree, with a matchless view of the Saint John River far below. The moment came when the university wanted to build a new residence on that very spot. Colin approached Mr Neil. The answer was a firm no. After an interval, Colin tried again. 'Now, Fred, I know what Dr MacKenzie said, and of course I stand by that absolutely. But I have a suggestion to make. However, there are two conditions.' 'What are they?' 'The first is that the new residence will be named after you.' 'After me?' 'Yes; but if you won't accept that, we'll say no more about it.' 'Well! What is the second condition?' 'That you should turn the first sod.' 'Turn the first sod? Like Lord Beaverbrook?' 'Just like Lord Beaverbrook. But if you refuse, then that's the end of it.' 'Dr Mackay! What is the suggestion?' 'That we should move your house to the other side of the pine tree.' Done.

Carlyle Allison, who on Duhamel's resignation became Vice-Chairman, was highly knowledgeable, very hard-working, and an expert at getting action from the Treasury Board and the Department of Public Works. There were long delays in getting our staff and equipment. Without Carlyle, and his close friendship with John Diefenbaker, they would have been longer still.

Yvan Sabourin was remarkable in more ways than one. He had been a champion wrestler. He had swum the Hellespont. He was one of the finest cooks in Quebec. He was a great traveller. It was said that Mme Sabourin never knew, when he left the house in the morning, when he'd be back. She might get an afternoon cable saying he was on his way to Helsinki or Istanbul!

Andrew Stewart was an admirable Chairman. At one of our first hearings he set the tone. Jack Kent Cooke was before us. He owned a popular and lucrative radio station in Toronto and was used to calling the tune, no matter where or with whom. Andrew asked him a very relevant question. He replied haughtily: 'Now, Dr Stewart, you wouldn't expect me to answer that question!' 'Yes, Mr Cooke,' said Andrew, 'I would.' He got his answer.

Andrew worked like a Trojan and his patience was almost inexhaustible. I realize in retrospect what a very difficult time he had, and what a difficult team to lead. He had a very soft voice. So had our counsel, Mr Pearson. Both must have had exceptionally keen hearing. Most people's statements I could hear well enough without my hearing aid. But these two I often could not. Andrew, opening a public hearing in a large hall, would say something in such dulcet tones that I am sure many of the audience were in the same plight as I. I formed the habit of bringing out my hearing aid rather ostentatiously; Andrew, catching sight of it, would raise his voice to what for most people would have been normal. With Mr Pearson I had to adopt a different method. When he was questioning an applicant or a witness, to me inaudibly, I'd intervene by saying, 'Mr Chairman, I was under the impression that this was a public hearing, not a confidential exchange between counsel and the applicant (or witness).'

Emlyn Davies was brilliant, gentle, and witty — a delightful companion.

Leslie Marshall became one of my closest friends, perhaps partly because neither of us had any use for Joey Smallwood.

Guy Hudon, one of the great lawyers of his time, was said to have taken twenty-nine cases to the Supreme Court of Canada and won twenty-eight of them. He was at first somewhat diffident about expressing his views, pleading that he distrusted his English. This was complete nonsense because his English was superb. He and I found ourselves in close sympathy almost from the first, especially when he said after one hearing, disgustedly: 'Not one of them has the faintest concern with the public interest. All they care about is making money.' So I kept at him to speak up. His word would have far more effect than mine: as I was a trade unionist and a CCFer, my opinions would be heavily discounted. He was an eminent Conservative, of vast knowledge and high reputation; no one would dream of writing him off as a socialist. After some hesitation he decided to take the plunge, and from then on he was one of the most valuable and articulate members of the Board. He was an ardent supporter of the Quebec credit union movement, the Caisses Desjardins, doing all their legal work without fee.

The one thing all the members of the Board had in common was concern for the public interest, though of course we did not always see it in the same light. We faced three major tasks, all of them made more acutely difficult because television was comparatively new. We had to set standards of Canadian content. We had to recommend the grant or refusal of broadcasting licences, especially TV — notably 'second stations' where a place already had one station. We had to consider a private TV network.

On Canadian content, I think we were reasonably successful. I do not recall any serious adverse criticism, except once when the French version of a decision to stiffen the Canadian-content requirements left out a line or two. Our original regulation had stipulated that from 1 April 1962, 55 per cent of all programs should be Canadian. Later we decided that this general regulation was inadequate: the prime time was getting a very slim part of the 55 per cent; Canadian programs were being shuffled off into the earlier hours, or the small hours. So we proposed to require that 40 per cent of prime time should go to Canadian programs. This was, as it were, on top of the general 55 per cent.

But the proposal produced a storm in Quebec. Furious protests poured in. The Board, particularly the Chairman, was perplexed and outraged: here we were, imposing stricter requirements and we were being accused of a disastrous watering down of the existing standards. We held an *in camera* meeting in the Board's office in Ottawa, and were drafting an indignant defence when a possibility suddenly struck me. The text before us was in English. I asked for a French version, as it seemed to me that something might have gone askew in the translation. This suggestion was greeted with protests that our translators were experts, that any mistake by them was inconceivable. I agreed that they were indeed experts; but accidents could happen. We got the French version that had been given to the newspapers and lo and behold a couple of lines had got left out, so that it appeared that the Board was proposing to cut the 55 per cent to 40! Our indignant reply to the critics was of course thrown into the waste-basket and replaced by a most apologetic explanation.

The hearings on licences for new stations, especially TV, meant that we travelled to almost every part of the country. The four cases I remember particularly are Toronto, Halifax, Vancouver, and Calgary.

The Toronto hearings caused a good deal of a dust-up. The Toronto li-cence was, of course, a prize, popularly described as 'a licence to print money'. There were several competitors, all formidable.

One was Jack Kent Cooke. The other applicants all appeared flanked by technical experts and financial backers and advisers. Mr Cooke had only a row of empty chairs on either side of him. When it came time for questions, Emlyn Davies (the kindest and gentlest of men) said: 'Mr Cooke, I notice that while all the other applicants have come here with a number of technical and financial advisers, you have come entirely alone.' 'Yes, Dr Davies. I do not need any technical experts. I have all the technical knowledge needed for this enterprise. I do not need any financial advisers or supporters. I have myself all the financial resources that can be needed.' Emlyn said: 'Yes; but Mr Cooke, has it ever occurred to you, has it ever crossed your mind, that a day may come when you will not be there?' Great was the deflation of Jack Kent Cooke. He was speechless. I said afterwards to Dr Davies: 'Emlyn, it had never occurred to him that he was not immortal.' 'No,' said Davies, in his musical Welsh lilt, 'Jack Kent Cooke does not think theologically, but Emlyn Davies does.'

Cooke was not the leading contender. The *Toronto Telegram* group (John Bassett, Joel Aldred, and others) was. Its members were all Conservatives, and some of them had let their tongues wag, boasting that their licence was in the bag. When we recommended that they get the licence there was an uproar, led by the eminent Toronto lawyer, Joseph Sedgwick. The fact was, however, that the *Telegram* presentation of its case seemed to all of us unquestionably the best. I still think so, and my opinion was endorsed very recently by a friend who remembered the whole affair and is certainly not a Conservative. As it turned out, the *Telegram* people were, to say the least, overconfident about what they could do in the way of programs. But this was true of everybody who got a TV licence. I suppose if we had known more we might have been skeptical about their promises; but we should probably have had to be skeptical about all the applicants.

Mr Sedgwick's attack on us was so abusive that I thought the Board ought to have remonstrated when he appeared before us in another matter.

My colleagues thought otherwise, so I simply absented myself whenever he appeared. I was near enough once, however, to gather that he made a magnificent rhetorical display. A noted member of the Ontario Bar, he was listened to in what in India they call 'pin-drop silence'. But one member of the Board was not impressed. Guy Hudon began his questioning, in his splendid organ voice, with: 'Mr Sedgwick, you talk a great deal, but you say absolutely nothing.' I think most of the Ontario people there must have felt as Sydney Smith did when someone 'spoke disrespectfully of the Equator.'

Our decision in the Halifax case produced fresh charges of partisanship. There were two applicants, one headed by the present Senator Finlay MacDonald, the other by someone whose name escapes my memory. Both made excellent presentations: we were hard put to it to decide which was the better. But there was one aspect of the case presented by MacDonald's competitor that worried us: its financial capacity to carry out its undertakings. We felt it necessary to call this applicant back on the point. The answers we got to our detailed questions did not satisfy us and we recommended that MacDonald's group get the licence. The allegations that our recommendation had been a foregone conclusion were wholly unfounded.

I do not recall any charges of partisanship in the Vancouver or Calgary cases. In Vancouver we had a number of applicants. One was a personable young man who gave us a most attractive presentation. Most of the Board were quite bowled over by him. I was not. I liked him, but I did not think he had the ability, or the financial strength, to make good. I voted against giving him the licence. So, I think, did Edward Dunlop. But the majority were all for him. As it turned out, the misgivings were well founded: he had to sell out within a relatively short time.

The Calgary hearings remain in my memory because of an absurdity. One of the applicants was a group consisting almost wholly of multi-millionaire oil tycoons. They had one non-tycoon, a local radio-station owner, who made their presentation. It was an impressive effort. Its highlight was this: 'Dr Stewart, Dr Connell, Mrs Gilbride, gentlemen: our group is so profoundly moved by the overwhelming importance of this medium—its cultural importance, its social importance, its political importance, its economic importance—that, regardless of whether we get this licence or not, we have *already* made a *grant* to the University of British Columbia for research in *depth*.' At the thought of a grant for research in depth from the massed millionaires in front of us, I was almost awestruck. So, I dare say, must have been most of my colleagues. But not Dr Connell. When it came time for questions, she pulled the microphone towards her and in her frail voice asked: 'Mr ——, did I understand you to say that your group had already made a grant to the University of British Columbia for research on this subject?' 'That is correct, Dr Connell,

Dr Stewart, Mrs Gilbride, and gentlemen. We are so profoundly impressed by the importance . . .' (and he went through the whole thing again). 'What was the amount of the grant?' I was already having trouble with deafness and I thought my ears, in Wodehouse's words, had 'handed in their portfolio'. At the coffee-break I asked Carlyle Allison whether the man had really said what I thought he had said. Carlyle looked at me with an indescribable expression: 'He did.' The amount was $500.

Our hearings on the second network passed off uneventfully as far as I can recall.

From time to time we had to hold hearings on changes in control of a station. At one of these an important TV station offered a proposal that in my opinion would have given the Americans far too substantial an influence. I objected, and went to so far as to say, in a letter to the Chairman, that if the Board approved the proposal I should feel compelled to resign. The applicant dropped the objectionable feature, but not before Emlyn Davies had presented me with an elaborate written remonstrance saying that it was most improper for me to threaten resignation: it was my duty to accept the decision of the majority. My recollection is that he likened the Board to a Cabinet, and argued that a Minister could not properly threaten resignation. It did not take me long to deal with that one. I quoted chapter and verse, notably Lord Hartington's threat to resign if Gladstone did not send a relief expedition to rescue General Gordon.

Frank Peers, in his book *The Public Eye: Television and the Politics of Canadian Broadcasting: 1952-68* (1979), reproduces most of my letter of objection to my colleagues. I think it is one of the best things I ever wrote, except for one ludicrous and disastrous misprint—probably my own fault. I had meant to say that what the station's proposal actually said was only the visible part of an iceberg. In the printed text 'visible' is replaced by 'hidden'! The context makes clear enough what I meant, but readers of Peers' book must wonder whether I had taken leave of my senses. Only a short time ago I discovered in the same book that the TV station and its American friends nominally accepted the Board's final decision, but then did an end-run around it that gave them all they had wanted.

The Board had two special joint committees: one with the CBC, one with the association of private broadcasters. I was on both. The chief spokesman for the CBC was, of course, its President, Alphonse Ouimet. The chief spokesman for the private stations was their Association's president, Don Jamieson, afterwards a Minister in the Trudeau Cabinet. Both were exceedingly able, indeed formidable. I did my best to support the CBC. I don't think anyone expected me to do less. My views were well known.

On the private-broadcasting committee I once had occasion to make a stand in defence of the BBG's position and duty. We had had a meeting of the committee, at which Mr Jamieson and his colleagues discussed with us a draft regulation we were considering issuing. They did not like it and suggested some changes. The committee adjourned, and in due course the Board met and issued the regulation without the changes the private broadcasters had wanted. At the next meeting of the committee Mr Jamieson was irate. What was the use of having a committee, he said, if, when we had reached an agreement, the Board went back on it? I waited for the Chairman or some other member to reply to this. No one did. But this kind of statement could not be allowed to pass unchallenged. So I intervened.

'Mr Jamieson, in the circles in which I move, the word "agreement" has a very definite meaning. The employer and the union negotiate. They come to an agreement; they sign it. It becomes binding on both of them. You have said that the Board apparently attaches no importance to what your Association says. That is not so. We listen most carefully, as we should, to what you say. We are most grateful for the information and opinions you give us. But we do not negotiate. The joint committee is a purely advisory body. Having listened to you, the Board decides what it should do. The Board was not set up to negotiate with you. It was set up to regulate you and the CBC alike. We listen to you. We thank you. We do not make an agreement with you.'

An uncomfortable silence followed. But this was the last we heard of that preposterous notion.

As time went on, however, both Guy Hudon and I drew increasingly uneasy about the more and more informal relations between the Board and the private broadcasters. There seemed to us to be too much of the 'all boys together' atmosphere. We did not specifically raise the matter with our colleagues, because by the time we had got to that point we were already at odds with them on a much more specific and serious matter. But Guy let everyone see how he felt. We had been in discussion with an important and influential private broadcaster, whom most of the members had been addressing by his Christian name. When Guy's turn came, he said: 'Mr ——, if I may be permitted so to address you.'

Guy did not mince words. One applicant who had been before us several times, always full of sound and fury signifying very little, was before us again. We had already taken his measure, but he had not taken ours. He indulged in his usual palaver. I set to work to cross-examine him. I had a number of rather searching questions, but I could scarcely get through them all because Guy wanted to get at him. I had to keep saying, 'Yes, yes, Guy, but I've still got another question.' Then—having, I felt, laid bare a good deal of the nakedness of the land—I joyfully yielded to Guy. He asked a devastating question. The applicant replied: 'Well, Dr Hudon, my philosophy of broadcasting is—' He got no farther. 'Please, Mr ——. I do not wish to listen for the nineteenth time to what you are pleased to call your philosophy of broadcasting. Just answer my question.'

Guy had some trouble over his expense accounts. He drove to meetings in Ottawa instead of flying or coming by train. This, of course, saved the Government money. But the Treasury Board would allow him only 5 cents a mile for gasoline, and refused to pay parking fees for his car while he was attending meetings, which sometimes lasted several days. It also complained that his expenses for meals were not backed by sufficient vouchers. On the mileage allowance Guy pointed out that Victory Bond salesmen were allowed 9 cents a mile. The Treasury Board refused to budge. On the parking fees Guy asked whether he was expected to keep his car in his bedroom. The Treasury Board remained adamant. 'Very well,' said Guy. 'From now on I shall leave my car at home. It will cost the Government more money, but if that's what you want, that you shall get.' On the meals he retaliated by taking all of them in the Château Laurier cafeteria and submitting the cash-register slips. I remember him flourishing a fistful of them before me, saying: 'Let them question those!' Guy's great-grandfather (I think it was) had been an eminent Anglican divine, chaplain to the highest Masonic Lodge in England, and the Duke of Wellington had been one of his children's godfathers. Guy never forgot it, and in the face of the Treasury Board's exactions, said to Emlyn Davies: 'Dr Davies, I have Anglican ancestors and my Protestant blood is up!' Guy was of course officially a Roman Catholic, but not, I think, a very orthodox one. The Board held some of its meetings in a Roman Catholic church hall, where a lectern bore the words: 'Voie Vérité Vie.' Guy's sad comment to me one day was: 'La voie est obscure, la vérité douteuse, et la vie courte.'

Before the Edmonton hearing the Board held an *in camera* business meeting that dealt chiefly with the Chairman's annual report. Andrew Stewart read it aloud to us. It was a long document and necessarily not very exciting, being mainly a recital of the fact that the Board had held such-and-such meetings in such-and-such places, had heard such-and-such applications for this or that, had made such-and-such recommendations, had passed such-and-such regulations. Andrew paused to turn a page, and Mrs Gilbride's voice rang out: 'Well, what I want to know is [one of her two favourite ways of beginning], will this have to be read aloud to the House of Commons?' A stricken silence fell. Then: 'Because if it does, I'm telling you [another favourite phrase] they'll walk out!' Another stricken silence. Then I said: 'No, Mrs Gilbride, it does not have to be read aloud. It is just laid on the table.' 'Oh well, I'm glad of that.' Mrs Gilbride, alas, was unable to stay the course—not because of any flagging of energy or enthusiasm but simply because, as it turned out, she was beyond the Act's retirement age when she was appointed! Mr Pickersgill had discovered this and raised it in the House of Commons. We all missed her.

One extraordinary incident took place in 1961. The Broadcasting Act, Section 13 (4) (b), gave the Board power to grant or revoke permission for a station that was part of any network for the broadcasting of a particular program, or series of programs, for a period not exceeding one month, but with the proviso that if the station was operating as part of another network, no such permission should be granted without the consent of the operator of such network.

On 13 June the three full-time members of the Board appeared before the House of Commons' Broadcasting Committee with what the Chairman of that Committee called 'some recommended amendments to the Act which they have considered since we last met with them.' One of the amendments was to Section 13 (4) (b). It would have transferred the power from the full Board to the Chairman 'or his representative'. It would have lengthened the duration of the temporary network to not more than six months. It would have deleted the proviso requiring the consent of the operator of any permanent network the station belonged to, and substituted: '. . . subject to the conditions of affiliation between the station and the operator of such other network' — which, as Dr Stewart explained, meant that the contractual conditions of the affiliation agreement could not be touched (i.e. the temporary network could not take any of the permanent network's reserved time). This proposal was presented as coming from 'the Board'. Dr Stewart's precise words were: 'Now, in our view, that is, the Board's view . . . '

When I read this in the newspaper I was flabbergasted, for the amendment had never been before the Board at all! The President of the CBC was equally taken aback: it was evidently news to him also. He objected strongly to what he naturally thought was a decision of the full Board, and wrote the Chairman of the Broadcasting Committee that he wanted to be heard on it.

I had already protested to the full-time members of the Board; so, probably, had other members. At any rate on 14 June Dr Stewart told the Broadcasting Committee: 'In presenting the suggestion which we made . . . I should have prefaced my remarks by saying that this had not been considered by the full Board. We had prepared it in anticipation of the meeting of the Board which opens on 18 June, thinking that we would be called before the committee after that meeting. However, when we learned that we were to be called this week, we passed the recommendation to the chairman and asked to be allowed to speak to it. I am now making it clear that this has not been approved by the full Board and, after we have had a chance to discuss it with the Board next week, we may have further comments to pass on to the committee.'

They did. The discussion produced a markedly different amendment. If the temporary network was to be for less than two months, then the power to permit it would be vested in the Chairman of the Board or his representative; if for a period of two to six months, then in the full Board or its executive committee. The proviso requiring the consent of the operator of the permanent network was to be restored. And the Board said explicitly that it was 'not now in favour of the amendment proposed by the Canadian Association of Broadcasters' (the organ of the private stations). The three full-time members had apparently simply presented a CAB proposal as a BBG decision! As Alice in Wonderland said, 'curiouser and curiouser'. Dr Stewart sent the Board's decision to the Broadcasting Committee on 19 June.

The CBC had been applying for a French TV station in Quebec City. There was also a private applicant, who had a radio station and was reputed to be an influential Conservative. Guy Hudon had made a point of monitoring his radio programs and told me they were *'pourris'* (rotten). The applicant's presentation did not, to put it mildly, impress either of us. Both of us, on the other hand, were convinced that the time had come for the CBC to have its own station in the ancient capital, and the CBC's presentation confirmed our view.

But the Board did not make an immediate decision. On the contrary it put off, and put off, and put off. Guy and I were repeatedly assured that the next meeting would see the case dealt with. But we finally reached the limit of our patience. We decided that if our colleagues voted for another postponement, we'd resign; and we said so.

(At the last meeting we attended a fracas occurred that did nothing to soften our resolve. Yvan Sabourin made a virulent attack on Guy Hudon's integrity on a purely extraneous matter—I think it was the Caisses Desjardins. He had never made a bigger mistake. Guy's reply was a masterpiece of cold, precise refutation.)

We had a final interview with Dr Stewart, who tried to persuade us that the Board had to consider the Quebec City applications in the context of the whole national situation, not simply on the merits of this particular case. Guy replied that the Broadcasting Act required us to hear applications in each case on their merits, not in the light of some grand design, some general principle. 'The Judicial Committee of the Privy Council', said Guy, 'never laid down a general principle but once, when it laid down the general principle that it would not lay down general principles.' (Guy was a Civil Law lawyer, but he knew his Common Law.) Actually both Guy and I had been dismayed by a document the Chairman had sent to all members, setting out in detail what sort of program stations should broadcast at specific times of each day! Here we were being confronted by another example of the same sort of thinking. I said: 'Andrew, the trouble is that you're Scotch and I'm English. You, with Scottish logic, think we can lay down rules for our work, in detail, to last forever. I have the instinctive English distrust of general principles, and it is reinforced in this work by the constant, and swift, changes in broadcasting technology. I think we cannot plan everything ahead, in detail. I think we must decide each case on its merits.'

With characteristic generosity Guy said that though he must resign, there was no reason why I must join him. I did not come from Quebec City; I was not a French Canadian. I told Guy that as I had supported him all the way, I would support him now. 'I have taken the same stand on this matter as you, and for the same reasons.' So we both resigned in 1962.

I was very unhappy about resigning. I liked and respected my colleagues and I remained on friendly terms with, I think, all of them. Hudon's resignation created a considerable stir in Quebec, and of course especially in Quebec City. Mine, naturally, got less notice there, though there were some comments to the effect that everyone knew the English had strong stomachs but that this was too much even for one of them. It is probably the only time that Quebec nationalists have had a good word to say of me.

In its early years the BBG had its shortcomings; beyond question we made mistakes, and some of them were big ones. For example, we accepted far too readily the grandiose promises of applicants for TV licences. The job we had to do was wholly new, and we were all as green as grass. But on the whole I think we did about as well as could be expected. In the matter of Canadian content particularly, we laid foundations on which our successors could build—and have built, with varying degrees of success.

8

The Senate

During most of my years with the Labour Congresses I gave a course in Canadian government at Carleton University, usually in the evenings, but one year on Saturday mornings. A good many of my students were civil servants, some of them of mature years. They included East Indians, West Indians, Indonesians, and an occasional Chinese. I enjoyed the courses, and I think most of the students did. But by the time the age limit put me out of the Congress, in 1969, this sideline had come to an end. I think it was the younger members of the Department of Political Science who insisted I was too old. Anyway I was dropped.

I rather hoped some other university might find a use for me, but at first not much was forthcoming. I did small stints at Queen's and Trent, and one other institution offered me a course that I felt myself incapable of giving. Then suddenly Mrs Felix Walter, my old friend from McGill days who had become a member of the Department of French at the University of Waterloo, telephoned me. We had a lively and agreeable conversation, in the course of which she asked me what I was doing, now that I had retired. I said: 'Nothing.' She asked if I'd consider coming to Waterloo. I said yes, and she undertook to take the matter up with the university authorities. The result was that in the fall of 1970 I became a Visiting Professor, full time, in the Departments of Political Science (where I was to give courses in Canadian government) and History (where I was to give courses in labour history). This was financially a godsend; my new colleagues were delightful people, and I was soon thoroughly enjoying my return to academic life. There was, of course, some uncertainty about how long this happy state of affairs could last. So we kept our home in Ottawa and I took a flat in Waterloo, close to the university. My wife and daughters came up often, and of course I was often in Ottawa. Indeed, I was soon in Ottawa about half my time, for my appointment to the

Senate on 7 October 1970 did not involve giving up my professorship. Throughout that fall and winter, and the following spring, I commuted from Waterloo to Ottawa every Monday evening and was back again Thursday evening. But I found the constant shuttle just too much. So at the end of the academic year I very regretfully resigned my teaching post.

In Chapter 6 I described how Pierre Trudeau invited me to become a Senator. Paul Martin, the Senate Leader (who I suspect had something to do with my appointment), was disappointed that I chose to sit as a Liberal. He wanted me to be an NDP Senator. After what I had said about their Quebec policy this was of course impossible, and the NDP, which wanted to abolish the Senate, would have refused me with 'the pelt of a curse after my heels', to use an Irish expression. Thérèse Casgrain always insisted that Frank Scott declined Trudeau's offer of a senatorship because the NDP told him he must. Frank himself said it was because he wanted to devote himself to his poetry.

The Liberal Party was apparently not at all pleased to have me. When Martin's assistant asked party headquarters to give me a credential for a Liberal Party conference, he was coldly received: 'He's not a Liberal.' 'He says he'll sit as a supporter of the Government.' 'That doesn't make him a Liberal.' 'He's attending our caucus.' 'That doesn't make him a Liberal.' Eventually, grumpily, headquarters gave in. Trudeau himself told me the party was displeased by my appointment. When I suggested that they must feel better now that I was sitting as a Liberal, he replied: 'No. That makes it worse.'

In retrospect I realize that I ought to have done what Madame Casgrain did: sit as an Independent, supporting the Government's policy on national unity. In practice I behaved as an Independent, speaking and voting oftener against Government measures than for them. I must have been a nuisance to Trudeau and he must often have wished that I had stuck to the 'total silence' I had offered him when he made his first big speech on national unity.

My Conservative friends, of course, were appalled that I had chosen to sit as a Liberal. Mr Diefenbaker said he was 'shocked'. Mrs Meighen said: 'When I heard it, I wanted to put you over my knee and spank you.'

My acceptance of a senatorship surprised and disturbed a good many old friends. I had been a severe critic of the Senate, and had accepted and vigorously supported the unions', and the CCF's, demands for its abolition. Stanley Knowles, during my years in the Senate, delighted to circulate to all and sundry a philippic of mine on the subject. Fortunately for such reputation as I may have, some years before I was appointed I had come to the conclusion that abolition was impossible and campaigning for it a waste of time and energy. This was not because I believed it to be constitutionally impossible. On the contrary, I thought it could be done by ordinary Act of Parliament, which the Senate would probably find it impossible to resist. After all, the British North America Act, 1949, No. 2, empowered the Parliament of Canada to amend the Constitution, with the exception of provisions relating to (i) the powers of the provincial legislatures, (ii) 'rights or privileges by this or any other Constitutional Act granted or secured to the Legislature or the Government of a province', (iii) denominational schools, (iv) the English or French languages, (v) the annual session of Parliament, and (vi) Parliament's maximum duration. Manifestly no provincial *legislature* or *government* had any 'powers, rights, or privileges' at all in regard to the Senate; so for once I agreed with the Department of Justice that an Act of Parliament could do with the Senate whatever it saw fit. I had, perforce, to give up this belief when the Supreme Court of Canada, in the Senate Reference case of 1980 (in one of its more bizarre decisions), ruled that this could not be done without provincial consent!

But in spite of my view of the actual law on the subject, I had realized well before 1970 — and said so in print — that if the existing Senate were abolished, we'd have to create another to take its place. Every federation in the Western world had an Upper House representing in some fashion the constituent units. So did India. The Canadian provinces, and the Canadian Parliament, would never accept unicameralism. Senate reform was another matter. Its possibility did not preclude my becoming a member of the Chamber as it stood.

I was immediately placed on the National Finance Committee, but my commuting made it utterly impossible for me to serve. I was also placed on the Transport and Communications Committee, where I served for some time, and took part in the decisions on two important bills.

One, a Government bill introduced in the Senate, would have given certain creditors powers that in my opinion fell squarely within the exclusive provincial jurisdiction over property and civil rights and was therefore beyond the powers of Parliament. Every lawyer on the Committee said so. I kept quiet until, to my astonishment, several of them looked at me and asked what I thought. I said: 'Well, as you all know I am not a lawyer, and if all of you had thought this was *intra vires* I should certainly not have dared to contest your opinion. But I think you are all quite right. We cannot pass this bill.' We circularized all the provincial Attorneys-General, who agreed with us. We reported that the bill 'should not be further proceeded with' and it was dropped.

The second was the Maritime Code Bill, dealing with the law of shipping. It was highly technical, and the House of Commons had passed it in a single day, doubtless convinced that the Department of Transport would have thoroughly vetted all the purely transport parts, and the Department of Justice all the purely legal. In fact, however, the bill was a masterpiece of bad drafting. We were presented with two bulky volumes, inches thick, of technical amendments: one volume from the Dominion

Marine Association, the other from the Admiralty Law Committee of the Canadian Bar Association. We made 82 drafting amendments and one that was not. Up to this time ships could be registered at a whole series of ports across the country. But some landlubber, presumably in the Department of Transport but perhaps in Justice, had had an inspiration. The bill provided that from the moment it came into force there should be just one port of registry for all shipping: the great, active, bustling seaport of Ottawa, Ontario! Every member of the Committee from the two coasts and the shores of the Great Lakes at once went into orbit, closely followed by this expatriate Newfoundlander. The Senator whom the Government had placed in charge of the bill told the Minister that this section would have to go or the Senate would throw it out. The Minister caved in. The amended bill went back to the House of Commons just before prorogation and died on the Order Paper.

These are examples of the work the Senate does in revising bills, sent up to it from the House of Commons in what is technically called 'a blank and imperfect state'. Another, and major, example in my time was the Income Tax Reform Bill of 1971. This did not come to the Senate till just before Christmas, and it was to come into force in January. It was a massive document, some 700 pages of infinite complexity and staggering ramifications. It was clearly impossible for the Senate or its Banking, Trade and Commerce Committee to do anything effective in the face of this 'Christmas closure'. After sending it to the Committee, which had of course to report back on it after very brief hearings, the Senate passed it unamended.

Immediately the welkin rang with denunciations of the set of lazy old good-for-nothings who had given only the most perfunctory consideration to perhaps the most important piece of legislation in Canada's history. The *Globe and Mail* printed a cartoon showing a crowd of Senators leaving the Chamber in festive mood, with the caption, 'Here we go a-wassailing'. It looked like a damning indictment. In fact it was totally wrong-headed, the product of gross ignorance. The press seldom attends sittings of the Senate or its committees. The Senate's treatment of this bill was actually a massive display of hard work.

The bill was based on a Government White Paper. When that was published the Senate Banking, Trade and Commerce Committee, having had long experience of bills reaching the Senate at the eleventh hour, undertook a preliminary study of the Paper. (This was done by virtue of a practice known as the 'Hayden formula', because it had been introduced by Senator Salter Hayden, the Chairman of the Committee. Before a Government bill or preliminary White Paper ever reached the Senate, the Chairman of the appropriate Committee could move that its 'subject-matter be referred' to his Committee.) This study lasted from 28 January 1971 till 24 June. The Committee held 31 meetings, heard 118 witnesses, and received 225 written briefs. It suggested 44 changes in the Government's proposals, every one of which the bill incorporated.

The Committee then undertook a preliminary study of the actual bill. The Committee held fourteen sittings, from 29 September 1971 till 13 December. It heard 129 witnesses, received 36 written briefs, and made three reports, dated 4 and 24 November and 13 December. It made nine suggestions for amendments, all of which the House of Commons adopted. So by the time the bill reached the Senate, the lazy old good-for-nothings had put in over seven months' intensive work on the subject, and had secured 53 changes in the bill.

There were still a few provisions the Committee thought should be changed. But they involved redrafting of some complexity, which could not be done in the few days remaining before the bill would come into effect. Of course the Senate could have deferred further consideration till it came back in January. The difficulty with that was that certain provisions, changing the existing law, were to come into force on 1 January 1972. So if the Senate passed them some time in January or later, anyone obeying the existing law would be violating the new law, which would be retroactive to 1 January, and anyone obeying the new law would be violating the existing law! The Minister of Finance and his officials assured the Committee that its further suggested amendments would be brought forward in an amending bill or bills. The Committee and the Senate accepted this. The amending legislation duly came and was adopted.

The Senate does most of its work in committees and, in my experience of them, generally without partisanship except for the occasional highly controversial bill. Even on those (as, for example, the Drug Patent Bill and the Immigration Bills of 1988), its committees hear a host of witnesses, receive voluminous written evidence, and propose amendments that are based on solid facts and responsible arguments from people and organizations with considerable knowledge and experience of the subjects at issue. But for many of its critics, if the Senate does anything it's defying the will of the people as expressed by the House of Commons (this, though until 1988 it had not rejected a bill sent up from the Commons for nearly half-a-century); if it does nothing, it is simply eating its head off in luxurious idleness. It can all be summed up in a simple formula: 'The Senate is always wrong.'

Most of my work in committees was in Joint Committees of the Senate and the House of Commons, notably the Special Joint Committees on the Constitution in 1971-2 and 1978, and the Joint Standing Committee on Regulations and Other Statutory Instruments, from 1973 till my retirement (see Chapter 9). Both of these were fascinating and taught me a great deal, not least the stupefying ignorance, even of some lawyers and parliamentarians, of elementary facts of our constitutional law and history.

The first of the Committees on the Constitution had three excellent Chairmen: Senator Maurice Lamontagne and then Senator Molgat for the Senate, and Dr (now Judge) Mark MacGuigan for the House of Commons. We needed them, for we sometimes had weird or tumultuous witnesses in our progress across the country. A ludicrous example of the former came to us in Ottawa: a gentleman who wanted us to do something about what he considered the defective snow removal in his part of the city, and a lady who wanted us to do something about the inadequate and unreliable bus service in Hull! (This was almost too much for even Dr MacGuigan's superhuman patience.) Quebec separatists and assorted cranks (one of them brandishing a revolver) provided the tumult (most of which I escaped because I was fulfilling my academic duties at the University of Waterloo).

I took an active part in nearly all the hearings, and also in drafting our report. I had to cope more than once with people who suffered from the delusion that the British North America Act of 1867 had been imposed on us by the British Government when in fact it was based almost wholly on resolutions adopted at Quebec in 1864 and in London in 1866-7, by delegates of the British North American provinces, with not a single representative of the British Government even present.

There are only two things in the Act that owe anything to the British Government. One is the title of our country: 'Dominion'. (Incidentally, it is still there. It has never been changed.) The Fathers of Confederation wanted to call us 'the Kingdom of Canada'. But the British Government was scared this would upset the Americans, so it told the Fathers to come up with something else. They did: 'Dominion'. It was, Lord Carnarvon explained to Queen Victoria, 'a new title, but intended to give dignity' to Canada, and 'as a tribute to the monarchical principle which they earnestly desire to uphold.' The second thing that owes something to the British Government is the provision for the appointment of extra Senators to break a deadlock between the two Houses, which the British Government insisted on. The Fathers' original proposals had contained nothing on this subject, so they went back and produced Sections 26-28 of the Act, providing for two extra Senators from each of the three divisions of the country: Ontario, Quebec, and the Maritime Provinces. (The West got its two in 1915.) In both cases the Fathers decided what should go in.

The British Government also insisted that the pardoning power should be vested in the Governor-General, not the Lieutenant-Governors (as the Fathers had wished). But this was not in the Act, just in the Letters Patent and the Governor-General's Instructions.

This rubbish about the British North America Act's being 'foreign' and 'imposed' still keeps cropping up. I heard it from a Member of the House of Commons (a school teacher, God save the mark!) in 1987. Happily he was defeated in the last election.

It goes well, of course, with the nonsense that the Constitution Act of 1982 gave us 'a new Constitution'. In fact what it has given us is the old Constitution with knobs on: very important knobs—the Charter of Rights and Freedoms, five constitutional amending formulas, and some extra power for the provinces over natural resources, but still just knobs. Most of the Act of 1867 remains untouched, and the Act of 1982 lists no less than twenty-four Acts or Orders that are part of our written Constitution.

Our report was duly presented to both Houses. With most of its specific recommendations I agreed. With others I did not. I set forth my views at some length in the Senate, indeed at a length some of my colleagues clearly thought tedious. I spread my speech over parts of three sittings. I might just as well have saved my breath to cool my porridge. The report had called upon Canadians to 'press with us for the writing of a new Constitution' (this was one of the things I did not agree with). They didn't. Our report disappeared into limbo.

In 1971 a Dominion-Provincial Conference in Victoria hammered out a constitutional revision that came to be known as the Victoria Charter. Brief life was here its portion, brief sorrow, short-lived care. The Quebec government, having given a tentative consent, withdrew it, just as a previous Quebec government had withdrawn its consent to the Fulton-Favreau formula for constitutional amendment in 1964.

In 1978 Trudeau tried again in Bill C-60. This elaborate and ill-drawn measure aroused a storm of controversy. I fought it as hard as I could, especially its proposals on the monarchy and the Senate. In the first week after the bill was brought down I broadcast ten attacks on it, four in French and six in English, and that was only a beginning. Telephone calls even pursued me to Prince Edward Island, where my wife and I were on holiday.

The bill would have replaced the Senate by a House of the Federation, whose members were to be chosen partly by the House of Commons, partly by the provincial legislatures on the basis of proportional representation of the various parties in each legislature. The Liberal Senators were almost unanimously against this. But they were also almost unanimous that Senators must say little or nothing lest they be accused of merely wanting to hang on to their jobs, which the bill would have wiped out. The night before it was to come before the national caucus (Liberal members of both Houses), we held a meeting of Liberal Senators, where almost everyone counselled silence. I listened uneasily. Then the chairman called on me. I said: 'Well, I had meant to argue strongly against this measure at tomorrow's caucus. But after hearing what the rest of you have said, I think I had better keep quiet.' Chorus of protest: 'Oh, no! You must say what you think. No one can accuse you of self-interest. You'll be out next year anyway.' Accordingly, next morning I put my case to the national caucus and got a good hearing, even some applause. In the discussions that followed over the next few weeks I urged upon my fellow-Senators that while they might feel they could not attack proposals for the disappearance of the Senate, there were many other provisions of the bill that we found highly objectionable and there was no reason why they should not criticize these. They did.

Even among the Liberal members of the House of Commons there were doubts and dissent. One local MP who was well aware of my views invited me to be part of a panel at a meeting of his riding association. The other panelists included Dr Mark MacGuigan, MP. On that evening I took aim especially at a section of the bill which said that if a Prime Minister were defeated in the House of Commons he could resign (making way for a different government in the existing Parliament; correct); or he could ask for a dissolution (a fresh general election; correct); if the Governor-General refused the dissolution, the Prime Minister could advise the Governor-General to invite him (or her), the defeated Prime Minister, to form another administration. This last made every hair on my head to 'stand on end like quills upon the fretful porpentine.'

I pointed out to the audience that it meant that a defeated Prime Minister could 'prance into Rideau Hall and say: "Well, Your Excellency, I have just been censured by the House of Commons. I now advise you to invite me to form a new Government."' Dr MacGuigan interjected: 'Oh, the House of Commons would defeat him.' I said: 'Yes; and he could then march into Rideau Hall and say: "Well, Your Excellency, I have now been twice censured by the House of Commons. My claim therefore to be asked to form a new government is twice as strong as it was the day before yesterday."'

This concoction displays an ignorance of responsible government that passes all understanding. If it was drafted by a lawyer, it provides a good illustration of the fact that lawyers, even constitutional lawyers, may be very ill-acquainted with constitutional usage.

The bill was referred to a Joint Committee of both Houses, of which I was a member, and by no means a silent one. The Committee gave particular attention to the clauses on the monarchy and the Senate. On both it had the benefit of the expertise of the Department of Justice. On the monarchy, it had the word of one of that Department's officials, now a judge, that the Queen could not herself give assent to a Canadian bill. He was disconcerted when I pointed out to him that King George VI had done precisely this with nine bills in 1939. My faith in the Department of Justice was somewhat shaken. On the Senate, I have discussed on pages 152-3 the belief of the Department of Justice, which I shared, that Parliament could abolish the Senate by a simple act. The Conservatives moved to have the sections on the monarchy and the Senate referred to the Supreme Court of Canada for an opinion. Except for the Liberal

Whip, every Liberal Senator on the Committee (even the Deputy Leader) voted for the motion. The government referred the Senate sections to the Court, which said the Department of Justice was wrong. That pretty well finished the bill.

I became Senate Chairman of the Committee on Regulations and Other Statutory Instruments for the same reason that I had four times become a candidate for elected office: they couldn't get the man they wanted. But this committee must have a chapter to itself.

During my time in the Senate I almost always worked six days a week, from 9:30 or 10:00 in the morning till 5:30 or 6:00 in the evening. Sometimes I started earlier and stopped later. When there was emergency legislation (such as back-to-work bills) I was there in the small hours of the morning. Once, awaiting a bill that did not come to us till 5:00 a.m., I spent most of the night on a couch in my office; then, when the bill arrived, got up and made a speech. Technically this sleeping in the office is against the rules. But I declined to go home at the normal hour and be routed out of bed in the middle of the night. (The rule against sleeping in the building is said to have arisen from the rather bizarre behaviour of a member of the House of Commons, many years ago, who used his office as his dwelling place and hung his laundry outside the window. The authorities felt obliged to tell him this was not part of his parliamentary privileges.)

In the Senate itself, as distinct from the committees, I took an active part. I spoke often. Running my eye recently over the *Debates*, I was depressed to find how often I was both long-winded and dull. Fortunately some few of my speeches still struck me as sensible and well expressed. None of them were read. For a few I used very brief notes, which really *were* notes: a few words to make sure I did not leave out something I thought important. I never had a ghost-writer, and never served as anyone else's, except once, very reluctantly, when I was with the Canadian Labour Congress. It was after that one lapse from virtue that I wrote, for the *Toronto Star*, a blistering attack on the practice.

My speeches covered a wide variety of subjects. Many, of course, were on the Constitution: the monarchy (which, like the Fathers of Confederation, I 'earnestly desire to uphold'); the rule of law; the position of the Senate; Senate reform; patriation of the Constitution; the amending process; the Official Languages Bill of 1969; a fixed date for elections (which my friend Jim Macdonnell properly described as 'the end of responsible government'); and the possible limitation of the provincial power over education by the words 'in and for each province'. But I by no means confined myself to these. I held forth also on national unity; on Quebec separatism; on the deficiencies of certain CBC programs; on the folly of joining the Organization of American States; on the James Bay Agreement with some of the aborigines in the area, but extinguishing the rights of them all; on the danger of undermining the merit system in the public service; on the scandal of long delays in filling Senate seats; on the necessity of appointing more Opposition Senators; on the virtues of obstruction in the House of Commons; on the inordinate powers granted to the bureaucracy by a new Immigration Act; on the report of the Committee on the Mass Media; and on indiscriminate privatization (which might sell off what was profitable, leaving the state with the 'dead or dying ducks').

A few of the speeches are perhaps worth brief comment, sometimes for serious reasons, sometimes for frivolous.

A prize example of the latter is the one on the mass media where, dealing with the private broadcasters, I burst into song: 'Oh, I am a pirate king, Yes, I am a pirate king, And it is, it is a glorious thing to be a pirate king.' I believe only one other Senator ever sang in the House. It is perhaps hardly necessary to add that he also was a Newfoundlander: Jack Higgins. What he sang I do not know. From my recollections of him, he also may have quoted Gilbert and Sullivan.

On the monarchy, I emphasized that it was our own deliberate choice at Confederation. Sir John A. Macdonald had been eloquently explicit on this, and Sir George Cartier if anything even more so.

On the rule of law, I expatiated on the curious (and dangerous) apparent belief of many officials and some Ministers that administrative convenience is a basic principle of our Constitution, the law hardly more than a minor nuisance. (This always reminds me of Theodore Roosevelt's story of the Irish New York Assemblyman who sought his support for a bill that would have violated the State Constitution: 'Ah, Mr Roosevelt, what's the Constitution between friends?') I shall have more to say of this in the next chapter.

The position of the Senate came up when we considered a bill providing for wire-tapping. The Senate made a safeguarding amendment, which I voted for. The House of Commons threw it out. When the bill came back to us a considerable number of Senators wanted to insist on our amendment. Senator Goldenberg moved, and I seconded, that we do not insist. That we had the power to insist was as incontestable as that we had the power to veto the bill outright. That we should exercise the power in this case was another matter. To do so would undoubtedly kill the bill: the House of Commons would not accept our amendment. Senator Goldenberg and I, and a majority of our colleagues, thought that the bill, even without our amendment, was better than no bill at all. I argued that only in very rare circumstances should we exercise our power to veto, or our power to insist on amendments. For example, if the House of Commons, in the last year of its mandate, passed a bill that had never been before the electors and was strongly opposed by one or more of the regions, the Senate might properly refuse to pass it until it had been submitted to the people in a general election. This, in fact, the Senate had done with the Borden Naval Bill of 1913, and was to do again with the Free Trade Agreement Bill of 1988. (By that time the case for the Senate's action was even stronger than in 1913, because changes in the rules of the House of Commons had so whittled down its power of obstruction that the Opposition in that House could no longer force an election, as it had in 1911 on Reciprocity.)

On Senate reform I took the position that in a federation there had to be an Upper House representing, in some fashion or other, the constituent units as such. I was somewhat skeptical of the chance of reform. (In 1925 Mr Meighen, on Mackenzie King's vague pledge on the subject, said: 'So that old bird is to be provided with wooden wings and told to fly again!') Appointment by the provincial governments, leaving the Senate's existing legal powers intact, would give the provinces enormous power in federal matters and would never be accepted by the House of Commons whose consent, by custom, would be necessary for any constitutional amendment.

On Quebec separatism I argued that Quebec could not secede except by a constitutional amendment, which would need the consent of all, or nearly all, the provinces. Such an amendment would involve very tough bargaining.

Joining the Organization of American States I called a first-class recipe for winning enemies and not influencing people. The United States would always expect us to toe its line. The Latin-Americans would expect us to support them against the United States. (M.J. Coldwell, who had originally favoured joining, changed his mind. He told me why. He had been a delegate to the Economic and Social Council of the United Nations. Someone moved a motion he agreed with. When the 'yeas' were called for, he held up his hand. The United States delegate frowned fiercely and waved imperiously for him to lower his hand. That was enough for M.J.: no more OAS for him!)

The Senate Committee that considered the James Bay Agreement reported the bill without amendment, but with a pious recommendation to the Government to do something for the aborigines whose rights were extinguished but who were to get no compensation. Senator Flynn, the Leader of the Opposition, moved an amendment on third reading to remedy this defect. In a masterly and very witty speech he pulverized the Government's position, making game particularly of Senators Croll and Robichaud, the great champions of minority rights, and of Senator Langlois, the Deputy Leader of the Government in the Senate who, in the committee, had used strong language on this very subject. I supported the amendment by voice and vote. So did several other Liberals. The huge Liberal majority defeated it.

When the Chairman of the Public Service Commission made a speech calling for a 'more representative Public Service', and referring to some (of course unnamed) public servants as 'slobs', with a derogatory epithet, I saw an attempt to undermine the merit principle and rose to its defence in an impassioned speech. I am old enough to remember what things were like before the Union Government took the stuffing out of patronage in the public service. I recall my grandfather's story of a member of the House of Commons staff who, for years before the election of 1896, never lost an opportunity to proclaim his devotion to the Conservative Party. After that election he was heard proclaiming his devotion to Liberalism. One of his colleagues taxed him with his change. The answer was: 'Yes, I was a Conservative. But no Government can change faster than I can.' I remember, after the election of 1911, discussions at the family dinner table about what might happen to members of the House of Commons staff who had been known as Liberals; and Charles Ritchie has told me of questions in his family about 'when R.L. [Borden] will do something for Willie' (he did). The prospect of something like quotas in the civil service for particular groups in the population horrified me, and I said so. Indeed, I damned the Chairman's speech.

I went overboard again (as it proved, this is all too accurate a description) on the Immigration Bill. It was open to very strong attack for the page after page of powers it gave to the executive. I listed them, with searing comments, and wound up with an amendment striking down many. This was seconded by Senator G. Isaac (Ike) Smith, the former Conservative Premier of Nova Scotia. Neither of us noticed that it might be out of order because it would have touched on the expenditure of money, which had to be recommended to the House of Commons by Message from the Governor-General. When the Law Clerk, Raymond du Pléssis, gave it as his opinion that it *was* out of order, as beyond the powers of the Senate, I was appalled. I had to leave Ottawa for a longstanding speaking engagement in Calgary so could not even be present to confess my fault. All I could do, when the Speaker ruled the amendment out, was to ask Senator Smith to read aloud my letter to him in which I lamented I could not be there to don a white sheet and repent in sackcloth and ashes. I added that I hoped this might have some effect in stopping people from calling me a constitutional expert. (Henceforth any such label might well produce only the response: 'Oh, Forsey! That's the fellow who fell downstairs with the coal-scuttle and the tea-tray with his amendment to the Immigration Bill!') Senator Flynn moved a brief amendment that was unquestionably in order. But my unavoidable absence deprived me of even the consolation of being able to vote for that. (Du Pléssis has since revised his opinion.)

One other philippic I delivered was on the bill setting up the office of Comptroller-General. It was a very brief bill, and in my judgement gave him or her no real power whatever. Quoting a phrase of Arthur Meighen's many years before on a very different bill, I called it 'a roaring farce and a resounding fake', adding a good many scathing phrases of my own. I think it was one of the best speeches I have ever made. It was perhaps on this occasion that a friend, sitting in the Senate Gallery beside a Minister and his executive assistant, heard the Minister say to his assistant: 'That God-damned son of a bitch! We ought to throw him out of the caucus.'

What I suppose I might call my swan-song in the Senate came on the Unemployment Insurance Bill in December 1978. The New Democratic Party had proposed in the House of Commons a whole series of amendments, all of them as far as I can recall amply justified and all defeated. When the bill reached the Senate, the Conservatives also condemned various features. So did I. But the Government was determined to get the bill through, and nearly all the Conservative Senators had gone home for Christmas. One who had not was Senator Duff Roblin, whom I am proud to call an old friend. I moved up to the front benches beside him and together we set to work. He moved amendments, I seconded them, or vice versa, by turns and by agreement. Of course they were all defeated, resoundingly. We had the support of the two or three other Conservatives still in town, and on one amendment the support also of Senator Florence Bird, Liberal. But usually there were only four of us. A sour Liberal wit called us 'the Gang of Four'.

Part-way through my time in the Senate a very Conservative friend denounced me, to my face, as 'the most complaisant Liberal in the place'. I told him he should look at the *Debates* and the record of divisions. I thought I had spoken, and voted, as often against the Government as for it. Recently I took my own advice. I found that, as the years went on, I spoke oftener and oftener, and more and more strongly, against the Government. Then I checked the division lists. In a total of twenty-four cases where a Government proposal was at issue, there were fifteen where I voted against it; and this does not count cases where a motion was carried 'on division' but without a recorded vote, or votes in Committee of the Whole where names are not taken down. I have often wondered whether my performance may have made Pierre Trudeau sorry he ever appointed me.

I ought probably to have sat in the Senate as an Independent. But if I had I'd have missed some fun. For example, I'd not have discovered that in the room where the Liberal caucus met there were photographs of every Liberal leader except Edward Blake! I called attention to this and was staggered to find that some members of the caucus had never heard of him. One, a professor of law and now a judge, came up to me and said: 'Eugene, who *was* Edward Blake?' My reply enlightened him: 'One of the greatest constitutional lawyers Canada has ever had; Laurier offered him the Chief Justiceship; and he was leader of the Liberal Party from 1880 to 1887.' The Senate *Hansard* reporters were equally at sea on the subject, or more so. When I referred in a speech to Blake without his Christian name, they asked me if I meant William Blake!

If I'd sat as an Independent I should also have missed my chance to take part in the 1972 general election, campaigning for Trudeau (see pages 120-1).

It might have been supposed that, with my background, I'd have something to say in the Senate about foreign affairs and might have been a member of delegations to the United Nations and to other countries. Actually I don't think I uttered more than two or three sentences on foreign affairs. As for parliamentary delegations, I never thought of applying, except once. I felt I had no competence, except on that one occasion in 1973 when I did apply, and was chosen to go to Chile. But the thing fell through. I knew something about the situation there, and my younger daughter, who had married an Ecuadorian and was working for CUSO in Ecuador, had kept me abreast of South American affairs. I planned to stop over with her and her family on my way to or from Chile. Then President Allende was murdered. I did get to Ecuador for a fortnight, but strictly on my own and at my own expense.

I had visited the United Nations the previous year, but only as an observer. As this was immediately after the election of 1972, most of my time in New York was spent working on the constitutional questions that might arise if, as seemed likely at first, Mr Stanfield got more seats than Mr Trudeau and no one got a clear majority. I was on the telephone for hours with Gordon Robertson, then Clerk of the Privy Council. I was physically present at a number of conferences of the Canadian delegation and a number of meetings of the UN General Assembly. But my heart was in Ottawa, a-chasing the returning officers.

My going to New York at all involved a curious bit of by-play. I had to have a passport. I had one already but was told it wouldn't do: I had to have a 'special' one. For this, of course, I had to produce a birth certificate. I proffered what I had and what had hitherto always served: a document signed by the Methodist minister in Grand Bank and the Resident Magistrate (who happened to be the doctor who brought me into the world). It said that according to the baptismal register of the Methodist church of Grand Bank I had been born on 29 May 1904. (I have never been able to understand how I could have been on that register, as I was in fact baptized in Mexico City.) The Canadian passport office said this wouldn't do: I must have an actual *birth* certificate. I said there probably were none in Newfoundland in 1904. 'Oh, well, write to the Department of Health in St John's and ask for one. And if they can't give you one, you can apply for a certificate of Canadian citizenship.' At this I took fire: 'I had ancestors in Nova Scotia more than two hundred years ago. I'll see myself dead in a ditch before I'll apply for a certificate of Canadian citizenship!' (As I often say, I am both a new Canadian and a native-born Canadian, having, at the age of 45, performed the monstrous and unnatural feat of becoming a native-born Canadian by virtue of Newfoundland's entry into Confederation.) To my surprise the Department of Health in St John's sent me a certificate. It stated, correctly, that I had been born in 1904, but that my birth had been registered in 1907! I simply cannot believe that either my mother, in Ottawa, or my grandparents, in Grand Bank, when I was nearly three years old, suddenly decided to inform the authorities of my existence. The only explanation of this peculiar document I have ever been able to think of is that my letter to the Department of Health landed on the desk of a relative, or a friend of the family (which is by no means impossible), who said: 'Oh, we all know Eugene was born in Grand Bank in 1904. Fill in a certificate and put on it any date you like.' The upshot, I suppose, is that there is really no legal proof of my existence, let alone of my age.

The first figures for the 1972 election gave the Conservatives 109 seats and the Liberals 107, with the NDP holding the balance of power. This produced a crop of nonsense in the press: the Liberal Government should resign; if it didn't, the Governor-General should call on Mr Stanfield to form a government. I told Gordon Robertson that this was wholly wrong, adding: 'Tell Pierre to hang on.' I had no doubt that this was not only his constitutional right but his duty. The Conservatives' flirtations with the 'two nations' policy had convinced me that national unity would not be safe in their hands.

In my eight-and-a-half years in the Senate I made only occasional speeches in French, chiefly because the English translations were so bad. They never made me say the opposite of what I had tried to say, but they simply were not English; they verged on pidgin. I protested, repeatedly, with no result. So I gave up. Before I did so I encountered, in the West Block cafeteria, a formidable-looking gentleman who, in slightly accented English, said he had read my protests in the Senate about the English translations of my efforts. He added, 'I am a translator myself,' and I prepared myself for a scorching condemnation. What I got was: 'You are quite right. They are very bad. Keep it up! The people who do this job are Francophones with what they think is an adequate knowledge of English. They ought to be Anglophones with an adequate knowledge of French.' The French translations, however, of my English speeches were superb (except for rare instances where the translator was unfamiliar with some out-of-the-way English idiom I had used). When I read the original transcript (the 'blues') I usually found myself saying, 'I didn't think I had put that so well,' and then finding that indeed I hadn't: the translator had rounded off all the sharp corners and produced something much better.

I used the earphones constantly, but only because my failing hearing made it hard for me to hear either language without them. Several of my English-speaking colleagues twitted me with what they considered proof that my assertion that I was tolerably bilingual was pretty thin. I was obliged to confess that it was my ears that were feeble, rather than my French.

The only speeches I regret are the ones I didn't make. One was an oversight. Just after I took my seat we had a bill from the House of Commons amending the Weights and Measures Act. I glanced at the title and decided it was some minor technical change in a matter in which I had no competence and that I needn't look into. Actually, it introduced the metric system, which has embittered my declining years by forcing on me incessant mental arithmetic. But I was preoccupied with the October Crisis and the invocation of the War Measures Act, so I let slip the chance of expressing my strong feelings on the subject.

The Senate has a special device called an 'Inquiry'. The name is misleading, for it has nothing to do with asking questions. A Senator simply gives notice that on a particular day he or she will 'draw the attention of the Senate' to a specific question. Occasionally the discussion leads to the appointment of a Special Committee, or a sub-committee, to investigate and report. I had wished to put down an Inquiry on the dangers of nuclear energy; a second on the multiple threat to the environment; and a third on rail transportation. But the Constitution and the Statutory Instruments Committee absorbed almost all of my time and energy—which was perhaps just as well. I hope that in spite of my failure to address these three subjects I earned my keep. Apparently some people thought I did. For when the age limit was about to retire me from the Senate in 1979, Geoffrey Stevens, in his column in the *Globe and Mail*, said I might be too old for the Senate, but I was not too old for the House of Commons: I should run in the election that was about to take place.

This was flattering, and surprising. What followed was more so. Senator Royce Frith, who was managing an important part of the Liberal campaign, actually pressed me very hard to become a candidate. He told me I was 'a Campbell's Soup Candidate. Nobody ever asks what's *in* Campbell's Soup. They just buy it.' I pointed out what fun the other parties would have quoting speeches of mine in the Senate denouncing this or that Government bill, but he made light of this.

What took me aback even more was an approach by Ed Broadbent in the Parliamentary Restaurant: 'Is there anything in this story that you might be prepared to run for the House? We'd be delighted to have you as a candidate.' This nearly bowled me over. For, some weeks before, at a private luncheon, he had waxed rhapsodical over the Report of the (Pépin-Roberts) Task Force on National Unity and I had cursed it just as heartily. I felt a little like an Orangeman listening to a Pope saying: 'We'd be delighted to have you as a priest.'

If my wife had been well, instead of in her ninth year of Parkinson's disease, I might have been foolish enough to succumb to Royce Frith's persuasion. As it was I never even asked him where he was thinking of putting me up. I have little doubt that if I *had* run I should have added one more to my list of ignominious defeats.

My memories of the Senate are nearly all very happy ones. My colleagues were almost always to my faults a little blind, to my virtues very kind. Some of my Senate friends are dead; Louis Beaubien, for one; Nancy Bell for another. Most of those I knew best are still in the Senate: Dan Lang, Hartland Molson, Charles McElman, Duff Roblin. Dan and Hartland are among my closest friends. George McIlraith and Florence Bird, retired by the age limit, are still flourishing and have not cast me off. Muriel Fergusson, voluntarily retired, is the same keen mind and the same delightful person as ever, though now somewhat handicapped physically. As Speaker she was an indefatigable, and invincible, champion of the Senate's rights against the encroachments of the House of Commons and the Department of the Secretary of State. I still cherish memories of her accounts of her battles and triumphs. We occasionally write or telephone each other. Paul Martin was a good friend as long as he was in the Senate, but I have seldom seen or heard from him since he left. Some people think of Paul as just a very smart politician who knows all the angles. He was certainly that. But he was, and is, very much more: a fine and amply stocked mind and a generous spirit to whom the people of Canada owe a great deal. Allan MacEachen I have known since he was a professor at St Francis Xavier University. He is most certainly still flourishing, still adding to a long and distinguished career of public service. John Stewart, also of St Francis Xavier, was appointed after I retired. I have known him for a good many years. He is among the most learned and valued members of the Upper House, a genuine expert on constitutional matters, and a friend whom I have the good fortune to see often when Parliament is sitting. Ray du Pléssis rounded off, as far as he could, my education in public law and added to my consciousness of how little I know.

I often think Carl Goldenberg, who was retired by the age limit in 1982, almost deserves Voltaire's verdict on the prophet Habakkuk: '*Capable de tout*'. The *Parliamentary Guide* takes two pages of small print to list his achievements: royal commissioner for the Dominion and for Manitoba, Ontario, Quebec, and Newfoundland on a variety of subjects; similar work for the Governments of Jamaica and Trinidad; labour arbitrator; wartime mandarin; permanent umpire for the Canadian Labour Congress in inter-union disputes; special constitutional adviser to the Prime Minister at the Victoria Conference and in the proceedings that led up to it; and of course Senator. It is a signal honour to have been his friend for two-thirds of a century. Indeed, our friendship speaks volumes for his tolerance, since he is a devotee of Mackenzie King, whom I have spent much of my life denouncing.

One distinguished journalist has said recently that the Senate is made up of 'has-beens and never-weres'. As an authentic has-been, and probably a never-was, I am hardly an impartial witness. But I think if the Senate's detractors were to go down the list they would find very few 'bagmen' or party hacks, but a great many men and women of knowledge and experience and judgement in a variety of fields of activity. If they watched carefully enough they would find that at least a good half the members (not the often-stated thirty per cent) do a solid week's work in the Senate itself, in its committees (which often sit for prolonged periods when the Senate is adjourned), and in their home communities. One of the most silent Senators of my time in the House has recently received an international award for his prolonged and fundamental work in scientific agriculture. The late Senator McGrand, who in his seventies and eighties, while he worked at his senatorial job six days a week, was responsible for a pioneer report on childhood experiences as a cause of criminal behaviour — the first of its kind in the world. Anyone who listens to the speeches in the Senate, or even reads them, will find that they are generally well informed, well organized, well thought out, well expressed.

Very few of the journalists in the Press Gallery ever come to the Senate. I doubt if many read the debates. Most of them are content to repeat clichés, without the faintest attempt to find out whether they are justified. Their reaction to anything the Senate does (or doesn't do) is Pavlovian: they bark and snap. When Mr Joe Clark appointed Senator Jacques Flynn Minister of Justice, one of these gentry called me on the telephone: 'This is a terrible appointment. Flynn's no good.' I said: 'If you fellows ever came up here and listened, you'd know that Jacques Flynn is a first-class lawyer, a first-class parliamentarian, and a first-class speaker in both languages. It is an excellent appointment.' And so it proved, though unfortunately Jacques's work was cut short by the Government's defeat.

Of course one of the clichés is that the Senate is just a bulwark for the rich and their interests. The sessions of 1987, 1988, and 1989 have provided a curious commentary on this one. According to the journalistically received wisdom the Senate, when it got the Drug Patent Bill, should have passed it like a shot, whooping it up for the drug multinationals. But it didn't. It took quite the opposite line, subjecting the bill to the closest scrutiny, hearing all sorts of objections from people of undoubted knowledge and experience in the field, and proposing a string of amendments that were anathema to the multinationals. Again, according to the received journalistic wisdom, on the Immigration and Refugee Bills, and the Unemployment Insurance Bill, the Senate should have passed them, unamended, in jig-time. Why bother about the poor and the persecuted? But instead the Senate also subjected these bills to intense scrutiny, to prolonged hearings of experts in the field concerned, and proposed a string of amendments to make the legislation more effective, more humane, and better able to stand up to what promised to be formidable challenges in the courts. Apparently the collection of has-beens and never-weres has not understood the infallible pronouncements of the press. It is clearly dead and damned. But, being dead, it yet speaketh; being the tool of the big interests, it stands up for the small man and the ordinary citizen, the poor and him that hath no helper.

But the journalists, with a few honourable exceptions, possess convictions that are above and beyond being shaken by anything so trivial as mere evidence. Perhaps the saddest thing about it all is that many of those who simply reel off the ancient clichés are on other subjects well informed — clear, logical, and sensible. Is it a case of what the Roman Church calls invincible ignorance?

9

Preserving the Rule of Law

The Joint Committee on Regulations and Other Statutory Instruments was a new one, created under the Statutory Instruments Act, 1972, for the express purpose of examining and reporting on regulations and other defined subordinate legislation.

Why was it set up, and what is meant by subordinate legislation?

A very large part of the law that governs us is made up not of Acts of Parliament but of regulations or orders issued by the executive Government under authority conferred by Acts of Parliament upon the executive. The sphere of government has become so wide, so pervasive, covers so many possible sets of largely unforeseeable circumstances, that it is impossible for Parliament to legislate in detail. All it can do is confer on the Governor-General-in-Council (the Cabinet), or a Minister, or a Board, or a Commission or Committee, power to make regulations or orders to accomplish certain specific purposes, within limits set by the Acts. The results of this delegated rule-making power are described as 'subordinate legislation' because they are subordinate to the delegating, the enabling, Acts. They are valid and binding only if they fall within the limits of the power the relevant Act has conferred.

The mass of this subordinate legislation is enormous, and it is often of crucial importance to the daily lives and fortunes of thousands, or even millions, of ordinary people. The enabling sections of, for example, the Unemployment Insurance Act or the Immigration Act may run to pages, and the regulations or other 'instruments' issued under them to volumes. The enabling sections of such Acts need to be carefully drafted so that they do not confer powers that should be exercised only by Parliament itself, or more power than is necessary, or leave the executive with uncontrolled discretion to do pretty much as it pleases. The 'instruments' (rules, orders, proclamations) must be carefully scrutinized to see that they fall squarely within the powers conferred by Parliament, and are not so exercised as to trench unduly on the lives, rights, and liberties of the Queen's subjects.

The drafting of the Acts is of course the business of the Departments, especially the Department of Justice. The scrutiny of the enabling sections is the business of the two Houses (and here the Senate plays a very important part). The scrutiny of the subordinate legislation cannot be effectively done by individual members of either House, nor as a rule by either House in plenary session. The members are too busy; there is not enough time in the parliamentary time-table. There has to be a committee expressly charged with this task.

It is no light one. When our Committee was set up in the winter of 1973, it faced not only a daily flood of 'instruments' but a two-year backlog that had piled up since the Statutory Instruments Act came into effect. The backlog, and the daily flood, reached into every nook and cranny of our common life.

We elected our Chairmen: Gordon Fairweather for the House of Commons, myself for the Senate. Fairweather was soon called upon to undertake other pressing duties and I cannot remember that he was able to take more than an initial, formal part in our work. He was succeeded by Robert McCleave, QC, MP. After he left Parliament, Gerald Baldwin, QC, MP, took on the job. Both were first-rate. Both had brains, legal expertise, and what Sir Robert Borden called 'nerve and backbone'; which meant that they could, and did, stand up to the Department of Justice and Privy Council Office wallahs in the numerous battles we had with those gentry.

Then we had to get a staff. The Parliamentary Library Research Branch supplied us with two excellent counsel: Graham Eglington and Lise Mayrand. Graham, an Australian-Canadian, is the best consitutional lawyer I know. He has a thorough knowledge of British, Australian, and Canadian constitutional law and practice, experience in all three countries, a mastery of terse, nervous English, and the courage of a lion. Lise brought us equal courage, legal expertise, a mastery of both official languages and both Civil Law and the Common Law. She and Graham and I, and McCleave and Baldwin, enjoyed one of the happiest, and I think most fruitful, relationships I have known. We were also blessed, in Helen Leroux, with an administrative secretary of superlative ability.

We had our staff, who were well able to cope with the daily flood of documents. But we needed also half-a-dozen senior law students, taken on for the summer, to deal with the backlog.

This looked simple. It wasn't. We found the students easily enough. But the people who had to authorize their employment dragged their feet, week after week, leaving us on tenterhooks and the wretched young people hanging in mid-air, not knowing whether they were going to get summer jobs or be left high and dry. This went on till almost literally the eleventh hour. By that time Fairweather had had to go to England on other official business and I was left alone to handle the situation. I had been, uncharacteristically, very patient, very polite, and had got nowhere. Finally my West Country English temper blazed up. I was sure that Fairweather, if he were there, would back me. So I issued a peremptory order that the students were to be taken on at once. They were. No sergeant-major could have got prompter results.

All this, however, was only the beginning of our troubles. We still had to get the money we needed, and we had to get it from the two Houses. This of course complicated matters and took extra time. Then the Circumlocution Office got to work again. Delay succeeded delay. Eglington had to buy, out of his own pocket, some essential volumes. He had to go to Hull to get them, and the officials at first refused even to pay for the taxi! (He ultimately got the taxi fare and was reimbursed for what he had spent on the books, but 'not without dust and heat'.) After some further tribulations of a like kind, we got our budget voted and were able to start work.

Our first task was to draw up a list of the criteria by which we'd judge the documents submitted to us and make our reports. In this we had the invaluable help of the then Law Clerk of the Senate, Russell Hopkins, who entered on the work with zest, and of course knowledge and skill. Both Houses unanimously approved our list.

Our next step was to go to Westminster to see how the corresponding Committees of the Lords and Commons handled their work. Graham, Lise and I, and Russell Hopkins made the journey. We worked hard and learned a great deal, especially from Mr Speaker's Counsel, Sir Robert Speed, who had for some thirty years been counsel to the Commons Committee. It was Sir Robert who was later to enable us to 'vanquish and overcome all our enemies' in the Department of Justice, as I shall tell.

We got home and started work. Our list of criteria had fourteen items, three of them with two sub-items. None had anything to do with the policy of any instrument, which we felt was not our business. All were concerned with defending the Queen's subjects from the unlawful or improper use of authority. The first laid the foundation and set the tone: to report 'Whether any Regulation or other Statutory Instrument within its terms of reference that, in the judgement of the Committee (a) is not authorized by the terms of the enabling statute, or, if it is made pursuant to the prerogative, its terms are not in conformity with the common law, or (b) does not clearly state therein the precise authority for the making of the instrument.'

So the first question we had to ask ourselves when any instrument came before us was: 'Is it within the power of the Governor-in-Council (that is, the Cabinet), the Minister, the Board, Commission, Committee or other body which purports to have enacted it?' To use the technical legal term, is it *intra vires* or *ultra vires* — within their powers or beyond them? This, of course, meant that we had constantly to be in contact with the Department of Justice; the more so because we had to have, in every Department, a 'liaison officer' who in almost every case was an officer of the Department of Justice. So every time we had doubts about *vires*, the legal validity of an instrument, we came smack up against the Department of Justice. Whenever we asked the Department why it thought the thing was valid, over and over and over again the liaison officer replied with what I came to call 'the recorded message': 'I am not allowed to give a legal opinion.' In one case we got this five times in a single letter.

When we remonstrated, the Department of Justice replied that it was the legal adviser of the Crown, not of Parliament or any Committee of Parliament; that the solicitor-client relationship precluded any disclosure of its opinion. This, of course, was just dodging: the client, the Government, could easily have given permission. Eventually, by going direct to the Minister of Justice himself we got what was in fact all we had ever asked for: a statement, in each case, of the reasons why the Department concerned thought the instrument was valid. The reasons were, to put it mildly, not always convincing. But at least we could then report the Committee's decision without being accused of having failed to hear the other side.

At the very outset of our consideration of *vires*, Elmer Driedger, the excellent former Deputy Minister of Justice, confronted us with the contention that we had no business doing anything of the sort. We were not a court of justice.

Our reply was fourfold. First, our criteria, adopted by both Houses, said we must. Second, neither is the Department of Justice a court. Its opinions, usually invested with an Olympian and more-than-papal authority by being described as 'rulings', are neither infallible nor enforceable. They have often been rejected by the courts. In the Senate Reference case of 1980, the Department argued that Parliament could abolish the Senate by simple Act. The Supreme Court of Canada said it could not: it must have provincial consent. It is, of course, the Department's right to offer its opinion on the validity of any bill, Act, or regulation or proposed regulation, and it is its duty to do so when asked by the Government. But what it produces is still only an opinion.

Third, a cat may look at a king. Any parliamentary committee is entitled to raise questions as to the legal validity of any measure, and to express its opinions on the point. Senate committees, in my time, certainly did. One that I was a member of reported to the Senate that a certain Government bill was a matter of provincial jurisdiction, beyond the powers of Parliament, and should therefore not be further proceeded with; the Senate concurred and the bill died. Of course the Senate Committee's report did not settle the law (neither did any report of our Committee), nor did the Senate's adoption of the report. But I am certain that no Senate committee, nor indeed any committee of the House of Commons, would ever accept the proposition that it could not consider, and report on, the legal validity of any bill or regulation.

Fourth, the citizen ought not to be forced to bear all the trouble and expense of going to the courts to prove that what purports to be law is not law at all; and this applies just as much to subordinate as to substantive legislation. If, while a bill is before Parliament, a Member, a committee, or even a witness can convince the House that a particular provision is *ultra vires* and should therefore be struck out, citizens may be saved much toil, trouble, and expense, and perhaps the courts much needless work. If, when a regulation is promulgated, a parliamentary committee can report that, in the committee's opinion, it is *ultra vires*, the Government may be induced to withdraw it, or amend it to remove the offending provisions; and if it does, it should not be overborne by any tenderness for the *amour propre* or delusions of grandeur of the Department of Justice.

This whole question of *vires* goes straight to the heart of the rule of law, one of the cornerstones of our system of government. The rule of law means that everyone is subject to the law; that no one, no matter how important or powerful, is above the law: not the Government; not the Prime Minister or any other Minister; not the Queen or the Governor-General or any Lieutenant-Governor; not the most powerful bureaucrat; not the armed forces; not Parliament itself, or any provincial legislature. None of these has any powers except what are given to it by law: by the various Constitution Acts and their amendments; by a law passed by Parliament or a provincial legislature; or by the Common Law of England, which we inherited, and which—though enormously modified, added to, subtracted from by our own Parliament or provincial legislatures—remains the basis of our constitutional law, our criminal law, and even, except for Quebec, our civil law (property and civil rights).

If anyone were above the law, none of our liberties would be safe. What keeps the various authorities from getting above the law, doing things the law forbids, exercising powers the law has not given them? The simple answer is, of course, the courts. If Ministers or officials try anything of the sort, the courts will bring them up short. But what's to prevent them from bending the courts to their will? The great principle of the independence of the judiciary, which is even older than responsible government.

Well, someone may say, we know that. Does Forsey think he has to teach his grandmothers to suck eggs? If the courts are there and have the power to maintain the rule of law, what need have we of more? But if the courts can protect us against parliamentary breach of the rule of law, *a fortiori* they can surely protect us against breach of that rule by the executive: by the Cabinet, by individual Ministers, by officials; and we can 'Give all our days to dreaming, And all our nights to sleep.'

No, we cannot. The protection offered by the courts, though ultimate and indispensable, is not by itself enough for several reasons.

First, because the sheer mass and scope of subordinate legislation is so enormous that very little of it is likely to get before the courts at all.

Second, because getting it before the courts takes time and money, often a great deal of both.

Third, because some subordinate legislation doesn't get published (or at least didn't, down to 1979, when my time on the Committee ended; I hope this has since been remedied. We asked for remedy repeatedly.)

Fourth, and worst, because so many Canadian officials (and, apparently, Ministers, their formal masters) have little or no notion of law, or of the place of law in society. For many of them, administrative convenience is a basic principle, even *the* principle, of our Constitution, and the idea that subordinate legislation *is* subordinate is novel, strange, a nuisance.

This is a hard saying. Unfortunately the records of our Committee provide ample evidence of its truth, and are supplemented by evidence from very different sources.

Barnabas de Laky—a close friend, a former high official of the royal Hungarian government, a lawyer and graduate of the London School of Economics—was a member of the Department of Health and Welfare. On one occasion officials of that department presented to an interdepartmental committee, of which he was a member, a proposal of some kind (he never told me what). He looked at it and said: 'Well, I am just a Hungarian lawyer. But I can tell you at once that this violates at least five Acts of Parliament.' Startled, his colleagues consulted the departmental solicitor. He said it violated eleven! On another occasion a committee, of which de Laky was a member, was confronted by a specific proposal for action under the Canada Pension Plan. De Laky looked at this one and said: 'We cannot do this.' 'Why not?' 'It violates Section —— of the Canada Pension Act.' 'Oh, that's a very silly section.' 'It *is* a very silly section. When it was in draft I pointed this out to the Deputy Minister and the Minister. But Parliament enacted it. We cannot violate it.'

This second tale brought me up short. I said: 'Where in the world did this proposal come from?' 'You'd be surprised.' Knowing de Laky's position in the Department (he had helped draft the Pension Act), I could only assume it had come from pretty high up. 'But, Borna, I *know* these people! They are highly educated.' 'Please, Eugene. They are not highly educated. They have frequented educational institutions. They are excellent technicians. But they have no idea of law or of its place in society.'

When the engagement of the Prince of Wales was announced, there was one of the rare meetings of the Queen's Privy Council for Canada with the Governor-General present, and also one or more members who were neither Ministers nor ex-Ministers. This meeting was formally notified of the engagement. An official of the Machinery of Government Section publicly, and portentously, announced that this had been absolutely essential; that under the Royal Marriage Act the Sovereign had to secure the consent of the Canadian Privy Council; that without that consent the succession to the Throne would be in jeopardy. Eglington and I looked at this in the newspaper and our eyes almost started from our heads. First, the Royal Marriage Act was passed in 1772, almost a hundred years before there was any Canadian Privy Council, and of course it referred to the Imperial Privy Council. Second, it did not require the consent of that Council, only that it should be notified. Third, the succession to the Throne could be dealt with only by an Act of Parliament.

After John Turner's voluminous and much-criticized 'patronage' appointments in 1984 a veteran retired Deputy Minister, and a longtime and very able executive assistant to a Minister, told me that they had had dealings with the Privy Council Office for many years and each had found that there was no one there who knew anything about the Constitution.

Even the courts can be frustrated in dealing with subordinate legislation. Maurice Wright, the lawyer for the Labour Congress and various unions, had one case of a client who had applied for a position in accountancy in the Department of National Revenue. There was a competition and he won, hands down. He got the job. After a few months there was a competition for a better job, for which he was professionally qualified. He applied for it. The Public Service Commission refused to accept his application, saying he had to have spent a full year in his existing job before he could apply for another. He asked for the authority on which this decision was grounded. 'Bulletin No. 12.' On examination it turned out that Bulletin No. 12 was *ultra vires*; it had no legal basis whatever! But the Commission took the man who had come second in the other competition, far behind the winner, and plunked him into the new job. Mr Wright's client went to the courts and won, with costs.

There was a very curious sequel. The federal court said: 'This man is entitled to a certain sum of money.' The Government wouldn't pay up. So back he went to the federal court to compel payment. The judge said: 'Mr Wright, I cannot understand this. I thought this Court had already pronounced on this case.' 'Yes, my Lord. You are being asked to sit in appeal on your own judgement.' The man eventually got his money, but it took two court cases to do it. As I said to the Senate: 'We do not feel that these people should be able to play ducks and drakes with employees of the public on the basis of something they have dreamed up out of their own inner consciousness.' I might have added that it shows how far recourse to the courts can be from being a sufficient safeguard for the rights of the Queen's subjects.

I ought to have been prepared for official disregard of the law for I had witnessed, and denounced, a flagrant and notorious example. F.A. McGregor, Commissioner of the Combines Act, made a report under that Act dated 28 December 1948. The Act required that it be published within fifteen days, which meant 13 January 1949. The Government did not in fact publish it till 7 November, whereupon a storm broke in the House of Commons. The Government unashamedly produced twelve defences of its breach of the law, all of them worthless and some of them contradictory. Anyone who thinks this is exaggeration, or embroidery of the facts, can look up the details in my article in *Public Affairs* (Dalhousie University, Winter, 1953). The excuses, plus a couple of 'explanations', are all there, verbatim with my comments, garnished with quotations from *Iolanthe, Alice in Wonderland,* and E.OE. Somerville and Martin Ross's *All on the Irish Shore.* The defences and explanations can be checked against *Hansard.*

Did the Government say a word of contrition? It did not. Did it introduce a retroactive Bill of Indemnity 'deeming' its actions 'to have been' legal, despite the express words of the Combines Act? (That is what Mr Ramsay MacDonald did in Britain when he had inadvertently broken a statute.) It did not. Did any Minister resign? No. Just Mr McGregor! What did Ministers do? They laughed.

My article wound up with this:

'Freedom depends on law. But law which can be set aside whenever the Government sees fit, for as long as it sees fit, without Parliament or the people hearing a word about it, is not law at all. It is a shadow. It leaves the citizen utterly defenceless. Such liberties as he still appears to have are no longer rights, just favours of the Government in office. What the Government did to Section 27 (5) of the Combines Act it can do to any section of any Act. No law is safe, and when no law is safe, no citizen is safe.'

Our Committee had plenty of examples of the official cavalier attitude to the law. Perhaps the most conspicuous had to do with the repeated increases in the first-class letter rates by Order-in-Council in flat defiance of the Post Office Act. I say 'flat defiance' because it seemed clear to Graham, Lise, and me that the Act said the increases could be made only by Act of Parliament. The majority of our Committee thought otherwise, and in its several reports on the matter merely expressed doubts as to *vires*, adding that the Order-in-Council constituted 'an unusual and unexpected use of the powers conferred by the enabling statute.' Our counsel and I had no doubts whatever. Nor did Elmer Driedger, who telephoned me at breakfast to ask, in a fury, what was the matter with our Committee: 'Eugene, this Order-in-Council is totally illegal. You ought to have said so.' I replied: 'You are preaching to the converted. Eglington and I told the Committee precisely that, but they got cold feet.'

Even so, the Committee's several reports were censorious, and one of them was unanimously adopted by both Houses, with Ministers present! But the Government paid no attention whatever. On the contrary, rebuked once, it repeated the offence a second time, and a third.

The Government of course flourished in our faces a statement by the Department of Justice that the impugned Orders were all valid. Eglington and I were totally unimpressed; so much so that when the Clark Government came in we approached the new Postmaster-General, John Fraser, to take the only action that was then possible to vindicate our position without enormous confusion and expense: the passing of a retroactive Act of Indemnity stating that the Orders should be 'deemed' to have been valid. Fraser saw our point at once and acted. The resulting Act was one of the very few the Clark Government got through Parliament.

Second example: a committee of officials took action to dispose of a stock of feed grains. The action was urgent because of market conditions. But the instrument purporting to make the action legal was passed over a year before the committee of officials had any legal existence! The officials concerned seemed genuinely puzzled by the questions we raised. The necessity for the action was plain. They had not looted the till: the sale had brought a profit to the Government. Our asking where they got the legal authority to act just baffled them.

Third example: the Public Service Commission passed a regulation for which Eglington could find no basis in law. He was introduced to a high-level committee that included several lawyers. He said: 'I cannot find any statutory authority for this regulation.' 'Oh, there is none.' 'Then you are relying on the prerogative?' 'Oh, no.' 'Then what *are* you relying on?' 'The ordaining power.' When Eglington told this story to me, I exclaimed: 'I never heard of the ordaining power.' 'Oh, yes; there was an ordaining power in the Crown, last actively claimed by Richard II. James I wanted to use it, but Sir Edward Coke, in the famous Case of the Proclamations, ruled that it had lapsed.' Eglington explained this to the officials. They replied blandly that they were not relying on any ordaining power of the Crown. 'Then on what?' 'The ordaining power of the Cabinet.' 'What is that?' 'A long-standing Canadian tradition which has now hardened into law, by virtue of which the Cabinet can do anything which is not inconsistent with a statute.' Eglington argued them out of that one and it never surfaced before our Committee.

But the regulation itself did. It involved an appointment that we were inclined to think beyond the powers conferred on the Commission by the Public Service Employment Act and inconsistent with two sections of that Act. One of these provided for appointments by 'a process of selection designed to establish the merit of candidates.' The regulation had provided for a different process, which had been used to make an appointment of some importance.

We asked the Commission Chairman to tell us why the Commission considered this valid. He said he would ask their Director of Administration to explain. The explanation was that the process provided for in the regulation had allowed the Commission to appoint the person it thought best qualified for the job. He expatiated for about half-an-hour on this person's superlative merits: no person equally qualified could have been found by the process laid down in the Act. We said: 'This gentleman may be all that you say. We are not questioning his ability or his knowledge. Nor are we questioning that you might not have been able to get him by the process laid down in the Act. But where did you get the authority to pass this regulation?'

'I shall ask our Director of Personnel to explain.' We had another half-hour of eulogy of the appointee. Again we said: 'Yes, yes. But where is the legal basis for your regulation?' To that question we got no answer except that the Department of Justice said it was legal; which passed us by as the idle wind, which we respected not. My own opinion was that the Commission could have made this appointment legally by using another section of the Act, which it had apparently overlooked and certainly did not invoke. Perhaps the reason it didn't was inadvertently revealed by one of the Commissioners at lunch, just after the hearing. The Commission had just got rid of its legal adviser, and, she said, they were all so thankful: 'He was always raising points of law!'

Our Committee reported to Parliament that 'the Commission appears to have accepted the force of the Committee's views,' and 'is currently preparing amendments to the Act.' We added: 'What is required is a retroactive amendment . . . validating the appointments made . . . under the Regulation (which is still purportedly in force) and indemnifying all involved in the paying of salary and fringe benefits to all those so appointed.' We felt this warning was needed, because in a letter to us the Commission had said similar regulations had been adopted, and the totality would affect 'thousands' of cases. In my speech to the Senate on our report, I commented: 'Thousands of officials have been appointed, by express confession of the Public Service Commission, illegally; they have been receiving their pay illegally; they have been getting fringe benefits illegally; they have been dispensing public money and taking public actions illegally.'

We had a battle royal over the Government's assumption that it had the power of dispensing with regulations in favour of individuals. Parliament can, of course, expressly confer this power on a regulation-making body. But without such express provision, no such power exists. Two examples of this insolent assumption are notable: a proclamation purporting to be issued under the Navigable Waters Protection Act, and a Special Parole Board Regulation.

The Navigable Waters Protection Act contained two sections prohibiting dumping of certain substances in navigable waters, and a further provision empowering the Governor-in-Council, by proclamation, to exempt from the operation of those sections, 'in whole or in part . . . any rivers, streams or waters' covered by those sections. We were confronted by a proclamation purporting to exempt Denison Mines Limited from the prohibitions 'for the area shown on the attached map.'

The Committee promptly objected on two grounds. First, the Act provided for exempting 'rivers, streams or waters', not an 'area' shown on a map, attached or unattached; and all previous proclamations of this sort had duly specified which rivers, streams or waters were being exempted. Second, and more important, the Act provided for exempting waters, not persons. It did not provide for removing the prohibition for a particular person or corporation, leaving it in full force and effect for everyone else. Therefore, the proclamation was *ultra vires*.

'Why?' said the officials. 'Because it is an exercise of the dispensing power.' This appeared to mean absolutely nothing to the departmental lawyer. So Eglington explained that the dispensing power of the Crown had been made unlawful by the Bill of Rights of 1689. (I added my twopennyworth: that its exercise was one of the things that had cost James II his throne; I had learned this before I was in high school; I can produce the book I got it from.)

This fluttered the official dovecotes to an extraordinary degree. Eglington had a series of telephone calls from departmental lawyers, all officials of the Department of Justice, wanting to know what the dispensing power was and in what Bill of Rights its unlawfulness was to be found. They had looked in 'Mr Diefenbaker's Bill of Rights' (1960) and couldn't find it. Eglington replied disgustedly that it was not in Mr Diefenbaker's Bill of Rights. Well, was it the American Bill of Rights? No, it was not. Well, what Bill of Rights was it? 'The Bill of Rights which followed the Glorious Revolution of 1688.' 'What Revolution was that?'

But worse was in store. Government lawyers at a much higher level told us that the English Bill of Rights of 1689 was no part of the law of Canada. When I heard that I went right through the roof. I shall come back to this presently.

We had the same song-and-dance with Special Parole Regulations No.1, of 1973. This had been suggested, and drafted, by one of the legal advisers of the Privy Council Office. The Parole Act authorized only general rules, not particular rules applied to particular inmates of prisons. The special regulation applied only to one Jacques Leblanc. It purported to shorten the period he had to serve in prison before he could be paroled.

When the Committee raised the question of *vires*, it was told that Jacques Leblanc, who was not very bright, had been convicted of a crime in which the principals, who were juveniles, had got off more lightly than he. The Quebec Court of Appeals rejected Leblanc's appeal from his sentence, but recommended that the authorities take some action to reduce the disparity between the sentences. The Government obliged by the Special Regulation. There were, of course, other, and perfectly legal, ways in which poor Jacques' hard fate could have been mitigated. But apparently they just did not occur to the officials. Their method was easy and convenient. What further justification could the most captious critic require?

The Committee replied that this was another exercise of the dispensing power, and therefore totally illegal. The Parole Act conferred no power of dispensation on anyone.

Our remonstrances produced no effect. So we played our trump card. We sent for Sir Robert Speed.

The Department of Justice had thought it could brush aside the Committee's objections. I strongly suspect that it cherished the illusion that Eglington and I were the fountain and origin of its troubles with the Committee. Eglington was the person it most often came up against, and I was a very vocal Chairman, with decided opinions and no hesitation in expressing them in very plain language. At any rate, when I described myself to an audience of Government lawyers as 'probably the Department of Justice's Public Enemy No. 2', adding that I could scarcely hope to occupy the position of No. 1, which was undoubtedly filled by Mr Eglington, there was a shout of laughter. Fortunately we were both negligible. Eglington was a young whipper-snapper and, worse, not a member of any Canadian Bar (he soon became so) — just an Australian lawyer. I was old, not a lawyer, described by an Australian Senator as 'an obscure Canadian Senator'.

Sir Robert Speed was a different matter. No one could call him a young whipper-snapper; he was on the verge of retirement. Nobody could say he was an old duffer who knew no law and had no experience. He was a senior English QC, a veteran high servant of the House of Commons. So when he appeared before our Committee it was not surprising that officials of the Department of Justice filled every seat around our meeting-room, with their eyes goggling, their ears flapping, and their tongues hanging out.

We placed before Sir Robert one of the choicest specimens of the exercise of the dispensing power and asked him what his Committee would do if confronted with such a document. He read it and then said, in tones of astonishment: 'But nothing of this sort could ever come before us!' 'Why not?' 'It's completely unlawful.' 'Why is that?' 'It was made unlawful by the Bill of Rights of 1689.' We were never presented with any more attempts to exercise the dispensing power.

The Department of Justice never ventured to repeat the assertion that the Bill of Rights of 1689 was no part of the law of Canada. But after the age limit had put me out of the Senate, I was reading a quotation from an eminent Canadian professor of law, writing on an important constitutional subject, and was flabbergasted to find him saying that the preamble to the British North America Act, which speaks of 'a Constitution similar in principle to that of the United Kingdom', had brought into Canadian constitutional law such enactments as the Bill of Rights and the Habeas Corpus Act. I felt obliged to tell the young lawyer who was citing this as an authority that it was nonsense. The phrase 'a Constitution similar in principle to that of the United Kingdom' meant simply 'responsible government'. The Quebec resolutions had said that the executive government was to be vested in the Queen, to be exercised by Her Majesty personally, or by her representative duly authorized, 'according to the well understood principles of the British Constitution'. The phrase in the preamble to the Act was simply the Colonial Office legalese for what the Fathers had proposed. It had nothing to do with the Bill of Rights or the Habeas Corpus Act. Those enactments became part of the law of Canada by virtue of the reception of the English law in the various parts of Canada long before Confederation. There is no ground whatever for dragging them in by any preambular back door. The dates are given in the late Chief Justice Bora Laskin's Hamlyn Lecture, *The British Tradition in Canadian Law*. It is disquieting that a legal scholar should be ignorant of this fact. It is doubly disquieting that other scholars, and of course students, will not unnaturally assume that he was correct and look no farther and that, accordingly, this theory will in due course become one of the fairy-tales of the Canadian Constitution to which I once rashly, and publicly, promised to devote a book in my declining years. That was decades ago. I said then that the volume would have to be loose-leaf, since there was a fresh fairy-tale almost every day. Alas, their proliferation has known no surcease (this one has recently made its reappearance in a judgement of the federal court). If I were to write the book now there would have to be a series of chapters, probably written with Eglington, from our experiences on the Committee we both served; it might not be the least horrendous part of the whole.

(Even some academic works have their howlers. A published doctoral dissertation I read on a certain part of the Constitution had twenty-six on a single page: names, dates, positions held. It did not rise to this height all the way through, but the rest of the book had an abundance of cases of the same sort. I immediately warned the publisher about any possible second edition. The assistant editor replied that the work had been read by four academic authorities. I gave it a searing review, citing some of the howlers and offering to send a complete list to anyone who wanted it. I thought this might sting the four to some kind of reply. One—I think the supervisor of the dissertation—wrote me that he thought I had been 'rather hard' on the author. He did not attempt even to question the accuracy of anything I had said. Not a peep from the other three. The whole lot, as I said in the review, obviously just had not done their homework. A very distinguished historian wrote a short history of the

Canadian Constitution, 'And lo! Ben Adhem's name led all the rest!' I sent him forty pages of double-spaced typescript on the errors of fact, and once more I emphasize *fact*. I never received a syllable of reply. These are not hazy recollections of my dotage. I have a fat file marked 'Errors'. I have chosen only a few of the gems it contains. I could have produced dozens. It is hard to say which does the most damage: lawyers ill-acquainted with history, historians ill-acquainted with law, or political scientists ill-acquainted with both.)

The state of affairs in Canadian officialdom that I have described may sound scarcely credible. What explains it? Canadian Ministers and civil servants (and both seem sometimes to forget that 'minister' means 'servant', and that the servants of a servant are no less servants) have not been given a double dose of original sin. I have known a great many of them over something like half-a-century, some of them very well, and have almost invariably found them decent, kindly, hard-working, and knowledgeable within their own fields. Why did they behave so oddly (to use no harsher term) in regard to the matters I have been discussing?

One reason is that from the schools of English-speaking Canada English history (and in this context I say 'English', not 'British', advisedly, as most of what is involved antedates the Union of England and Scotland) has largely disappeared. The consequence is that young people coming out of these schools often have no more notion of the great struggles between King and Parliament in seventeenth- and early eighteenth-century England than if they had spent their formative years in the jungles of the Congo. But those struggles are crucial for Canadians. Their results are a fundamental part of the working Constitution. The independence of the judiciary is about a century older than responsible Cabinet government, even in Britain, and is essential to its survival. Habeas corpus, a cornerstone of our individual rights, goes back even farther. Of course lawyers know this (or ought to). But not all officials or Ministers are lawyers; some who are are sometimes too complaisant; and some lawyers are more equal than others.

Until recently, in most Canadian law schools constitutional law seems to have meant Sections 91 and 92 of the Constitution Act of 1867 referring to the division of legislative power between the Dominion and the provinces — little if anything more. But whether today's law students are taught basic facts of English constitutional law — which are equally basic facts of Canadian constitutional law — I do not know. I hope so. They should be.

The sorry saga of the attempted use, by what one constitutional lawyer has called 'these latter-day Stuarts', of a long-dead power to dispense from the law in favour of individuals, is the most spectacular part of the story of the obstacles our Committee faced as it tried to do its job.

In the first place, all statutory instruments, except those lawfully kept secret, were to stand 'permanently referred' to our Committee. But the definition of a statutory instrument was a masterpiece of complexity, ambiguity, and obscurity. The Legal Advisers to the Privy Council Office furnished us with interpretations that our report described as 'incomprehensible and unworkable, and productive of inconsistency in approach even by the Legal Advisers' themselves. But it was these same Legal Advisers who actually applied the definition, 'and whose views are therefore complied with by Departments of State and regulation-making authorities.' Certain classes of documents had to appear in the *Canada Gazette*. But it was not at all clear which, and the Legal Advisers 'declined to identify' those they considered to be statutory instruments. Publication, even where the Legal Advisers admitted that it must take place, did not have to be within any time limits. We had cases where a statutory instrument was not published for months (in one case, eleven months) after it came into force. This sort of thing, we told the two Houses, 'makes a mockery of the permanent reference of all statutory instruments to the Committee'. Some documents that even the lay Popes of the Privy Council Office agreed fell within the definition were never published. Some, our *Second Report* said, we 'occasionally [stumbled] across.' Some were volunteered by a department concerned. We had 'neither the time nor the resources to step into the twilight world of unpublished . . . instruments.'

Then there was the question of sub-delegation. Parliament had delegated to the Governor-in-Council, or a particular Minister, Board, Commission, or Committee power to make certain rules. But, as we reported: 'The principle of *delegatus non potest delegare* (a delegate cannot delegate) is fundamental to our law. It was with surprise that the Committee discovered that sub-delegation of rule-making power was achieved by statutory instrument and that the Department of Justice considered the practice quite proper, even in the absence of statutory provision authorizing a delegate to sub-delegate his rule-making power.' This was based on the use of the word 'respecting', or the phrases 'in respect of', or 'in relation to'. Eglington told me that this kind of phrasing did not occur in British or Australian statutes. Our report said: 'The Committee views the attempt to give to a delegate under an enabling power cast in terms of subject matter an automatic right to sub-delegate as simply another attempt to subvert the most fundamental proposition of all, namely that subordinate legislation is subordinate. The delegate of law-making power, whether he is a Minister, a Commissioner or the Governor-General in Council, is a *subordinate* law-making authority and is not in the same position with relation to the subject matter as is Parliament.' This use of 'respecting' was intertwined with the issue of the dispensing power: '168 instances have come to the Committee's notice.'

Another problem was the use of items in Appropriation Acts to confer rule-making authority. 'From 1st January 1972 to 30th June 1976 at least one hundred and four items of delegated legislation have to the knowledge of the Committee been made pursuant to Votes. . . . The Committee fears that many, many more examples exist which have not been cast by the Crown's legal advisers as statutory instruments and of the existence of which the Committee has neither knowledge nor the means of knowledge . . . . Moneys are voted by Parliament to be disbursed for a stated purpose but *all* the rules governing that expenditure, the determination of eligible recipients and so on, are left to be made by a subordinate authority. Parliament simply hands a sum of money to a subordinate authority with authority to spend it for a particular purpose, often vaguely stated, as that authority sees fit. The authority then makes a set of rules, often very elaborate, governing the expenditure . . . and, in effect, defining the purpose and objects of Parliament's bounty. Often the financial basis which gives the legal justification for the use of a Vote in an Appropriation Act is a fiction since the money voted is only one dollar.' Often the enabling power was so stated as to exclude the delegated legislation from the definition of a statutory instrument, and hence from parliamentary scrutiny.

To compound the offence, the rule-making power was often to be exercised 'subject to terms and conditions approved by the Governor-in-Council.' This, said our report, 'is completely lacking in specificity as to whom the power is given [to]. Who is it who is to set or make the terms and conditions which His Excellency in Council may approve?'

The Committee objected also to the practice of 'filling up' and extending old Votes and old enabling powers, 'under a series of Votes commencing at some point in the intermediate or distant past which are then amplified in scope or altered in some one or more particulars by succeeding Votes.' These were often expressed 'to extend the purpose' of an earlier Vote, and the extensions were sometimes 'barely related to the particular objects of the original Vote. The combination of the accumulation of extension and the extreme generality of language in which almost all enabling powers in Votes are expressed renders the task of the Standing Joint Committee so difficult as to negate any effective scrutiny. To the extent that scrutiny is rendered ineffective, Parliament's control of the purse is subverted.' Piling Ossa upon Pelion, 'the enabling powers were often not found in the Votes themselves, but in items in the Estimates to which individual Votes related.'

We wound up our report on this aspect of the subject by noting that power to make subordinate legislation is not granted in Votes in Appropriation Acts in Britain or Australia, and by recording our 'opposition, as a matter of principle', to the use of the device here.

Our catalogue of defects in the Statutory Instruments Act, and in instruments, and of obstructiveness to revealing what was going on ran to fifty-five pages, with chapter and verse and specific instances throughout.

My own speech in the Senate on the report occupies ten pages in the Senate *Hansard*; and for once I think I was concise, not verbose.

During Mr Baldwin's Chairmanship, the House of Commons thrust upon the Committee a task wholly beyond our original terms of reference: freedom of information. This was a cause dear to Baldwin's heart, and we went into it thoroughly. I was myself initially rather skeptical about an Access to Information Act. I played the Devil's advocate.

Some of the changes the Committee recommended in the law and practice relating to statutory instruments have been made; not, I think, all. To find out which, and how many, is utterly beyond my physical (and intellectual) strength. I am now, in the crisp words of a great-aunt in Moncton, 'old and infernal', or, in the language of the distinct society of my native province, 'wonderful slow'. A very lively contemporary describes himself as 'in the prime of my senility'. He has kindly given me permission to apply the description to myself.

10

Illegal Legal Opinions
and
Constitutional Writings

Years of teaching Canadian Government at McGill and Waterloo, and many conversations with Frank Scott (the Faculties of Arts and Law were in the same building at McGill), gave me rather more than a superficial knowledge of Canadian constitutional law. One of the somewhat bizarre aspects of my career is that even though I'm not a lawyer, I have on occasion been asked for legal opinions, and have several times drafted petitions for the disallowance of provincial Acts.

For example, on the Rentals Reference case — on whether the Government could continue rent control when the war had in fact ended — Maurice Wright, counsel for the Canadian Congress of Labour, asked me to prepare a memorandum on the economic background of his submission to the Supreme Court. I did him 18,000 words. I shall never forget his comment when he had read them: 'Well, I don't mind admitting that this is a lot better than I expected.' He used almost the whole thing.

When the first Official Languages Bill was brought down in 1969 Gordon Fairweather, former Attorney-General of New Brunswick, called me to ask whether I thought it was within the powers of Parliament. I said yes. Had I written anything on it? I said no. He said he wished I would. I remonstrated that my opinion was not worth much. 'I think you might allow other people to judge the value of your opinions. I'd like you to do it, and allow me to show it to Stanfield.' So I did. It appeared later in the *Globe and Mail*.

When the Auditor-General, Kenneth Dye, got into his dispute with the Government over Petro-Canada's purchase of Petrofina, two of his officials came to see me to ask whether I thought he was on solid ground (he suspected the price was unwarrantably high) in seeking certain information the Government was refusing. I said, 'Yes', bolstering my opinion by citing Section 13 (1) of the Auditor-General Act, 1976, which entitled him to any information he required, 'except as provided by any other Act of Parliament that expressly refers to this sub-section.' I could find no such 'other Act'. Some weeks later a very eminent constitutional lawyer who had been consulted by the Government called me, wanting to come to see me. Of course I was highly flattered. He had been looking at the sub-section and 'could see no way out of it'. I said: 'Nor can I. You, of course, may know of some other statute that contains such provisions. I don't.' 'No, there is none.' 'Well, I had already reached the same conclusion.'

I may add that I was wholly unshaken by the fact that the Department of Justice took the opposite view. I have had too many occasions, notably during my Chairmanship of the Joint Committee on Regulations and Other Statutory Instruments, to question its 'rulings' (i.e., opinions); not to mention the occasions when the Supreme Court of Canada said the Department was wrong. Once, in a moment of exasperation, I said to Senator Salter Hayden, one of Canada's foremost lawyers: 'I am not impressed by the legal opinions of the Department of Justice.' To my astonishment and gratification he replied: 'I congratulate you on the restraint of that statement!'

The Labour Congress asked me for several opinions. One was on the British Columbia Act of 1961, which virtually forbade union contributions to political parties. Andy Andras, director of our legislative department, brought me a copy. I read it. He said: 'A bad law.' 'Yes.' 'What can we do?' 'Elect a new government in British Columbia.' 'What about disallowance?' 'Save your breath. I know more about disallowance than anyone else in Canada except Gerry La Forest [now Mr Justice La Forest of the Supreme Court of Canada] and you haven't a chance, especially now that Diefenbaker has knocked the stuffing out of the power by refusing to disallow those Newfoundland Labour Acts two years ago.' (I deal with this below.) 'Can we take it to the courts?' 'Yes, but you'll lose.' 'Why?' 'Because they'll say it's "property and civil rights in the province", an exclusive provincial jurisdiction.' The officers then asked me to write them an opinion. I did at some length, saying that the Act was within the powers of the British Columbia legislature. But I urged them to get a proper legal opinion from Professor Frank Scott. They did. He said I was wrong. His opinion, of course, was a beautiful piece of work: learned, eloquent, elegant, and ingenious. But I shook my head: 'Too clever by half. The Supreme Court of Canada will never buy it.'

The officers were disturbed. They insisted I go to Vancouver to meet the union lawyers there. I protested that this was a waste of the Congress's time and money; but no, go I must. So I went. On the way I saw Andrew Brewin, QC. He told me that all the lawyers said I was wrong. I met the unions' lawyers in Vancouver and was appalled. One of their arguments was that the Act was discriminatory. I said: 'Of course it is. But that is totally irrelevant. If you were in an American state, with a state constitution that forbade discrimination, you could plead this with some hope of success. But you can't here. [This, of course, was long before the Charter of Rights and Freedoms.] All our courts will look at is one question: "Has the province jumped the fence into the Dominion garden?" And they'll say, "No, and the Act is therefore valid."' But the unions' lawyers were like the deaf adder that stoppeth her ear. They went ahead with their case. After losing in the Supreme Court of British Columbia and in the Court of Appeal, they went to the Supreme Court of Canada. I had forgotten the whole thing till one day Andras reappeared in my office with a long face: 'The Supreme Court of Canada's decision in that British Columbia case has come down.' 'What did they say?' 'The Act is valid.' 'Andy, you see I'm not such a fool as I look.' 'There's no answer to that. I'm going.'

Under the Constitution Act, 1867, the Dominion Government can disallow, wipe off the statute-books, any provincial Act within one year of its receipt at Ottawa. It has been done 112 times, for every province except Prince Edward Island and Newfoundland; the last time in 1943. But from 1922 to 1937 the practice had fallen into disuse and was widely believed to be obsolescent or constitutionally dead. In 1937, however, it was abruptly resuscitated to nullify three Alberta Social Credit Acts eleven days after they had been passed. This was unexampled celerity and the Prime Minister, Mackenzie King, set another precedent by issuing, with great fanfare, a ringing denunciation of the legislation's denial of recourse to the courts, and of the Alberta Government's refusal to agree to a reference to the Supreme Court of Canada: 'To take away the right of any citizen of Canada to appeal to the courts of the land against the exercise of arbitrary power is opposed to the whole spirit of our institutions and the liberties we cherish.'

Also in 1937 the Premier of Quebec, Maurice Duplessis, passed his 'Act Respecting Communistic Propaganda', better known as the Padlock Act. This legislation has to be seen to be believed. First, it made it 'illegal for any person who possesses or occupies a house in the province to use it or allow any person to make use of it to propagate communism or bolshevism by any means whatsoever.' But it contained no definition of communism or bolshevism. The Premier (who was also Attorney-General) told the legislature that a definition was unnecessary: 'Communism can be felt'; and 'Any definition would prevent the application of the law.' A legislative councillor suggested a definition that would include as Communists 'those who daily vilify public men'. Another would have accepted a definition that 'Communism meant those actions which sap the foundations of the things dear to the province.' One of the Ministers told a service club that the Act had to be wide enough to cover 'the many who are Communists without knowing it'. The Premier denounced the CCL as 'a movement of Communist inspiration', and branded the American CIO (Congress of Industrial Organizations) and the American Newspaper Guild 'Communistic'. In the words of R.L. Calder, 'the definition of Communism reposed in the cranium of the Attorney-General.'

In the second place the Act gave the Attorney-General, 'upon satisfactory proof that an infringement . . . has been committed', the power to order a 'house' closed 'for any purpose whatsoever' for 'not more than one year'. 'House', unlike Communism, was elaborately defined to mean 'any building, penthouse, shed, or other construction attached to the ground or portable, above, or below ground, permanently or temporarily.'

Against this, there was no recourse to the courts, except that the owner could petition a Superior Court judge to have the closing *suspended* if the petitioner could prove that he did not know the house was being used for propagating Communism (undefined), or *removed* if he could prove that it had not been so used during the previous year! From the judge's decision there was no appeal; and the tenant had no recourse to a court at all.

The Act also forbade publication or distribution of 'any newspaper, periodical, pamphlet, circular or writing whatsoever propagating or tending to propagate communism or bolshevism', on pain of imprisonment for three to twelve months and payment of costs, or, in default, an extra month in jail; and there could be no appeal. Moreover, any constable could seize and confiscate any such writings, upon instruction of the Attorney-General or anyone authorized by him, and the Attorney-General could order the material destroyed.

A group of outraged citizens (of whom I was one) promptly formed the Montreal Civil Liberties Union to fight this monstrosity. It plainly fell within the canons for disallowance set forth by a series of Ministers of Justice in a long list of cases. It was arguable that it was invalid as an invasion of the exclusive Dominion field of criminal law (the Supreme Court of Canada so found in 1957). It was in 'conflict with Dominion legislation and policy'. It produced 'confusion and private injury'. It conferred 'arbitrary powers'. It was 'extraordinary', 'without parallel in the history of Dominion or provincial legislation'. It 'denied recourse to the courts', or 'left no adequate remedy in the courts'. It was 'contrary to reason, justice and natural equity'. It was 'opposed to principles of right and justice'. It was 'confiscatory'.

I drew up the petition the Civil Liberties Union presented for disallowance. The Government refused, giving two main grounds. First, the Act had been passed unanimously by the provincial legislature. (This was, of course, totally irrelevant.) Second, the protests against the Act had 'come almost exclusively from persons in other provinces unaffected by the Act.' This was simply untrue. No less than one hundred and eight organizations in Quebec had protested.

And where was Mackenzie King when the ink was hardly dry on his denunciation of denial of recourse to the courts, his anathema against 'arbitrary power'? There was not so much as a peep from the great champion of the people, the proud grandson of the revolutionary of 1837. 'The trumpet's silver sound was still, / The warder silent on the hill.' Worse, the warder had gone over to the enemy. Nor were the opposition parties in the House of Commons of much use.

The decisive fact, of course, was that the Padlock Act had the enthusiastic support of the Quebec Roman Catholic Church and of the Quebec business community. No one wanted to challenge the Quebec élites. The Alberta legislation had the fervent opposition of the business community across Canada, and the support only of impoverished farmers — everyone in power was ready to listen to the business interests. Marx, in his grave, might have smiled.

My next work on disallowance was on behalf of the Canadian Congress of Labour, the Trades and Labor Congress of Canada, and the Railway Operating Brotherhoods when they jointly petitioned for the disallowance of the Prince Edward Island Trade Union Act of 1948. This stated that, except on the Canadian National Railways, there could be no union in the Island other than purely local bodies made up of Island residents. Even these would be forbidden to strike without arbitration (to which the provincial government would be a party), and would have to have a licence to do so from the Provincial Secretary — who could refuse a licence, or cancel one at any time, thus holding a sword of Damocles over the heads of even the most purely provincial unions.

This stirred up the union movement like an egg-whisk. The Canadian Congress of Labour asked the Dominion Government to instruct the Lieutenant-Governor to reserve the bill for the Governor-General's pleasure. (The Constitution Act of 1867 empowers the Lieutenant-Governor to refuse assent to provincial bills, which has been done twenty-eight times, or to send them to Ottawa, unassented to, in a state of suspended animation; this has been done seventy times, the last time in 1961. Such 'reserved' bills come into effect only if the Governor-General-in-Council — the Dominion Government — assents. The Act also empowers the Dominion Government to instruct the Lieutenant-Governor.) This would have prevented the proposals from becoming law, at least until the Dominion Government saw fit to accept them.

I drew up the petition for reservation, citing reasons given by Ministers of Justice for not giving assent to reserved bills, notably that the legislation was discriminatory. It discriminated between railway workers and other workers. It discriminated among citizens of the Island by preventing them from belonging to national or international organizations, while Rotarians, Masons, and others were free to do so.

We did not get reservation. The three central bodies then got together and petitioned for disallowance. I drafted this petition also. Despite an excellent legal opinion from the Dean of the Faculty of Law at the University of Toronto (the redoubtable 'Caesar' Wright), which we incorporated in the petition, it might not have been easy to get the Act thrown out by the courts, and the process would probably have taken more than the year within which disallowance could take place. We recited the litany of reasons given by Ministers of Justice over the years for recommending disallowance, noting how many of them applied to this Act. A Cabinet committee consisting of the Minister of Justice, the Solicitor-General, the Secretary of State, and the Postmaster-General heard a delegation of three from the Trades and Labor Congress, two from the Railway Operating Brotherhoods, and five from the Canadian Congress of Labour (of whom I was one).

We did not get disallowance, but we did get substantially what we wanted. The Dominion Government sent to Charlottetown the senior Maritime Minister, Mr Ilsley, to tell the Premier the Act must be repealed or the offending sections taken out or it would be disallowed. In 1949 the legislature took the stuffing out of it.

In 1959 Mr Smallwood passed through the legislature of Newfoundland two of the most horrendous anti-union Acts Canada had ever seen. This provoked a more formidable battle. Where most of the unions in the province were concerned the provincial legislature could do anything it liked, provided it did not invade some field of exclusive Dominion jurisdiction, and provided it was not stopped by reservation or disallowance. The refusal to disallow the Padlock Act and the Prince Edward Island Trade Union Act (no one knew then of Mr Ilsley's mission), and the increasing power of the provinces in Dominion-provincial relations, had convinced nearly everybody that no Dominion Government would dare to disallow any provincial Act. Many people also believed that the provinces had become more enlightened, or had learned a lesson from the Supreme Court's invalidating the Padlock Act in 1957. Moreover, Mr Smallwood was an old union organizer and socialist orator, surely the last person to sponsor anti-union legislation.

By this time the Trades and Labor Congress and the Canadian Congress of Labour had merged in the Canadian Labour Congress. There was now, except for the former Catholic unions and some of the Railway Operating Brotherhoods, a united labour movement. Early in the CLC's career one of its unions, the International Woodworkers of America, went into Newfoundland and organized the loggers employed by the two big companies there, or their contractors: the Anglo-Newfoundland Development Company and the numerous contractors for Bowaters Newfoundland Pulp and Paper Mills. Local 2254 took on Anglo-Newfoundland and Local 2255 Bowaters.

Local 2254 went through all the processes prescribed by the Newfoundland Labour Relations Act, including accepting the report of a Conciliation Board that the company rejected, before it finally took a strike vote and struck. Nobody has ever questioned that this local followed to the letter everything in the Act. Local 2255, perhaps discouraged by 2254's failure to get anywhere by following the legal course, lost patience and struck without going through the process at all. The one strike was legal, the other illegal.

The provincial government could have proceeded against Local 2255 for breaking the Act. It did not do so. It could have applied, or had the employers apply, to have 2255 or both locals decertified by the Labour Relations Board. It did not do so; it took no steps available to it under law. But the two companies—incensed by having to deal, for the first time, with a real union and a strong one—applied pressure on the government, which responded handsomely.

It brought in two bills. One, the Trade Union Emergency Provisions Bill, simply wiped the two locals out.

But having tasted blood, the government was not satisfied with this. It wanted to have power to make sure that no union, national or international, would be able to do anything the government did not like. Hence the second bill, which applied to all unions except those in industries under Dominion jurisdiction. It was 'something lingering, with boiling oil in it.'

First, it provided that if it 'appeared to the Lieutenant-Governor-in-Council [that is, the provincial government] that a substantial number of the officers, agents, or representatives of any union or body of unions outside the province had been guilty of a heinous crime (such as perjury, embezzlement, manslaughter, trafficking in narcotics, and so on), then the Lieutenant-Governor-in-Council might cancel the union's certification.

Note the vague and sweeping terms. If it 'appeared' to the government that a 'substantial' number of officers, etc., of the union, elsewhere in Canada, or more likely in the United States (if it was an international union) had been guilty, that was enough. (This, of course, was an attempt to make Newfoundlanders' flesh creep by reminding them of the misdeeds of American union officials like Jimmy Hoffa, and tarring all unions and union officers with the same brush.) What was a substantial number? The government would decide. Would the accused have had to be convicted? No; the government's say-so would be enough. Was there any provision for a hearing, even by the Cabinet, let alone the courts? No; the government could cancel the certification of any union (except in industries under Dominion jurisdiction) by mere fiat, without a shred of legal proof.

The provision was so broadly worded that it would have applied to an extraordinary number of individuals and organizations. For even affiliation of a union to a 'body' the government declared guilty was enough. Most of the national and international unions were affiliated with the Canadian Labour Congress, and the Congress was a member of the International Confederation of Free Trade Unions. So that if it 'appeared' to the provincial government that any of the officers, agents or representatives of the CLC or the ICFTU were guilty of any of the 'heinous' crimes, bang would go the certification of a union local in Newfoundland, which might never have heard of the person or persons concerned. The government could go over the newspapers with a fine-tooth comb till it found some union official in British Columbia, or the Northwest Territories, or the United States, or Western Europe, or Central or South America, pluck out a rumour of embezzlement or drug-trafficking by a minor union official, and presto the Newfoundland local would be swept into limbo.

The bill forbade various union practices, such as secondary boycotts and secondary picketing; and some of its provisions applied not only to officers, agents, and representatives of unions but also to ordinary members. For example, if an injunction (other than interim) had been issued against an officer, agent, representation, or member, the Government could decertify the union. The injunction did not have to have been violated; just issued.

Similarly another provision made unions and their officers, agents, representatives, or members suable for tortious acts, but gave them no right to sue anyone who had committed tortious acts against them. Still another provision said that if the Labour Relations Board was *considering* decertification for any of the perfectly legitimate reasons specified in the Labour Relations Act (for example, if the union had lost its majority), the government could decertify by mere fiat, ousting the Board's jurisdiction. If that happened, that union could not be certified in any future proceedings without the express permission of the government.

Also, the government could take possession of the assets of a dissolved union and dispose of them as it saw fit: hand them over to the Salvation Army, or the poor of St John's, or the Anglo-Newfoundland Development Company, or simply add them to the provincial Consolidated Revenue Fund. There was no restriction at all.

In the whole bill there were no judicial safeguards whatever. For all practical purposes it gave Mr Smallwood the power of life and death over every union in Newfoundland except those in industries under Dominion jurisdiction. He'd be monarch of all he survey'd, his rule there'd be none to dispute. That was what we were faced with.

I was even more in the middle of this affair than in the Prince Edward Island case. The government of Newfoundland kept the bills under wraps, except of course from the legislature. It gave no notice, allowed no representations. No one except the Assemblymen knew what was in the legislation. There were reports in the newspapers, but they were not of much use. If we were going to ask the Dominion Government to act in the matter we had to know exactly what the bills said. So I became a sort of animated telephone. I rang the union lawyer in St John's (who, fortunately, was a member of the Assembly). He read me the texts over the phone and I took them down. Then I called the Minister of Justice, Davie Fulton, a close friend, and said: 'Do you know what's in those Newfoundland bills?' 'No.' So I read them out to him.

I think we asked, first, that the Dominion Government instruct the Lieutenant-Governor to reserve them for the Governor-General's pleasure. I have since been told that this was done, but he ignored the instructions. The bills went through with lightning speed and received assent.

This plunged us again into the whole business of disallowance and I drew up the petition. It recited the history of the use of that power. Sir John A. Macdonald had laid down on 18 June 1868 criteria that were supposed to guide all subsequent Ministers of Justice. He made it perfectly clear that the issue was not simply the power of a province to pass a particular bill. It might be well within the power of the province but still objectionable because it was unconstitutional in the broad sense of the word; because it was an invasion of private rights; because it was inequitable and unjust. We argued that the Acts 'comprised discriminatory legislation', that they were 'unjust and oppressive', that they 'formed part of a scheme for the oppression' of workers (all phrases taken from previous disallowances). We went through the whole thing, point by point.

In most cases where disallowance had taken place on the ground of invasion of rights, those concerned had been property rights. We suggested that the Government of Canada should not seem to be giving property rights priority over the rights of workers. We hinted that this would enable Marxist critics to portray the Government as simply the instrument of the employing class, staunchly defending the interests of that class but oblivious of the rights of workers.

Our petition dealt also with the theoretical alternatives to disallowance. One was to let somebody appeal to the courts in a test case. But this would take far too long, and in the absence of a charter of rights and freedoms it was very doubtful that the courts would find the Acts were beyond the powers of the province. Also, the unions would be compelled to spend a lot of money to defend what was really a public, not a private, right. A reference case (the Government asking the Supreme Court of Canada for an opinion as to whether the Acts were valid) would be quicker, but still expensive, and the result very doubtful. Our objection to the legislation was not, essentially, that it was a matter of jurisdiction but a matter of public policy. The province was doing something that was contrary to one of the standards that a series of Ministers of Justice had laid down: it was contrary to Dominion policy and Dominion legislation. The Dominion Parliament had passed one Act after another clearly indicating that unions were legitimate and proper. It had passed an amendment to the Criminal Code that penalized employers for violating certain rights that this Newfoundland legislation destroyed for most of the workers of Newfoundland. It was a question of the general interests of Canada, not of jurisdiction.

All this ought to have touched, even twanged, a responsive chord in Mr Diefenbaker, the great champion of civil liberties. Perhaps it did, but he gave no sign. He was in the midst of an acrimonious dispute with the Government of Newfoundland over other matters.

There was a further complicating factor. When the two local unions struck, there was a good deal of violence on the picket lines and a constable was killed. This undoubtedly influenced the response of both the Newfoundland government and the Government in Ottawa.

The Diefenbaker government faced a situation with two aspects, and where two courses of action presented themselves. The RCMP, which by contract with the provincial government was doing most of the policing in the province, asked for reinforcements. The CLC asked for disallowance of the Acts. The Dominion Government then did what still seems to me exactly what it ought not to have done: it refused the reinforcements and refused to disallow.

Throughout this sorry affair the Liberal Opposition in the House of Commons supported the Liberal government of Newfoundland. This, of course, helped to make smooth the rough places for Mr Diefenbaker.

Fortunately the story does not quite end there. Apparently our remonstrances produced some effect, little by little. The Trade Union Emergency Provisions Act was 'spent' the moment it was passed and it decertified the two locals. The other Act remained, unchallenged in the courts (where it would probably have survived) and untouched by the Dominion Government. But in 1960 the legislature removed or modified some of the most offensive sections, and in 1963 one more. In 1977 a new and comprehensive Labour Relations Act threw out the whole sorry mess.

Yet it had taken some time to achieve these happy results, and in the meantime the Acts of 1959 had achieved their objects. The two union locals had been destroyed and their parent union eliminated from Newfoundland and replaced by a tame 'union' nearer to the heart's desire of the Smallwood government. Also, by 1977 that government had been replaced by a different one, nearer to the heart's desire of the electors of Newfoundland.

My own part in all the turmoil did not escape comment from four quarters. I wrote, for the *United Church Observer*, an article setting forth the objections to the two Acts. A United Church minister in Newfoundland took the other side, in a tearful and bleating effusion, which said nothing at all abut the merits or demerits of the legislation but rang the changes on the theme that 'Newfoundlanders were poor, but proud'. That was the first response.

The second was like unto it, though more dignified. It came in a personal letter from a very highly respected minister. This also paid no attention to the legislation but remonstrated that 'Mr Smallwood is a sincere and loyal Newfoundlander.' To this I replied: 1. I never said, or even hinted that he wasn't. His sincerity and loyalty are wholly irrelevant. If it comes to that, Hitler was probably a sincere and loyal German. In both cases, what was at issue were policies and actions. 2. I attacked not Mr Smallwood but his legislation, and gave reasons.

Next came the Attorney-General of Newfoundland, Leslie Curtis, when I met him some years later. He told me my article in the *Observer* was 'all wrong'. I replied that he was entitled to his opinion. He responded, with the utmost bonhomie: 'But we don't blame you for that. We know you're just a paid public relations man and write what you're paid to write.' At this I took fire: 'Mr Curtis, I am not and never have been a "public relations man". I have never written one syllable that I did not believe. I may have been mistaken, but I never wrote anything I did not believe. That article was written from white-hot conviction.' This produced no effect whatever. The Attorney-General merely repeated what he had said.

Finally many years later, when I was in the Senate, one of the Newfoundland Senators, a former Minister in Smallwood's Cabinet, said to me one day: 'When you attacked our Labour Acts of 1959 weren't you a paid official of the Canadian Labour Congress?' 'Yes.' 'Well, don't you think that meant you weren't altogether impartial?' My answer was: 'When you supported those Acts, weren't you a member of the Cabinet that sponsored them? Don't you think that means that you weren't altogether impartial?' No reply.

I was particularly irritated by the stuff about 'sincerity', which I have encountered in the context of other battles. When the separatists were riding high in Quebec I gave my reasons for disagreeing with certain statements by Mr Lévesque. After my speech a dear elderly lady, an English-speaking Ontarian, plaintively remonstrated that 'Mr Lévesque is very sincere.' I said: 'I never suggested he wasn't. But what's that got to do with it? If someone wants to burn my house down, the fact that he really believes that this is for the public good will no doubt weigh in his favour at Judgement Day. But I am not interested in his motives or his "sincerity". All I want is to stop him burning the house down.'

My last disallowance case was on Quebec's Bill 22, passed in 1974. This Act severely restricted the rights of English-language Protestant schools. The Protestant school authorities decided to fight it. First, they set up a committee of lawyers to deal with its validity. The chairman was T.P. Howard; Jean Martineau (former *bâtonnier* of the Quebec Bar) and Frank Scott were other members. The lawyers prepared a massive report demonstrating conclusively, in their opinion (and mine), that Section 93 of the Constitution Act of 1867 preserved inviolate the school boards' jurisdiction over the language of instruction. The legislature could not touch it. On the strength of this the Protestant school authorities decided to ask the Dominion Government to refer the Act to the Supreme Court of Canada for an opinion as to the validity of the provisions on this subject. They decided also to ask, alternatively, for disallowance.

The talk of disallowance stirred the Montreal *Gazette* to a stupid editorial. Frank Scott wrote me that it must be answered and I was the man to do it. I did. Frank was much pleased. I then suggested that if he and his colleagues were proposing to ask for disallowance, I might be of some use to them. He promptly invited me to the next meeting of the lawyers' committee.

I had a grand day. At the end of it I thanked the members and incidentally apologized for having ventured opinions on points of law, which as a layman I had no business doing. (Mr Martineau exclaimed: 'But what a layman!') I then said that, having made such contribution as I could, I would be of no further use. Palmer Howard replied: 'Eugene, you are a member of the team. You will come to our next meeting.'

I spent seven full days with the lawyers. I drafted the part of the petition that asked for disallowance, going over the familiar ground, and personally presented the petition in the Privy Council Office. Of course nothing came of it. The Government would not disallow; nor would it refer the matter to the Supreme Court. By the time it did get to the courts on a test case the Act had been repealed and the court refused to consider it. The repeal brought no relief, for Bill 22 gave place to the much more drastic Bill 101.

Because of what I had written on the reserve power of the Crown or its representatives, the Australian constitutional crisis of November 1975 — when Sir John Kerr, the Governor-General, dismissed the Whitlam government — aroused my liveliest interest.

Most of what I had written was on the grant and refusal of dissolution of Parliament. Dismissal of a government, of course, is a perfectly distinct point, though Gil Rémillard, the present Quebec Minister of Intergovernmental Relations, in his evidence before the Joint Committee on Senate Reform, totally confused the two. He said that Gough Whitlam had asked the Governor-General to dissolve Parliament and Kerr had refused. The fact was that Mr Whitlam had adamantly refused to ask for dissolution and Sir John Kerr had insisted that there must be one. Rémillard had got the facts upside down.

The Australian High Commissioner in Ottawa and the Department of External Affairs both provided me with ample documentation, and I had at my elbow Graham Eglington, who knows the Australian Constitution down to the last detail.

The Australian Senate, which had undoubted legal power to refuse to pass money bills, had refused to pass two Appropriation Bills unless there was either a general election or a half-Senate election. Mr Whitlam, with a majority in the House of Representatives, refused both conditions The Senate stood firm. The result was that in a matter of weeks the Government would have had no money legally available to pay about 40 per cent of its obligations. The only way to get the Senate to pass the bills was to have an election. As Mr Whitlam wouldn't call one, the only recourse was for the Governor-General to dismiss him and commission the Leader of the Opposition as a caretaker Prime Minister, who would advise a dissolution. Under the Australian Constitution there is in certain circumstances provision for dissolution of both Houses. The caretaker Prime Minister promptly advised this; the Senate passed the two bills; the election took place.

It was clear to me that not only had Sir John Kerr acted constitutionally, he had taken the only course possible to secure the normal functioning of parliamentary responsible government. I wrote a letter to the *Globe and Mail* saying so and giving my reasons. I also took the liberty of writing Sir John Kerr and sending him a copy of my book of constitutional essays, *Freedom and Order*. (It turned out that he had already carefully read my *Royal Power of Dissolution of Parliament*.) From this beginning has developed one of my closest friendships, and a voluminous correspondence and interchange of documents and information. When Sir John wrote his account of this crisis, *Matters for Judgment*, he included a whole chapter on my work and asked me to write an Introduction. His English publishers, however, naturally wanted something better and they got it: a most admirable essay by Lord Hailsham. My effort appeared as an Epilogue.

This had a by-product. In 1984 a lawbook publisher in Australia wrote me that he wanted to bring out, in a single volume, a photo-edition of Dr H.V. Evatt's *The King and His Dominion Governors* and of my *Royal Power of Dissolution of Parliament* (both long out of print), with an Introduction by me on the present position of the reserve powers of the Crown and its representatives. I agreed (my Introduction ran to 30,000 words and 194 footnotes) and the volume came out in 1990.

In June 1987 I was involved in another matter rather nearer home. Léo Piquette, MLA, tried to ask a question in French in the Alberta Legislature and was stopped. The subject was referred to a Standing Committee, which heard a large number of witnesses on the status of French in the Assembly. I was one. I testified for two hours in support of the view that the legislature was in fact by law bilingual. The acting Law Clerk of the Assembly, purporting to summarize the evidence of all the witnesses, gave me a terrific and most contemptuous going-over. But the Supreme Court of Canada, in the Mercure case about a year later, backed every point I had made.

The Meech Lake Accord launched me into a fresh constitutional controversy, presumably my last. But that belongs in the next and final chapter.

I am sorry to have to add, as a coda to these recollections of my written opinions, something about battles long ago in which I took a minor and almost wholly unsuccessful part: a series of struggles against what I consider to have been attempts to rob Canada of her history.

One of them was over the adoption of our present flag in 1965. I felt it should be bicultural, with symbols—both British and French—to remind us of the origins of our nation. Instead, what we have is not even multi-cultural or agricultural; it is silvicultural. On the disappearance of any symbol of our British heritage, I said my say in verse—which no one would publish at the time and which there is no room for here.

The battle over the flag, in which I took only a very minor part, was at least fought honestly. There was ample discussion, and in general it respected both facts and logic. This was not true of the other two: the getting rid of 'Royal Mail' on the trucks and post boxes of the Post Office Department, where those who thought as I did were totally defeated; and the erasure of 'Dominion' from everything except, amazingly, our Constitution, where it still survives in the preamble and Section 3 of the Constitution Act of 1867, unrepealed and unamended.

The assault on 'Dominion' especially was characterized by bad law, bad history, bad logic; by chopping and changing, cringing, creeping, crawling (sometimes to Americans or other 'foreigners', sometimes to 'many good and loyal Canadians'—unspecified); by dodging, ducking, wriggling, squirming, backing and filling; by confusions (notably between the 'name' of our country, which is Canada, and its 'title', which is Dominion); by untruths and fairy tales. The perpetrators of this performance did almost all their work darkly, at dead of night, the sod with their bayonets turning. They took the word 'Dominion' off official documents and even out of the telephone book, surreptitiously, without any legal authority. Finally they changed the name of 'Dominion Day' by Act of Parliament—put through the House of Commons by something very close to sneak-thievery, when it is pretty certain there was not even a quorum. (Incidentally, one of the choicest examples of bad history in the debate was the assertion by an eminent journalist that 'it is safe to assume that the Fathers of Confederation in 1867 had no thought of using the word "nation"', when in fact the Confederation Debates of 1865 are sprinkled thick with it.) I have used very strong language here, but I can support every word. In fact I did so—in thirty pages of typescript, with chapter and verse—for this book. But a publisher's patience has limits, so I must be content with what Mrs Malaprop would have called 'a nice derangement of epitaphs'. I shall be glad to furnish a copy of the thirty pages to anyone who wants to read them.

11

Quebec Nationalism

This subject has taken a disproportionate amount of my time and energy for most of the last thirty years.

I think I know more about French Canada, Quebec, and Quebec nationalism than the average English-speaking Canadian. But this may merely be saying that one is greater than zero. Over and over I have approached some facet of the subject with reasonable confidence, only to discover that, to apply Churchill's words on the Soviet Union, I faced 'a mystery wrapped in an enigma'.

The Quebec nationalism I grew up with was of two kinds. One was the Canon Groulx dream of an independent Quebec state. This none of the rest of us took very seriously; nor, I think, did most French Canadians. The other was an orthodox, limited nationalism whose best exemplar, perhaps, was Maurice Duplessis. This we all did take seriously; we had to. It might be described as defensive nationalism. It concentrated on keeping what Quebec had, on fending off transfers of power from the province to the Dominion, on asserting and maintaining a Quebec veto on constitutional change.

With this the dominant forces in English-Canadian society had no real difficulty. The defensive nationalism was hardly even interested in economic questions, was quite content to leave the big decisions on these to the 'English', nationally and provincially. The 'English', naturally, were delighted. They controlled most of Quebec industry, and the French-Canadian majority in the provincial government and legislature was perfectly ready to co-operate in keeping wages down and blocking social legislation. The French-Canadian Roman Catholic Church was also ready to co-operate. As long as it could keep its flock unsullied by subversive modern ideas, keep their minds fixed on heaven, the money-grubbing 'English' could do pretty much as they pleased. This

This chapter incorporates some passages from the essay 'Our Present Discontents' in my *Freedom and Order* (1974).

is, of course, an over-simplification; but not quite as much as the innocent might imagine. The Quebec 'Catholic unions' were tame cats.

Some of the old-fashioned nationalists had dreams, springing from the French-Canadian birth-rate. 'The revenge of the cradles' would make New Brunswick a predominantly French province, and spread *la race* across eastern and northern Ontario to encircle the 'English' in the south of that province. I remember Frank Scott telling me how one of these people had said: '*Nous allons arranger l'Ontario*' (We shall arrange Ontario); and I recall an article in *Le Devoir*, when the Afrikaners took control of the Union of South Africa, that looked forward to the day when the *Canadiens* would do the same for Canada. No one was prepared for the sudden and drastic drop in the birth-rate that came with the Quiet Revolution. The dream of an expanding minority taking over gave place to the nightmare of a diminishing minority losing its political clout. To that nightmare Meech Lake is a response, and Bourassa is trying to convince us that it is a minimum response and inescapable. A good many of the English-speaking politicians and intelligentsia, mesmerized, have succumbed.

In Ottawa the defensive nationalism expressed itself by insisting that Quebec French Canadians must have three Departments: Justice (to protect the Civil Law), Public Works, and the Post Office (the two big patronage departments). Mackenzie King offered Sir Lomer Gouin the department of Trade and Commerce. Gouin wouldn't look at it. He insisted on being Minister of Justice.

But the new generation challenged the grip of the hierarchy, of St James Street, and of Maurice Duplessis. Father Lévesque founded the Faculté des sciences sociales at Laval University. The Catholic unions suddenly bared teeth and claws. Archbishop Charbonneau of Montreal supported their strike at Asbestos. Groups of young dissidents organized the Institut canadien des affaires publiques, a French-language counterpart of the Couchiching Conference. They also founded the Rassemblement, a miscellaneous collection of individuals united only in their opposition to Duplessis, and the brilliant periodical *Cité libre*. The Rassemblement faded out. *Cité libre* did not; it became a vehicle for the ideas of, notably, Pierre Elliott Trudeau.

When Duplessis died in 1959 a new spirit reigned briefly even in the Union Nationale, the party he had created and ruled. His immediate successor, Paul Sauvé, took as his watchword 'Désormais!' (Henceforth!). If Sauvé had lived the whole history of Quebec, even of Canada, might have been different. With his sudden death in 1960 the Union Nationale floundered and the provincial Liberals flung themselves into the struggle for what might now have been described as 'perestroika', the reconstruction of Quebec society.

Theirs was a new Quebec nationalism, symbolized in the slogan *Maîtres chez nous!* They were not content with keeping Quebec's traditional powers and its traditional portfolios in the Dominion Cabinet. They wanted their due share of the great economic decision-making portfolios, their due weight in Canadian national policies.

Nothing could have been more to my taste. As a CCFer, as a Canadian Congress of Labour official, as a consistent, vocal, even turbulent opponent of Duplessis and all his works, I not only welcomed the changes: I took a modest part in them. I spoke often (in French) at conferences organized by the Laval Département des relations industrielles. I was, from the beginning, a member of the Institut canadien des affairs publiques and attended its annual meetings (that was where I first met Pierre Trudeau, Jean Marchand, and Gérard Pelletier). I also joined the Rassemblement.

Our host at meetings of the Institut was often Hector Langevin, the wealthy treasurer of the Quebec Liberal Party. He gave us a vivid illustration of just what the prevailing orthodoxy could mean. His daughter was a pupil at a convent school, just across the street from her home. Every morning the nuns prayed 'for the soul of Monsieur Hector Langevin, Communist, whose house is across the street!'

This is a real-life parallel to the apocryphal tale of the teacher who was admonishing her class to be mindful of all the good things they enjoyed, and their source. 'Who gave us our beautiful school?' The class chanted: 'Maurice Duplessis.' 'Who gave us our fine new church?' 'Maurice Duplessis.' 'Who gave us the new highway that provides easy access to the school and the church?' 'Maurice Duplessis.' 'And who gave us the glorious blue sky above us?' One pupil piped up: 'Le bon Dieu.' The others turned on him with a shout of 'Communist!'

Many of the new nationalists wanted 'special status for Quebec'; that is, the transfer of powers from the Parliament of Canada to the legislature of Quebec. The list of powers was usually formidable and almost always began with 'for example', or ended with 'and the list is not exhaustive', or perhaps included both caveats. A variant was that the list was 'a minimum', or that its items were not negotiable.

My attitude to 'special status' was cautious. I pointed out that Quebec already had special status in certain matters, all of them constitutionally guaranteed: it was officially bilingual, it had its own Civil Law, and it had its own very special educational system. Other provinces also had special status in particular matters. The Manitoba Act appeared to guarantee official bilingualism and Roman Catholic separate schools in that province, though in fact the guarantees had proved worthless. The British North America Act gave New Brunswick power to levy certain export duties on lumber. The Terms of Union with Newfoundland provided special guarantees for that province's (then) four systems of denominational schools. Both Newfoundland and Prince Edward Island have guarantees of transport facilities connecting them with the mainland. So a special status for Quebec on some further particular matters could not be ruled out as a matter of principle. It was necessary to ask: 'Special status for what? What specific powers do you want? Tell us and then we can examine them and see what they would mean for you, and for the rest of us.' The almost invariable reply to this was: 'Oh, no. You must accept the *principle* of special status, and *then* we'll tell just what we want; and, having accepted the *principle*, you will be bound to give us the specific powers we shall then ask for.'

There were cries of outrage when I said this was asking us to sign a blank cheque. But what else could it be?

A few months later, in a public discussion, Andrew Brewin, MP, said he was surprised that with my trade-union experience I should be so perturbed by a 'bargaining position'. I was not quick enough to think of the obvious answer till some days afterwards. Then I wrote Andrew. Had he ever heard of a union going into negotiations with an employer with this proposition: 'We are not sure yet just what our demands will be. We may ask for a 50 per cent increase in wages, or a four-hour day, or a three-day week, or five months annual vacation, or fifty paid statutory holidays, or pensions of $500 a month at age 50, or some combination of any or all of them. But you must first accept the principle of our demands; then we'll let you know what they are.' I got a polite answer to my letter, but none to my question.

Some of the new nationalists wanted outright independence for Quebec. The Union Nationale wanted 'Equality or independence'—equality of Quebec with the rest of Canada, or, if that was refused, outright independence. This may have been the genesis of the 'two nations' theory, which the NDP adopted at its Founding Convention in 1961, and of the Progressive Conservatives' acceptance, at the Montmorency Conference, of the same notion.

That brings me to the Founding Convention of the New Democratic Party (NDP) in 1961. Politically speaking I am inclined to say that it 'brought death into our world, and all our woe'. A French-Canadian CCFer among my friends did not go quite as far as that. But addressing another CCFer (who stayed with the NDP) on this subject, he said: 'You people did not start this, but you certainly gave it a good hard push.' They did. And with honourable exceptions, they did it again over the Meech Lake Accord, and *fortissimo* in the Dominion election of 1988 when Mr Broadbent performed the ceremonial kow-tow to the Quebec nationalists at every opportunity.

I was a delegate to the NDP Founding Convention. I never saw the draft constitution of the new party, nor its draft program, till the Canadian Labour Congress gave me a credential to represent a local union in Moncton. I found myself almost at once the centre of a lively controversy. The draft constitution used the word 'national' seventy-six times. The committee chairman, J.H. Brockelbank of Saskatchewan, presented a report that struck out the word in every case. In exactly half the cases it was replaced by 'federal', in the other half it simply disappeared. Mr Brockelbank, in what I can only describe as namby-pamby tones, explained why: 'Some of us, especially in the West, have been proud to call Canada a nation, not realizing that when we did we were hurting and wounding our French-Canadian fellow-citizens. Now that we know it, of course we'll never do it again. Some of you may be surprised to hear me quoting Scripture, but I'm going to do it: "If meat make my brother to offend, I will eat no meat while the world lasts." '

This nauseating performance brought me to my feet instantly to move the reference back, calling upon the committee to bring in a report that 'would not be an insult to the intelligence of every person in this hall, English-speaking or French-speaking.' I quoted the French-speaking Fathers of Confederation George-Étienne Cartier, Hector Langevin, and Étienne Taché, who repeatedly spoke of the founding of 'a great nation', 'a single great nation'. Whether I quoted them in French or English I am not now sure, but quote them I did. The bulk of the delegates either did not get my point, or if they did were too eager for Quebec nationalist votes to pay any attention. I was, in P.G. Wodehouse's phrase, 'turned down like a bedspread'. The only visible result was an editorial in *Le Devoir* accusing me of having 'preached Anglo-Saxon domination'! I wrote to the paper, in French, pointing out that most of my argument had consisted of quotations from three French-Canadian Fathers; that perhaps it was possible that *they* were preaching Anglo-Saxon domination, but I thought it unlikely. *Le Devoir* climbed half-way down. I protested again and that honest man André Laurendeau, the editor, climbed down the rest of the way.

As I put it later: 'This is probably the only occasion in history when some thousands of people met to form a new national political party and began by resolving that there was no nation to form it in.'

The impression I got at the time was that a small section of the Quebec delegates had persuaded the rest of the Quebec contingent to adopt the two-nations doctrine, which even one of its own advocates later admitted was 'relatively new and little known', and the Quebec delegates then bullied or bamboozled the committee, and eventually the convention, into swallowing it.

I tried to argue, privately, with some of the leaders. I got nowhere. One of them assured me it was 'just words', it didn't really mean anything. Very flattering, that, to the intelligence of the French Canadians. But how often we have heard it since, the latest instance being the Meech Lake Accord! I told Tommy Douglas: 'You cannot build a party on a lie.' He chuckled and hurried up the steps of the platform. I warned the leaders the thing wouldn't even win Quebec seats, and it didn't. But in 1988 the party tried the same game, for the same purpose. Again I predicted it would not win seats, and it didn't.

Looking back, I am surprised that I did not leave the Founding Convention immediately after my motion for the reference back was defeated. I suppose I was reluctant to part from comrades of almost thirty years. Also, there were some things in the draft program that I thought needed to be changed, notably the proposal for a 'Guaranteed Full Employment Act'. Who had dreamed up that preposterous nonsense I had no idea. I was all for full employment. But to *guarantee* it, by Act of *Parliament*! I told the delegates that the day after the Act was passed the unfortunate NDP Prime Minister would be faced by a queue of unemployed stretching clear to Montreal in one direction and half-way to Toronto in the other. Again no one paid the slightest attention. I had meant to add that a Guaranteed Full Employment Act was as foolish and impracticable as a Guaranteed Perfect Health Act. As I sat down, a colleague reminded me of this. I was disgusted that I had forgotten. But he said, consolingly: 'You can do it when we get to the health plank in the platform.' Within minutes, however, I realized that I was just wasting everyone's time by staying. I went back to my office at the CLC where I could do something useful.

A few weeks later I turned in my NDP membership card. It had come to me automatically as a member of the CCF. It stated that by accepting it I accepted the constitution of the NDP. I wrote the 'federal' (not national! perish the thought!) secretary that I could not accept a party constitution from which the word 'national' had been deleted seventy-six times on the grounds stated by Mr Brockelbank. My resignation produced a small item in the newspapers, in which David Lewis 'regretted' my decision. It had no other result; it sank like a stone into a barrel of warm tar.

As a member of a CLC union I automatically paid a small monthly contribution to the NDP. I could have got out of it by a formal request. I didn't. In spite of everything I felt the NDP Members could and would play a useful part in the House of Commons, as indeed they did. In recent years, though not in 1988, I have occasionally voted NDP, and made small contributions to its funds for the same reason. But its stand on the Meech Lake Accord finished that. (While I was in the Senate I had the opportunity to hear Pierre Trudeau—speaking to a meeting of Liberals on the subject of the Quebec nationalists the NDP was trying to appease—say: 'Don't kid yourselves! What these guys want is two states. That's why Eugene [pointing at me] got out.')

That was the beginning of a battle that has now lasted almost thirty years and seems likely to last the rest of my life, and perhaps beyond. I have waged it in sundry places: in the Ontario Advisory Committee on Confederation, at meetings of the Learned Societies, in my 1962 presidential address to the Canadian Political Science Association, at the Conference on Canadian Unity at Banff in 1964, in countless public meetings, and in the newspapers.

There was one place where I did not wage it because I was not there, though I was invited: the 1967 Conservative Party's Montmorency Conference, which passed a 'two nations' resolution. Had I had any idea of what the Conference was going to do I might have accepted the invitation. There were at least two people at the meeting who were capable of tearing the two-nations resolution to ribbons. But one of them had laryngitis and neither, I think, spoke French. Had I been there I would have done a job on it — and in French, without notes (the angrier I get, the better my French becomes). I am not vain enough to think I could have defeated it. But I could at least have sounded a warning, and perhaps have revealed to some simple, kindly, susceptible souls where all this might lead.

In the course of my battles I was repeatedly confronted by glaring examples of pseudo-history. One I have already dealt with in Chapter 5: Bill Dodge on the Treaty of 1763. Here are five more.

The first, given currency in Dr Edwin Black's *Divided Loyalties: Canadian Concepts of Federalism* (1975), was Mr Justice Loranger's assertion in 1884 that 'At the outset of Confederation, no person had any idea of forming a political association; it was rather a commercial league of the nature of the Hanseatic league.' This is unadulterated nonsense.

My second example may well have owed its origin to the first. When I was in the Senate two schoolgirls from a French-language school came to ask me some questions on the Constitution. They began by saying they understood that the Fathers of Confederation had intended to form only a very loose union but that John A. Macdonald had got them all dead drunk, and when they came out from under the influence they discovered they had fashioned a highly centralized federation! I was, of course, thunderstruck. 'Where did you get this?' 'From our teacher.' I pointed out that the whole process had taken two years and four months, and that one of the Fathers, Sir Leonard Tilley, was a rabid teetotaler and prohibitionist. I told them that what the teacher had foisted on them was positively criminal. I should have complained at once to the Minister of Education.

My third example comes from a more authoritative source than the other two: the Honourable Guy Favreau, then Minister of Justice (in the *Globe and Mail Magazine*, May 1964): that Confederation was a 'pact, agreed in Charlottetown and finally in Quebec', between representatives of 'two founding peoples, two groups relatively evenly balanced, Quebec, the former Lower Canada . . . the people of French origin' and 'the other three provinces, or the other two plus Upper Canada . . . those who had English as their common language and similar cultural traditions.' This is a fairy-tale. In the first place the 'two groups' were not 'relatively evenly balanced'. Canada East, the future Quebec, had little more than a third as many people as Canada West, Nova Scotia, and New Brunswick combined; and almost 24 per cent of Canada East's population was of British origin. There were, of course, people of French origin in Canada West (the Census of 1861 showed they made up 2.6 per cent) and in Nova Scotia (6.3 per cent). The first figures for New Brunswick are for 1871 (15 per cent). Some of the 'British' may have been French-speaking Scots or Irish; some of the 'French' may have had English as their mother-tongue. But it is probably safe to say that in the original four provinces of the Dominion, the English-speaking outnumbered the French-speaking almost three to one.

In the second place, I cannot find the slightest evidence that at Charlottetown, Quebec, or London the delegates lined up on linguistic lines. If they had, the French-speaking would have been hopelessly outnumbered. At Charlottetown they were two out of 23, at Quebec four out of 33, at London two out of 16. The very incomplete records show little if any discussion of bilingualism, and the arguments over other matters seem to have been rather between the 'Canadians' as a whole and the Maritimers than between 'English' and 'French'.

I cannot resist the conclusion that most of those who talk about the 'pact' between 'two founding peoples' are unconsciously equating Canada East with 'French Canada', and the *pre*-Confederation *Province* of Canada with the *post*-Confederation *Dominion* of Canada. Canada East *was* 'relatively evenly balanced' with Canada West: their 1861 populations were about 44 to 56. But again, almost a quarter of Canada East's people were 'English', and the Dominion of Canada, even in 1867, was not merely the old Province of Canada writ large.

Once you grant the unfounded assumption, ignore the population figures and the membership of the Conferences, disregard the evidence of what was said and who said it, the Constitution Act of 1867 becomes simply a cozy arrangement between the French-speaking delegates from Canada East on the one hand, and the English-speaking delegates from the two Canadas on the other — with the Maritime delegates merely sitting on the sidelines, smiling sweetly, occasionally murmuring, 'and of course the Intercolonial Railway', and then signing on the dotted line what the 'Canadians' had already settled.

But the fact is that both at Quebec and London the Maritime delegates were very far from being yesmen or nodders. Why should they have been? The Canadas, by 1864, had got themselves into a political impasse, and had come to a Conference on Maritime union asking the Maritimes to get them out of it; which Nova Scotia and New Brunswick very kindly did. Both at Quebec and in London the Maritime delegates had a great deal to say, and said it forcibly and at length. The incomplete records show that they took up considerably more time than most of the 'Canadians' (after all, Nova Scotia had had thirty-three years' experience of representative government before Upper and Lower Canada came into existence), and far more than the French Canadians, and by no means exclusively on Maritime interests.

In short there is not, as far as I can discover, the faintest evidence of any pact, agreement, or bargain — in the Charlottetown, Quebec, or London Conferences or out of them — between two linguistic blocs. Anything of the sort must have taken place within the Cabinet of the Province of Canada before its delegates left for Charlottetown. The Maritime provinces seem to have accepted without question the arrangements the 'Canadians' had decided on for their purely local affairs.

The Maritime delegates seem also to have accepted without question the justice, the practical necessity, of the French Canadians' having the right to speak their own language in the Dominion Parliament, to use it in any courts the Dominion might create, and to have all the Acts and records of Parliament in both languages.

In an 1865 booklet (in both languages) on the Quebec Resolutions, the Honourable Joseph Cauchon devoted exactly 18 1/2 lines in 154 pages to the language provisions. The French Canadians, he said, were 'infinitely better off than men of our origin in the American Union where Federal and Local Legislation are exclusively English'; bilingualism in the Dominion Parliament and courts, and the Quebec Legislature and courts, had been 'cordially and spontaneously conceded, without discussion, without obstacle and without reticence.'

My fourth example of pseudo-history, the wildest of the lot, comes also from Mr Favreau in a speech given to the York-Scarborough Liberal Association on 25 January 1964. It was agreed in the Constitution of 1867, said the Minister of Justice, that 'French was to be recognized and applied in all federal fields on the same footing as' English; he went on to say that 'Quebec believes that the contractual provisions . . . that guarantee French as one of Canada's two official languages for affairs of state, for the federal Parliament and for the federal courts . . . have been allowed to lapse.'

Any such agreement would have covered much more than simply the federal Parliament and federal courts explicitly provided for in the Constitution Act, 1867; for example, Orders-in-Council. Is there one word of evidence that this was ever promised by anyone, let along agreed on? For quite other purposes I looked at the original Orders from 1 July 1867 to 19 May 1882 (there are thousands). I have found not one in both languages, and only one in French: P.C. 733 of 19 May 1881. If it was agreed by the Fathers that they should all be in both languages, is it credible that Cartier and Langevin, both Fathers of Confederation and both members of the first Dominion Cabinet, would have tamely submitted to such flagrant breaches of the agreement? Is it credible that their successors in Mackenzie's government and Macdonald's second government — men like Dorion, Laurier, Masson, Caron — would have remained mute?

Have the 'contractual provisions' of the Act of 1867, Section 133, that 'guarantee' French in Parliament and Dominion courts 'been allowed to lapse'? If so, where is the evidence? Silence.

The fifth example of pseudo-history is the assumption that French schools were guaranteed for the four original provinces in 1867, and for Manitoba in 1870. But there is not one syllable about school language in the Constitution Act of 1867, or in the Manitoba Act of 1870. Denominational schools, yes; but not French or English. (Incidentally, Manitoba did not abolish French schools in 1890: the 1895 *Sessional Papers* of the House of Commons contain the Report of the Manitoba Inspector of French Schools for 1894. It was Roman Catholic separate schools that were abolished.) A McGill professor of law, who later became a judge, once publicly argued that in 1867 'religion' and 'language' were co-terminous: that all the French were Catholics, and all the Catholics French, that all the English were Protestants and all the Protestants English. That the French Canadians in 1867 were nearly all Roman Catholics is no doubt true; the rest is demonstrable nonsense. The 1861 census figures for Canada West show that over 84 per cent of its 258,141 Roman Catholics were most certainly not French; and in Nova Scotia over 75 per cent of its 86,281. The 1871 figures for New Brunswick (the first I have been able to find) show that over half its 96,016 Roman Catholics were not French. There were large, and politically powerful, Irish Roman Catholic communities in both Canadas, and in Nova Scotia and New Brunswick — and, if we include all the colonies at the Quebec Conference, in Prince Edward Island and Newfoundland. (In Newfoundland the French-speaking were only a handful, and the Irish made up about a third of the total population.) There were also a good number of Scotch Roman Catholics in Canada West and Nova Scotia. The provisions for denominational schools in the Constitution Act of 1867 were the work of D'Arcy McGee, Thomas L. Connolly, and Alexander Tilloch Galt. It would have been very peculiar if two Irish Catholics and a Scotch Protestant had all said 'Roman Catholic' and 'Protestant' when they meant 'French' and 'English'.

I need hardly add that the terms of union with British Columbia in 1871, and Prince Edward Island in 1873, say nothing about language in the schools.

But of course the towering example of pseudo-history is the fable that Canada was intended to be 'two nations'. It was certainly not intended to be two political nations. The Province of Canada — Canada East and Canada West — had had something approximating two political nations. The two sections had equal representation in the legislature, and every government had two Prime Ministers: one 'English', one 'French'. They also had two systems of law, two Attorneys-General and Solicitors-General, and two systems of education. There is a legend that there was a constitutional convention that any legislation affecting only one section of the Province must have a 'double majority'; that is, the votes of a majority of all the members *and* of a majority of the members from that section—which, of course, would have meant that every Government must have a double majority to stay in office. This was in fact only a pet idea of John Sandfield Macdonald, who formally proposed it in 1856 as a solution to a ministerial crisis. It was defeated, John A. Macdonald voting against it. The Education Bill of 1855, which greatly strengthened the right of Roman Catholics in Canada West to separate schools, was passed by a majority from Canada East and a minority from Canada West.

The 'two-nations' Province of Canada broke down because it became ungovernable. That was what drove John A. Macdonald and George Brown to Charlottetown. 'Deadlock was the Father of Confederation.'

In the new Dominion, Parliament had 'rep. by pop.' in the House of Commons, not equal representation of Ontario and Quebec. In the Senate, Ontario, Quebec, *and the Maritimes* had equal representation; and there was one Prime Minister, not two. And over and over again—in Charlottetown, in Halifax, in Saint John, in Quebec City, in Montreal, and above all in the debates on Confederation in the Legislature of the Province of Canada—the 'Canadian' Fathers of Confederation, French-speaking and English-speaking, made it plain, emphatically and in both languages, that they considered they were founding 'a new nation', 'a single great nation, a political nationality independent of national origin' (Cartier). Macdonald spoke of 'joining these five peoples into one nation.' He added: 'We make the Confederation one people and one government, instead of five peoples and five governments . . . with the local governments and legislatures subordinate to the General Government and Legislature.'

The French Canadians of Quebec (nobody seems to have paid any attention to the Acadians) got guarantees for the survival of their own 'nationality', a word Cartier and Langevin used to describe them collectively, and a word everyone then applied also to 'Canadians' of English, Scotch, and Irish origin. The use of the French language in the Dominion Parliament and courts and the Quebec legislature and courts was also guaranteed. No French-Canadian spokesman, as far as I can discover, then asked for anything more. That all this was to exist within the framework of a single new political nation no one seriously questioned.

We English-speakers have been told *ad nauseam* that we do not understand French; that the French word 'nation' means 'a cultural and sociological group'. Yes. But it has also a political meaning. It is all very well to tell me that I don't understand French. But it would hardly have done to tell General de Gaulle that he didn't. Yet on 16 January 1964 he told Mr Pearson that he wanted Canada to be 'une nation forte et unie', a strong and united nation. Did he mean he wanted Canada to be a strong and united cultural and sociological group? If so he was expressing a wish that either French Canada or English Canada should disappear, which would be blatant nonsense.

The fact is that 'nation' has two meanings in both French and English: cultural and sociological on the one hand, political on the other. What some of our English-speaking learned men, and the poor innocents who follow them, apparently cannot get into their heads is the fatal ambiguity of the unqualified 'deux nations' and 'two nations', and the ease with which a skilled verbal juggler (and Quebec is full of them) can make it mean, at his or her convenience, either cultural and sociological 'nations' like Scotland, Wales, England, Wallonia, Brittany, Catalonia, French Canada; or political 'nations' like the United Kingdom, Belgium, France, Spain, and Canada. Daniel Johnson, then Premier of Quebec, actually performed this sleight-of-hand within two pages in his brief to the Federal-Provincial Structure Committee (September 1966). On page 2, French Canada was 'a nation, in the sociological sense of the term'; on page 3 he was demanding that this 'sociological' nation 'should have "juridical and political recognition" in a "new Constitution".'

As long as we allow ourselves to be fooled by this kind of legerdemain we shall be sitting ducks for every separatist or hemi-demi-semi-separatist in the country. We shall find ourselves, for one thing, agreeing that Quebec has a clear right to membership in the United Cultural and Sociological Groups, commonly known as the United Nations.

The Quebec nationalists have made this play on the word 'nation' a trump card in their games with the intelligentsia of English Canada ('though God knows why they're called so,' Healey Willan once said to me). An astonishing number of English-speaking public men (and women?), including eminent academics, have swallowed the palpable nonsense about the 'French' meaning and the 'English' meaning of 'nation'. They have apparently never heard of the English Common Law and Scots Law; of the Church of England and the Church of Scotland; of the National Gallery of Scotland and the Welsh National Symphony Orchestra. They have not noticed, or have forgotten, that there is no English, Scotch, or Welsh Parliament, no English, Scotch, or Welsh delegate to the United Nations; no delegate from Brittany or Wallonia or Catalonia.

The standard way of playing the two-meanings card has been, first, to get English-Canadian acquiescence that French Canada is a cultural and sociological 'nation' (this is easy); then, to equate French Canada with Quebec (not quite so easy, as there are well over a million French-speaking Canadians outside Quebec who have not one single vote in choosing the Quebec legislature or government); then, to insist that 'a nation' must have 'juridical and political recognition'. And there you are: QED!

Am I making this up? Listen to Daniel Johnson, again in 1966: 'We believe that there exists in Canada, in the sociological sense of the term, a nation of French speech.' Yes; just as there exists in the United Kingdom a Scotch nation and a Welsh nation (and, for the matter of that, an English nation). Then Johnson added: '. . . whose home is Quebec.' He had to. He was the Premier of Quebec, not of French Canada. He was presenting Quebec's demands, not French Canada's. But he wanted to speak for French Canada. So a page or so later he quietly dropped 'home', and substituted 'point d'appui' (base of operations).

Then came a formidable list of the things Quebec wanted, including power over 'relations with certain countries and certain international bodies' (a delightfully open-ended phrase). Some of the things were stated in vague terms (though none the safer for that). But the 'nation' was still, formally, cultural and sociological.

But turn the page: 'The new Government of Quebec has set itself a fundamental task: that of getting recognized, *juridically and politically*, the French-Canadian nation' (italics mine); and the 'nation' has of course become Quebec. The cultural and sociological nation, French Canada, disappears up one of Johnson's sleeves, and the political and juridical nation, Quebec, pops out the other.

Is this putting my own gloss on what Johnson really meant? Not in the least. In the same brief to the Structure Committee he said a 'new Constitution' must give 'equal *collective* rights [my italics again] to Canadians of English speech and Canadians of French speech' and 'give Quebec all the powers necessary to safeguard the Quebec identity' — precisely the words that turn up again in the Meech Lake Accord. In his book *Equality or Independence* (1965) Johnson drove the point home: Quebec must be politically and juridically equal to the rest of Canada or become a totally separate country. He had been careful to explain to the Structure Committee that the shared-cost programs, in which the Dominion gave conditional grants-in-aid (the 'spending power') to provinces in fields of their own exclusive jurisdiction, were well enough for a province; but 'for a nation, like ours' they just would not do. Quebec would have to opt out. The program would not apply to Quebec. But, he graciously added, Quebec would 'remain nevertheless willing to take part in the federal-provincial conferences which . . . might be summoned to discuss question relating to those programmes.' In other words the programs would no longer apply to us, but we shall be quite willing to help decide how they will apply to you. As Florence Nightingale said when the King gave her the Order of Merit: 'Too kind, too kind!'

Johnson's 'equality' for the French-Canadian 'nation' required an English-Canadian 'nation' for it to be equal to. But there wasn't any. Very well, then: it must be created. Mr Johnson was too polite to say so. But an English-speaking academic whose name escapes me, but who was quoted with whoops of enthusiasm by a prominent member of the Ontario Legislative Assembly, did: 'The French Canadians often say to us, "We know that we are a nation. Whether you English Canadians are a nation is for you to decide."' 'It is time', said the academic, 'to take up the challenge. If we are willing to make use of it for our own purposes, French-Canadian nationalism can help us to create a true English-Canadian nationalism. . . . The fact that the French-Canadians think of us as an English-Canadian nation . . . and address their demands to us as if we were such a nation, may encourage us to respond to their demands in their terms. French-Canadian nationalism can help to beget English-Canadian nationalism.' This tripe is part of what the prominent MLA described as 'the most brilliant succinct analysis of the crisis in Canadian Confederation.' The MLA himself added: 'Ontario's leadership could inspire the will to nationhood [not *Canadian* nationhood, perish the thought! *English*-Canadian nationhood] which English Canada has lost . . . the identity which English Canada lacks.' A second English-speaking professor added his twopennyworth: 'We lack, in English Canada, the will to evolve our national direction, at the very moment when Quebec is going forward in so dazzling a fashion.'

English-speaking Canadians do not consider themselves a nation. They never have. They do not want to; even the gentry I have just quoted admit that. Why should they be hectored or bullied into becoming one? Why should they be 'helped' to 'beget' a child they don't want? (Incidentally, it does not seem to have occurred to the 'helpers' that if they succeeded in forcing English-speaking Canadians to 'beget' an English-speaking nation, the parents, or the child itself, might insist on being totally English-speaking, bigotedly English-Canadian. The result of forced parenthood might be disconcerting.)

I had a good deal of exposure to English-speaking pundits of this kidney, notably at Senator Donald Cameron's Conference on National Unity in 1964 at the Banff School of Fine Arts, and in the Ontario Advisory Committee on Confederation, 1965-70.

My recollections of the Banff Conference are somewhat fragmentary, but perhaps not without significance. The French-Canadian delegation was made up almost wholly of Quebec nationalists, among them Professor Jacques-Yvan Morin, later a Minister in the Parti Québécois government, and Marcel Faribault, later the Conservatives' white (and very transitory) hope in Quebec. Morin was not then a separatist; he just wanted pretty well everything 'bi-national', half 'English', half 'French'. The English-speaking participants included Alex Corry of Queen's University and Andrew Stewart of the Board of Broadcast Governors. Most of the 'English' were earnestly anxious to show themselves 'open', conciliatory, broad-minded towards Quebec. They had plenty of opportunity. We listened to a perfect flood of Quebec nationalist oratory. The response of most of the 'English' was almost abject. I played the unenviable role of the little boy who points out that the emperor has no clothes on. In other words, I pointed out some of the practical difficulties that stood in the way of the wilder proposals. Stated in abstract terms these sounded plausible enough; applied to concrete situations, no.

One of the reiterated themes of Quebec nationalists was the necessity of Quebec's having some control over broadcasting. On that, Andrew Stewart asked the decisive question. The nationalists had been very insistent on the establishment and maintenance of a Canada-wide French TV network. 'Mr Chairman,' said Andrew, 'The maintenance of a nation-wide TV network is very expensive. The maintenance of two networks is even more expensive. Who will pay for the French network?' Consternation of the French participants. They huddled like a football team around Marcel Faribault, buzzing like a swarm of bees. Then after some minutes of agitated discussion Professor Morin rose, and in his beautiful Cambridge English said: 'We have asked Maître Faribault to state our position.' Faribault embarked on a magnificent oration. It fell into two halves. The first, which lasted about fifteen minutes, was on 'culture'—how vast it was, how far-reaching, how lofty, how profound, etc., etc. Then came part two: French culture—how vast it was, how far-reaching, how lofty, how profound, etc., etc. This also lasted about fifteen minutes. Then suddenly the answer: 'Quebec cannot pay. The federal authorities must pay.' (This was typical of Faribault. He was a Quebec nationalist, but he was also president of the Trust général du Canada. I once read an article of his on the changes he thought were needed in the Canadian Constitution. In alternate paragraphs the nationalist Pegasus soared into the Empyrean and the president of the Trust général came down to earth with a thump.)

The Ontario Advisory Committee was made up mostly of academics, some of whom were very distinguished. Most of them were acutely anxious to conciliate the Quebec nationalists. They were ably and ardently assisted by provincial civil servants who were like-minded but not always aware of the provisions of the British North America Act. In one case these zealous functionaries drew up an official Ontario proposal, to be presented to the Dominion Government, which was based on a gross legal howler. Fortunately, at almost literally the eleventh hour, they showed it to our Committee and one of the most distinguished academics, an eminent professor of law, was able to prevent its dispatch.

The civil servants sent us a great many clippings from the French-language press (none, as far as I can recall, from the English), and a steady flow of documents that illuminated at least their own preoccupations. We had also some reports from our own sub-committees. They needed scrutiny and got it, notably from Professor Donald

Creighton, Professor W.R. Lederman, and me. One sub-committee report proposed that Ontario should become constitutionally bilingual. To that, as a general proposition, I had and have no objection. But this document went into great detail on what should be bilingualized. Some of it was both foolish and impracticable and would have been fantastically expensive, with most of the money simply thrown away.

For example, all the municipalities were to be bilingualized. I jumped on that one: 'If you're proposing this for Ottawa, Cornwall, North Bay, Sudbury, and perhaps Windsor, where there are substantial numbers of French-Canadians, yes. That makes sense. But if you're talking about Toronto, Hamilton, London, Kingston, and a host of smaller places it is nonsense, and very expensive nonsense. Good interpreters and translators do not grow on bushes. There is already a great demand, from both public and private sectors, for their services. It will increase. Making the civic administrations of these and other cities bilingual would cost a great deal of money, and would do the Franco-Ontarians no good at all. If the government of Ontario has that kind of money to give them, I can tell them a dozen ways to spend it with real benefit to the minority.' This proposal had also come up at the Banff Conference and I made the same point. In both cases it was amended to conform with 'the commonplace quality of commonsense.'

Why do I rehearse all this at such length and in such detail? Because so much of the Quebec nationalist case, and so much of English-speaking acceptance of it, is based on unfact.

The proponents of the Meech Lake Accord have given us a fresh unfact: that Pierre Trudeau, during the Quebec referendum campaign of 1980, promised 'a renewed federalism' and then did not deliver. But he did deliver.

The Constitution Act of 1982 gave us the Charter of Rights and Freedoms, which limited the powers of both Parliament and the provincial legislatures and gave citizens some security against both; security that was enforceable against both. It gave us specific and enforceable aboriginal rights — insufficient, but at least a beginning. It gave us a constitutional commitment to reducing regional disparities. It gave us five specific, legally binding formulas for amending our Constitution.

One of those formulas provides that any province can opt out of any amendment transferring powers from the provincial legislature to the Parliament of Canada. That gives every province an absolute veto (for itself, but not for the rest of the country) over such amendments. It also provides that in any such amendment related to 'education or other cultural matters', the opting-out province would get 'reasonable compensation'.

Another of the amending formulas gives every province an absolute veto over changes in the composition of the Supreme Court of Canada. This guarantees Quebec at least three judges out of nine.

All these provisions were very important.

The 1982 Act took away Parliament's exclusive power to create new provinces and provided that any such change must have the approval of at least two-thirds of the provinces with at least half the population of the ten. That was entirely new, and very important, especially for the Territories (and apparently for the provinces, for in Meech Lake they stiffened the consent requirement to unanimity).

One section of the Charter of Rights and Freedoms guarantees certain linguistic minority rights in education; but part of this guarantee will apply to Quebec only if authorized by the legislative assembly or the government of the province. That also was entirely new, and very important.

Of course the Act didn't give the Quebec nationalists all they wanted. But Trudeau never promised it would. If he had, it would have amounted to abjuring the principles of a lifetime.

Most of what I have said about the unfacts has long been on record and is repeated here 'unrevised and unrepented' — except that in checking certain figures and quotations for this book I have found that I had slightly understated my case. What is also on record are my comments on the English-speaking appeasers who have swallowed the unfacts hook, line, and sinker. Usually highly intelligent and highly educated, they are ready to lie down on their backs and urge the rest of us to do likewise and join them in inviting the wildest Quebec nationalists to dance on our stomachs.

I say 'appeasers' advisedly. The drama of appeasement has been, and is being, played out on the domestic stage right under our noses. In her book *Unpopular Opinions*, Dorothy Sayers has a chapter on Britain between the wars and what made British politicians (with notable exceptions) and the bulk of the British people behave as they did. The chapter is headed: 'They Tried to Be Good', and it describes how 'the Voice of Enlightenment', 'the good and intellectual people', led 'the Flight from Reason', and, till almost the very outbreak of the war, persuaded the British people that resistance to German demands was 'naughty', until at last it looked as if Britain had become 'blind, deaf, dumb, paralytic and imbecile, without hope of recovery.' The same kind of people have been doing the same kind of thing here, and with a frightening degree of success. We have had, and still have, plenty of would-be Chamberlains. We shall be very lucky if we escape a Canadian Munich — an agreement, or 'accord', that would be hailed as a triumph of goodness, realism, moderation, and sweet reasonableness and might last no longer than the Munich agreement itself. This will no doubt be greeted with cries of outrage. I shall be denounced as a dinosaur, a living fossil, impenetrably anti-French, anti-Quebec. I have several defences against that.

In my Nowlan lecture at Acadia University in 1966 I addressed myself to 'certain things that we English-speaking Canadians need to have a firm grasp of':

'First, we must try to understand the position of French Canada [I should perhaps have said 'Quebec'] as a tiny island of people who speak French in a vast North American sea of people who speak English, and an island upon which that sea beats incessantly and thunderously. We should try to imagine what it would be like if *we* were the island and *they* the sea . . . Suppose that we found our English-speaking people spreading out into parts of Quebec and other predominantly French-speaking provinces, where English had no official status and English schools no constitutional guarantees. Might we not be asking for wider rights for the English-speaking language, and guarantees of English education for English-speaking children wherever the parents wanted it and there were enough such children to make it feasible? Might we perhaps feel that Ontario was not a province like the others; that it was the citadel of English-speaking Canada and as such had to have certain special powers? Mightn't we even have an English-speaking separatist movement?'

In the same Acadia speech I said: 'At least seven other provinces also already have, in one way or another, "special status" under the Constitution, and I can see no objection to giving any province a particular power or powers *merely* on the ground that this would make it different from the others. But I want to know first *what* power or powers, and why, and what the effect would be on the country as a whole. . . . But there is all the difference in the world between that and handing [the province] a blank cheque, especially as, if it fills [the blank] with a big enough figure, it will find it's NSF. . . . We should . . . be ready to examine and discuss, thoroughly, meticulously, any proposal bar none.' And I went into details about what English Canadians must do. Most of the things I specified have now been done. But I added: 'We should . . . be ready to *adopt* any proposals which can prove themselves. We don't want to spoil the ship for want of a ha'porth of tar, but neither do we want to punch holes in it to please people who prefer to put to sea in a sieve.'

These are not the words of a red-neck or a WASP bigot. But they were spoken almost a quarter of a century ago. Do I stand by them? I do. Can I prove it? I can. I have already recounted how I went clear to Edmonton in 1987 to support the legal rights of Mr Léo Piquette, MLA, to speak French in the legislative assembly.

Does this mean that I support the Meech Lake Accord? It does not. I argued against it before the Joint Committee of Parliament. I appeared four times before the Senate Committee of the Whole that was considering it. I gave the New Brunswick Legislative Committee 56 pages of denunciation, which I sent on to the Manitoba Task Force. I made a shorter submission to the Alberta NDP inquiry. Before a triple heart by-pass temporarily knocked me out I made critical speeches in Ottawa, Montreal, and St John's. The by-pass prevented me from appearing before the Ontario Legislative Committee, and from making speeches in Saskatchewan, Alberta, and British Columbia. Since my recovery I have repeated my arguments many times, in speech and writing. Here is an incomplete summary.

The Accord is a quagmire of ambiguities. It would produce a massive shift of power from Parliament and the legislatures to the Supreme Court of Canada, a very considerable shift from the federal Government and Parliament to the governments and legislatures of the provinces, and in a few years an appreciable shift from the House of Commons to the Senate. It would imperil the Charter of Rights and Freedoms in Quebec. It might well deal a body-blow to future shared-cost programs. It would give every province an absolute veto on the admission of any new province, and on an elected Senate, and on any change in the powers of the Senate and the number of Senators from any province. It would come very near establishing a new Third Order of Government, the mandatory annual Constitutional Conference of First Ministers, where every provincial Premier would have an absolute veto on even the *discussion* of any subject except Senate reform and the fisheries.

But the overmastering objection is the 'distinct society' clause.

No one can deny that Quebec is, culturally and sociologically, a distinct society. So is Newfoundland. We Newfoundlanders have a massive dictionary of Newfoundland English. We have our own peculiar school system, with distinctive constitutional guarantees. We once were an independent Dominion, equal in status to Canada, Australia, and New Zealand. We could amend our own Constitution, without going to the British Parliament, as Canada then had to do. But recognizing that is a very different thing from laying down, in the written Constitution, that the *whole* Constitution (bar the provisions relating to the aborigines and the Meech Lake clauses on immigration) and the *whole* Charter of Rights and Freedoms (bar multiculturalism) 'shall be interpreted in a manner consistent with' the distinct society clause.

The list of exclusive federal powers in the Constitution Acts that might be affected is a formidable one. Presumably the Supreme Court of Canada would give short shrift to any attempt to set up a separate army, navy, and air force, or a separate customs tariff, or a separate system of weights and measures on the plea that these were necessary to the 'distinct society'. But what about banking? Copyright? Patents? Interprovincial and international railways, telephones, highway transport? Atomic energy? Naturalization and citizenship? Unemployment insurance? The criminal law? (The Padlock Act was struck down because it invaded that exclusive federal jurisdiction; but Section 16 of the Accord might wipe that out.)

What about Parliament's paramount power over agriculture? The Accord itself explicitly shoots the paramount power over immigration full of holes. What about broadcasting? Air navigation?

The 'distinct society' clause could give the Government of Quebec massive new powers. The Government of Canada, and other backers of the Accord, say it will have only a 'marginal effect' in 'a few grey areas' of jurisdiction. No one can be certain which side is right until the Supreme Court of Canada brings down its decisions in specific cases. The clause may then turn out to mean very little. If it does, the Quebec nationalists will be furious: 'The damned English have swindled us again!' And they will ask for a string of specific new powers, so plainly and unequivocally stated that wayfaring judges, though WASPS, might not err therein. Or the clause may turn out to mean something very near 'sovereignty-association' for Quebec, and a substantial fragmentation of the power of the Government and Parliament of Canada right across the country. For the Accord contains a great deal that has nothing to do with Quebec's original five 'minimum demands' but applies to the whole country.

The 'distinct society' clause is just the old open-ended 'special status' with a wig and false whiskers. Even the name is borrowed from Daniel Johnson in 1966.

A friend of long experience in these matters has written me that there are two kinds of Quebec nationalists: the honest and the dishonest.

The honest are the separatists.

The dishonest 'want . . . an independent Quebec *in Canada* and they are demanding of the rest of us that we reorganize Canada to accommodate them.' Ultimately they want 'a situation in which all of the decisions that really count will be made for the Quebec people by their "national assembly" in Quebec City', but with Quebec still keeping 75 members in the Canadian House of Commons, 24 members in the Canadian Senate, and a dozen or so Ministers in the Canadian Cabinet, all playing a major part in decisions that would affect the nine provinces but would not touch Quebec in the least; making and unmaking Canadian governments; and, between times, drawing on the Canadian treasury for whatever money Quebec (Daniel Johnson's 'nation') wanted to supplement its own resources, and of course getting preferred access to lucrative Canadian contracts (what Mr Bourassa poetically calls 'booty'). Again: 'You stay *out* of our affairs; we stay very much *in* yours.' Quebec would have the powers of a nation plus the powers of a province. The rest of the country would be in a state of neo-colonialism, with Quebec as the imperial power.

And how would the Quebec nationalists attain this happy issue out of all their afflictions? By what Professor Al Johnson has called 'incremental sovereignty'. Jacques Parizeau, the present leader of the Parti Québécois, proposes getting power after power by a series of mini-referenda, each followed by a specific constitutional amendment, till a final referendum and a final amendment gave Quebec total independence. Mr Parizeau seems confident he would get all his amendments; no wonder, when he sees so many English-speaking 'intellectuals' and politicians ready to cut off their arms, their legs, and even their heads (though in some cases that might scarcely be noticed) to please Quebec nationalists.

Mr Parizeau, however, is an honest Quebec nationalist. What about the dishonest ones? They too believe in incremental sovereignty. Mr Bourassa, reproached by Mr Parizeau for not having got enough in the Meech Lake Accord, made it plain, in his speech to the Assembly in June 1987, that 'there will be a second round . . . another round of negotiations', for 'a number of areas not yet settled'. And he is muttering dark hints of a 'new political superstructure', perhaps modelled on the European Economic Community (or perhaps on Judge Loranger's 'Hanseatic League'): a regional international organization, an Organization of Canadian States, to parallel the Organization of American States (which, with incredible folly, we have just joined).

Mr Mulroney, in *The Parliamentarian*, July 1988, has told us that Meech Lake 'will help transform our constitution into a more authentically federalist document' (an old Quebec nationalist cliché, this). Ratification 'will allow us to move forward, with the knowledge that we are entering a new era in the history of our country. In those coming years we shall have an opportunity to refine further our constitutional process. For the Constitutional Accord of 1987 is not an ending. It is a beginning. It will set Canada's constitutional reform process on the road again.'

Meanwhile the dishonest nationalists, the pseudo-federalists, are trying to pre-empt the adjective 'national' for Quebec institutions. They were at this game even in the 1960s, objecting to the use of the word in the names of committees preparing for the Centennial of Confederation. Now their instruments in the federal government are taking the word off the names of most of our museums, and Mr Masse proposes to delete promoting 'national unity' from the statutory description of the CBC's mandate.

And each fresh Quebec 'demand' would be urged upon us as the only way to stop the separatists, to 'keep Quebec in the Canadian family'. Each demand granted, each increment of sovereignty surrendered, would leave Canada weaker and weaker, more and more at the mercy of the people who make the demands; the more so because each time a power is given up to Quebec, the other provinces would probably get it too (Quebec's threats would be supplemented by this bait dangled before the eyes of the other Premiers, and snapped up, as at Meech Lake). The process would end with the ghost of the deceased Canadian nation sitting crowned upon the grave thereof.

What the Meech Lake Accord ought to have shown us is that our whole process of constitutional amendment is wrong: out of date, undemocratic.

The Constitution belongs to the people, not the politicians. It is the people, not the politicians, who should decide what goes in, what stays in, what goes out.

What we need is a process as near to the Australian as we can get. In Australia an amendment must first be passed by both Houses of the Commonwealth (federal) Parliament. If they pass it, it goes to the *electors* in a referendum. If it gets a majority of the *electors* in the whole country, and a majority in a majority of the States, it goes into effect. The State Governments, and the State Parliaments, have *no part at all* in the process. If we had a similar process Canada would not be in danger of becoming just an eleventh province. But we cannot simply copy Australia for one very plain and conclusive reason: Australia has no Quebec.

Quebec's declining birth-rate, and its inability to attract enough immigrants, especially French-speaking immigrants, to make up for the decline mean that its proportion of the total population is going down and may well continue to go down. So in any vote on an amendment a majority of the electors in the whole country, plus a majority in a majority (even a two-thirds majority) of the provinces, would not give Quebec the security it needs, or feels it needs, for its distinctive institutions. Some amendments would therefore have to have the consent of a majority of the electors in each and every province. If the Meech Lake Accord fails to get the necessary unanimous approval of the provincial legislatures, we could have a real 'second round'. Not a fake, with many of the doors to a genuine reform banged, barred, and bolted by the unanimity requirement; but rather some prospect of meeting Quebec's needs without balkanizing the whole country.

Unfortunately, changing the amending process would itself, under the Constitution Act of 1982, require the unanimous consent of the provincial legislatures; and the provincial governments would look with a jaundiced eye on changing a process that would put them out of the picture. Perhaps the most we can hope for is what Trudeau originally proposed to put into that Act: provision for an appeal from a provincial legislature to the provincial electors. But a 'second round' with the present process would, I think, have to keep the existing provision that allows a province to opt out of any constitutional amendment transferring power from a provincial legislature to the Parliament of Canada.

There is one area in which I think the Meech Lake Accord is right. At present, if the amendment deals with 'education or other cultural matters', a province that opts out gets 'reasonable compensation'. Meech Lake would give it compensation no matter what subject it dealt with. This seems to me just and reasonable. Provinces that accept an amendment would be relieved of certain expenses that the opting-out province would still have to bear.

I think there would also have to be explicit guarantees that the Quebec Civil Law could not be touched by any amendment except with Quebec's consent, and that Quebec should have a minimum proportion of the seats in the Senate. It already has — under the Constitution Act of 1982 — a guarantee of at least one-third of the judges of the Supreme Court of Canada, and this would have to be maintained.

Parliament and the provincial legislatures should have the obligation to *promote*, not simply preserve, the *rights*, not simply the 'existence', of the linguistic minorities.

Provinces should be allowed to opt out of shared-cost programs in fields of exclusive provincial jurisdiction, but *only* if their own programs (not just *'initiatives* or programs') met *minimum standards*, criteria, conditions set by *Act of Parliament* (and were not just *compatible* with national *objectives'*, which could mean mere tokens), provided they did not fly in the face of something laid down in a speech or a White Paper. (President Reagan's 'program or initiative' on acid rain was 'compatible' with Mr Mulroney's 'objectives'.)

There would have to be special provisions for Quebec in relation to immigration; but most certainly not the preposterous, indeed impossible, 'guarantee' of a proportion of total immigration equal to Quebec's proportion of the total population, plus, if it chose, five per cent. Nor should there be room for the entrenched sweeping powers, notably over the integration of immigrants, nor the unspecified special methods of amendments of the immigration clause found in the Meech Lake Accord.

The 'distinct society' clause should go into the preamble (where Quebec originally proposed to put it). Placed there, it would not override the Charter of Rights and Freedoms or bind judicial interpretation of the Constitution. Other 'distinct societies' might join it there (for instance, the aborigines). But none of them would have the right to have almost the whole Constitution interpreted 'in a manner consistent with' its claims.

The Quebec nationalists of course might say: 'This won't do. All right for a province, perhaps, but [echoing Daniel Johnson in 1966] not for a nation like ours. Canada has rejected us. Very well, we leave.'

The claim that if two or three provincial legislatures reject Meech Lake, Canada is rejecting Quebec, is false. Rejection of Meech Lake is rejection of Meech Lake; rejection not of Quebec's five 'minimum demands' but of what Premier Clyde Wells rightly calls 'the dismantling of federalism'. However, the Quebec nationalist élite may persuade the Quebec people that secession, or Mr Bourassa's 'new political superstructure', is the only course open to them.

The separatists probably believe that secession would be 'roses, roses, all the way, with myrtle mixed in our path like mad.' If so they are suffering from a dangerous delusion. It is unlikely that the Canadian negotiators would be all sweetness, and there would be many tough problems: for example, a corridor to the Atlantic provinces; control of the St Lawrence Seaway (the Americans might be sticky about that); Quebec's share of the Canadian national debt; the right of the Indians and Inuit in northern Quebec to secede. (People sometimes forget that the Territory of Ungava, which till 1869 had been part of the Hudson's Bay Company's possessions, was given to Quebec in 1912 as a *province of Canada*, and that its population then consisted of 663 Indians, 543 'Eskimos', 46 'half-breeds', eight 'English', and two 'Scotch' —not one 'French' in the whole lot. The figures are in *Hansard*, 1912, p. 6161. The James Bay projects are all in Ungava.)

There would be other problems. The 'English' in Montreal, besides the aborigines, might claim the right to secede from Quebec. There would be the problem of federal property in Quebec, and of federal officials, and employees of federal Crown companies from Quebec who would have to decide whether to be Quebeckers or Canadians. If they chose to be Quebeckers, they would automatically become foreigners and lose their jobs. What compensation would they get, and who would pay it?

Mr Parizeau, to do him justice, recognizes at least some of these problems. But there are those in his party who may think the rest of Canada loves Quebec so much—or, alternatively, would be so sick of its incessant demands—that we'd cheerfully agree to any terms a separatist government would propose. The rest of Canada might indeed say, 'Go!' But it might not be ready to add: 'And take with you as much of the family property as you please.'

If the Meech Lake Accord fails,* it is perhaps more likely that Mr Bourassa will try to get the rest of Canada to accept his 'new political superstructure'. His chances of that may not be as good as he may fancy. The new superstructure would certainly involve giving Quebec very large new powers, plus a decisive voice in decisions that would apply only to the remaining nine provinces, and the ability to demand still more powers for itself, amounting to 'incremental sovereignty'. But the rest of the country might say: 'No, thank you. We can see the end of that road: neo-colonialism. If you want to get out, we are ready to negotiate the terms on which you do. But independent within Canada you cannot be. You cannot have dry water, boiling ice, sour sugar, or stationary motion.'

When the First World War broke out, Sir Edward Grey, the British Foreign Secretary, said: 'The lights are going out all over Europe.' They did. I hope the lights are not now going out all over Canada.

If Quebec separated, could a truncated Canada survive? Yes. It could even flourish. But there would be a new balance of political power.

---

*This was written before it actually did fail, on 23 June 1990.

As long as Quebec stays in, Central Canada (Ontario plus Quebec) has an overwhelming majority in the House of Commons: 174 to 121. If Quebec leaves, Ontario, bereft of its partner, would be in a minority. The West, plus the Atlantic provinces and the North, would have 121 seats to Ontario's 99. The eight provinces could carry any measure of Senate reform they could agree on. The necessary amendments — under the Constitution Act, 1982 — would have to have the consent of the legislatures of at least two-thirds of the provinces, with at least half the population of what would then be the whole nine. Eight is well over two-thirds of nine, and the eight would have over half the population of the nine.

There might have to be a 'new political superstructure', though very different from Mr Bourassa's. We might decide, for example, that we could not afford the luxury of nine provincial legislatures, cabinets, and bureaucracies. We might see a new and more functional division of power between the centre and the provinces. We might adopt an Australian-style formula for constitutional amendment where the people of each province, not the politicians, would give or withhold consent to changes.

In other words there is no reason why a new political entity, sans Quebec, need strike fear in our hearts — however much it is entered upon unwillingly. Any change of this magnitude, and its attendant complexities, would of course present an immense challenge, one not dreamt of by the Fathers of Confederation. But I have faith that Canadians, both English-speaking and French-speaking (of whom there would still be over a million), would be able to face the future united — 'One equal temper of heroic hearts / . . . strong in will / To strive, to seek, to find, and not to yield.'

Envoi

Religion has played a very large part in my life, though not the decisive part it should have played. I have been an unprofitable servant.

Brought up a Methodist, I had declared myself a candidate for the ministry, with some idea of foreign service. At McGill this simply wilted under pressure from 'the cares of this world' (which, however, did not mean filthy lucre, but activity as a layman for the Social Gospel). I should probably have made a very bad minister: impatient, hot-tempered, lacking in depth and in courage. It is perhaps significant that my change in direction cost me no internal struggle. I do not recall even praying about it. I just followed 'the devices and desires' of my own heart.

It would be exaggerating to say that I have lived my life on the fringe of religion. For most of my eighty-six years, I have been a pretty steady church-goer and contributor. For the last twenty-five years or so I have been an active member of the Église Saint-Marc, a French-language United Church in Ottawa; till I got too old and infirm I was an elder, steward, and treasurer; and I have conducted the whole service, in French, twenty-three times. But I doubt if I have ever turned anyone to Christ; I may even have turned some aside.

In my years in Montreal, and at Oxford, I enriched my religious heritage by frequent attendance at Anglican services, and became a devotee of the Book of Common Prayer. At Oxford my socialism took me to the Quakers (a great-great-grandmother had been a Philadelphia Quaker), and I joined the Society. I resigned from it during the Spanish Civil War, feeling that if I were in Spain I should certainly fight.

From Methodism, from Anglicanism, from Quakerism I have learned much (though not enough). From all three I have drawn great strength and comfort.

I end with Cardinal Newman's great prayer: 'Support us, O Lord, all the day long of this troublous life, until the shadows lengthen, and the evening comes, the busy world is hushed, the fever of life is over, and our work is done. Then, Lord, in thy mercy, grant us safe lodging, a holy rest, and peace at the last; through Jesus Christ our Lord. Amen.'

APPENDIX

Literary Allusions

My publisher thinks readers would like me to identify the numerous quotations and paraphrases sprinkled throughout this book. I offer the following list of sources:

Page

9	*He who is slow to anger is better than the mighty; and he who ruleth his spirit, than he that taketh a city.*	Proverbs, xvi, 32
24	*Surely this is to bring down the Holy Ghost*	Bacon, *Essays*: 'Of Unity in Religion'
26	*the glass of fashion and the mould of form*	Shakespeare, *Hamlet*, III, i, l. 162
48	*broke through language and escaped*	Browning, 'Rabbi Ben Ezra', xxv
48	*. . . slowly broadens down / From precedent to precedent*	Tennyson, 'You Ask Me, Why', iii
48	*The land where, girt with friends or foes / A man may speak . . .*	Tennyson, 'You Ask Me, Why', ii
48	*loyal passion for our temperate kings*	Tennyson, 'Ode on the Death of the Duke of Wellington', vii
49	*outward and visible sign*	*Book of Common Prayer* (Canada), Catechism
49	*noiseless tenor of their way*	Gray, 'Elegy in a Country Churchyard', 19
49	*blossomed like Aaron's rod*	*Numbers*, xvii, 8 ('the rod of Aaron . . . budded . . . and bloomed blossoms')
54	*. . . sondry folk, by aventure y-falle in felawshipe*	Chaucer, *Canterbury Tales*, Prologue

54	*City of Destruction*	Bunyan, *Pilgrim's Progress*
59	*more deadly than the male*	Kipling, 'The Female of the Species' ('For the female of the species is more deadly than the male.')
66	*Nothing venture, nothing win*	Gilbert, *Iolanthe*, II
66	*not by any to be entered upon*	*Book of Common Prayer* (Canada), Solemnization of Marriage
67	*state of life to which it shall please God to call us*	*Book of Common Prayer* (England), Catechism
80	*the voice of Jacob . . .*	*Genesis*, xxvii, 22 ('The voice is the voice of Jacob, but the hands are the hands of Esau')
104	*Not to know me argues yourselves unknown*	Milton, *Paradise Lost*, IV, 829
104	*tell forth thy tale*	Chaucer, *Canterbury Tales*, 'Summoner's Tale'
109	*his eye was not dim*	*Deuteronomy*, xxxiv, 7
117	*Thick as autumnal leaves that strow the brooks / In Vallombrosa*	Milton, *Paradise Lost*, I, 302
122	*monarch of all he surveyed*	Cowper, 'Verses Supposed to be Written by Alexander Selkirk ('I am monarch of all I survey, / My right there is none to dispute')
123	*Pitt is to Addington . . .*	George Canning, 'The Oracle'
127	*Who would true valour see*	Bunyan, *Pilgrim's Progress*

128   *painting the lily*   Shakespeare, *King John*, IV, ii, l. 11 ('To gild refined gold, to paint the lily')

140   *no dog barked*   Shakespeare, *Merchant of Venice* I, i, 94 ('And when I ope my lips let no dog bark')

144   *spoke disrespectfully of the Equator*   Smith in Lady Holland's *Memoir*, vol. I, p. 17

146   *sound and fury*   Shakespeare, *Macbeth*, v, v, l. 27 ('full of sound and fury')

157   *Brief life is here our portion,*
       brief sorrow, short-lived care   St Bernard of Cluny

158   *stand on end like quills upon the*
       fretful porpentine   Shakespeare, *Hamlet*, I, v, 1.20

160   *Oh, I am a pirate king*   Gilbert, *The Pirates of Penzance*, I

164   *my heart was in Ottawa, a-chasing*
       the returning officers   Burns, 'My Heart's in the Highlands' ('My heart's in the Highlands a-chasing the deer')

167   *to my faults a little blind . . .*   Matthew Prior, 'An English Padlock' ('Be to her virtue very kind; / Be to her faults a little blind')

169   *being dead, yet speaketh*   *Hebrews*, xi, 4

172   *not without dust and heat*   Milton, *Areopagitica*

172   *vanquish and overcome all our enemies*   *Book of Common Prayer* (Canada), Prayer for the Queen's Majesty

175   *Give all thy days to dreaming,*
       And all thy nights to sleep   James Elroy Flecker, *Hassan*

179	*which passed us by as the idle wind . . .*	Shakespeare, *Julius Caesar*, IV, iii, l. 68 ('. . . they pass by me as the idle wind, / which I respect not')
183	*And lo! Ben Adhem's name led all the rest*	Leigh Hunt, 'Abou Ben Adhem and the Angel'
185	*Piling Ossa upon Pelion*	Virgil, *Georgics*, i, 281
189	*the deaf adder that stoppeth her ear*	*Psalms* 58:4
191	*The trumpet's silver sound is still*	Scott, *Marmion*, viii
193	*something lingering, with boiling oil in it*	Gilbert, *The Mikado*
196	*nearer to the heart's desire*	Fitzgerald, *The Rubáiyát of Omar Khayyám* (ed. I, lxxvi ('Re-mould it nearer to the Heart's Desire')
200	*. . . darkly at dead of night / The sod with our bayonets turning*	Charles Wolfe, 'The Burial of Sir John Moore at Corunna', ii
201	*a nice derangement of epitaphs*	Sheridan, *The Rivals*, III, iii
205	*brought death into the world, and all our woe*	Milton, *Paradise Lost*, I, 3
219	*put to sea in a sieve*	Lear, 'The Jumblies' ('went to sea in a sieve')
221	*wayfaring judges, though WASPs, might not err therein*	Isaiah, xxxv, 8 ('the wayfaring men, though fools, shall not err therein')
221	*this happy issue out of all their afflictions*	Book of Common Prayer: Morning Prayer

222 *ghost of the deceased Canadian nation sitting crowned upon the grave thereof*

Hobbes, *Leviathan*, pt. iv, ch. 47 ('The Papacy is not other than the Ghost of the deceased Roman Empire sitting crowned upon the grave thereof.')

224 *roses, roses, all the way*

Browning, 'The Patriot' ('It was roses, roses, all the way, / With myrtle mixed in my path like mad')

226 *strong in will / To strive, to seek, to find, and not to yield*

Tennyson, 'Ulysses'

227 *devices and desires of our own hearts*

Book of Common Prayer, General Confession

Index